CULTURE SHOCK!

A Survival Guide to Customs and Etiquette

SHANGHAI

Sharol Gauthier

T0294124

Marshall Cavendish
Editions

Published by Marshall Cavendish Editions
An imprint of Marshall Cavendish International

A member of the
Times Publishing Group

Other Marshall Cavendish Offices:
Marshall Cavendish Corporation, 99 White Plains Road, Tarrytown NY 10591-9001, USA • Marshall Cavendish International (Thailand) Co Ltd, 253 Asoke, 12th Flr, Sukhumvit 21 Road, Klongtoey Nua, Wattana, Bangkok 10110, Thailand • Marshall Cavendish (Malaysia) Sdn Bhd, Times Subang, Lot 46, Subang Hi-Tech Industrial Park, Batu Tiga, 40000 Shah Alam, Selangor Darul Ehsan, Malaysia.

Marshall Cavendish is a registered trademark of Times Publishing Limited

National Library Board, Singapore Cataloguing-in-Publication Data

Name(s): Gauthier, Sharol.
Title: CultureShock! Shanghai : a survival guide to customs and etiquette / Sharol Gauthier.
Other titles(s): Shanghai : a survival guide to customs and etiquette | Culture shock Shanghai | Series: Culture shock!
Description: Singapore : Marshall Cavendish Editions, 2019. | Includes bibliographical references and index.
Identifier(s): OCN 1113858154 | ISBN 978-981-48-2873-4 (paperback)
Subject(s): LCSH: Etiquette--China--Shanghai. | Shanghai (China)--Social life and customs. | Shanghai (China)--Description and travel.
Classification: DDC 951.132--dc23

Printed in Singapore

Photo Credits:
All photos by the author except the following by Iman: x, 7, 8 and 232.
Cover photo by Zifeng Zhang on Unsplash.com.

All illustrations by Sukhbir Cheema

ABOUT THE SERIES

Culture shock is a state of disorientation that can come over anyone who has been thrust into unknown surroundings, away from one's comfort zone. *CultureShock!* is a series of trusted and reputed guides which has, for decades, been helping expatriates and long-term visitors to cushion the impact of culture shock whenever they move to a new country.

Written by people who have lived in the country and experienced culture shock themselves, the authors share all the information necessary for anyone to cope with these feelings of disorientation more effectively. The guides are written in a style that is easy to read and covers a range of topics that will arm readers with enough advice, hints and tips to make their lives as normal as possible again.

Each book is structured in the same manner. It begins with the first impressions that visitors will have of that city or country. To understand a culture, one must first understand the people—where they came from, who they are, the values and traditions they live by, as well as their customs and etiquette. This is covered in the first half of the book.

Then on with the practical aspects—how to settle in with the greatest of ease. Authors walk readers through how to find accommodation, get the utilities and telecommunications up and running, enrol the children in school and keep in the pink of health. But that's not all. Once the essentials are out of the way, venture out and try the food, enjoy more of the culture and travel to other areas. Then be immersed in the language of the country before discovering more about the business side of things.

To round off, snippets of information are offered before readers are 'tested' on customs and etiquette. Useful words and phrases, a comprehensive resource guide and list of books for further research are also included for easy reference.

CONTENTS

Construction began on the glamorous Pudong skyline a mere 30 years ago.

ACKNOWLEDGEMENTS

I have to admit in hindsight that one of my first thoughts about Shanghai was that it wasn't a very livable city. What did I know, then? Not much, it turns out. At that point, I hardly knew the city at all! Five years later, I see Shanghai through a very different lens. Clearly, I had culture shock. The truth is, Shanghai is a spectacular city. Better than that, it is a fascinating and exciting place to live.

During some of my time in Shanghai, I wrote a blog about China, which forced me to look closely at the city, its people, its culture, and our lives there. From the kernels of those observations, this book grew into something tangible and (I hope) helpful. Working on this project raised many questions, and I want to acknowledge the people who helped me find answers.

Thank you to Tracy Lesh of *Shanghai and Beyond* for answering language questions as well as food questions, and for being such a fantastic guide on a trip to Longmen Village. Thank you also to Allen Tan, not only for treating me to a delicious Chinese (and Malaysian) meal in Singapore, but also for helping parse the particulars of Chinese culture and language. My gratitude also goes out to Shanghai's most interesting expat, Betty Barr, who granted me time for an interview. What a pleasure it was to learn the fascinating story of Betty and her Shanghainese husband, George Wang, who were both born and raised in Shanghai during the 1920s and 30s.

Many friends at Shanghai American School were generous with answers as well. Sandy Hong and Serena Lu, members of the school's dedicated Chinese staff, offered helpful tips about Chinese culture. Serena also provided me with a long list of her favorite Shanghainese dishes. Iman Syah, whom I first met during a trip to the Lhagang (*Tagong*) Monastery—in the hinterland of the Tibetan Autonomous Prefecture—shared photos for the book and his thoughts on Shanghai's nightlife. Tiffany Kelley, colleague and good friend, was a regular go-to person whenever I needed help remembering details. Xiao Lin, our driver, deserves a shout out as well. He was always up for long conversations with me about our two countries; Xiao Lin taught me more about China and what it means to be Chinese than anyone else I know.

A hearty thank you goes out to my editor She-reen Wong at Marshall Cavendish International (Asia), who had the crazy idea, after reading my blog, that I should write a book. And I would not have finished *CultureShock! Shanghai* without the help of my mother, Harol Marshall, also a writer. Thank you for being my first set of eyes, and more importantly, for your encouragement in the very beginning, when reaching the end seemed far away.

Last, but definitely not least, thank you to my two daughters, Sophie and Colette, for offering perceptive insights into their own culture shock experiences in China. And finally, thanks to Marcel Gauthier for taking us all to Shanghai in the first place.

❝If you want to get more out of life . . . you must lose your inclination for monotonous security and adopt a helter-skelter style of life that will at first appear to you to be crazy.❞

**— Chris McCandless,
from Jon Krakauer's _Into the Wild_**

In the 19th century, Great Britain, along with France and the United States, invaded a series of Chinese cities that included Shanghai. Nicknaming Shanghai "The Paris of the East"—as much for the city's decadent reputation as for its proliferation of art, music, and entertainment—Westerners cordoned off the city and established their own outpost. They controlled it for nearly a century. During this era, Shanghai grew into a center of finance with an international reputation for extravagance. When the city finally fell to the Communists in 1949, it stepped away from the world stage and entered a state of hibernation and retreat from international affairs that lasted decades.

Enter the twenty-first century: Shanghai has finally resumed its position as the rising dragon of the East. Always something of a rebel, the city is once again China's crown jewel—one of the best examples of the country's successful and rapid modernization. As of this writing, Shanghai continues to hold title as the world's most densely populated urban metropolis. In just one-third of the physical space of Beijing, Shanghai

A close-up, vertiginous view of the iconic
Oriental Pearl Tower

is home to nearly 4 million more people. Its lofty cityscape rivals those of other modern cities. Shanghai has re-emerged as one of the 21st century's world-class financial centers. In 2017, CNN hailed Shanghai as "the greatest city in the world."

Shanghai's popular river promenade, the Bund, glitters with technological confidence as the city continues to improve and expand its stunning landscape. In 2019, the Centre Pompidou, a dazzling new branch of the esteemed French museum of contemporary and modern art, opened its doors on the Bund. Shanghai boasts some of the world's tallest buildings, largest businesses, longest bridges, fastest trains and elevators, and best restaurants. With abundant new wealth, it is now routine to see Porsches and Audis zipping down the Yan'an Elevated, shuttling young Chinese children to their weekend activities.

The city's prodigious metro system was built with stunning efficiency, and new metro lines pop up in the suburbs

The famous Bund glitters and captivates by night in one of the world's most glamorous cities.

at breakneck speed. At night, Shanghai's impressive network of freeways is backlit with blue lights, and the abundant skyscrapers play host to light shows beaming both Chinese and English advertisements to the crowds. The famous Pudong skyline is luminous, centered as it is around the neon Pearl Tower and a triumvirate of the world's tallest skyscrapers.

Contemporary Shanghai still resonates with visitors as something reminiscent of Paris. It is the world's newest City of Lights. In short, there is much to recommend Shanghai to foreigners, and more than 200,000 of them call this city home. As international expat populations go, it's a minuscule number, representing less than one-half of one percent of Shanghai's 24 million residents. Compare that to New York, where more than 37 percent of the population was born in a foreign country.

It's easy for new arrivals to be distracted by the outward glamour of the city. But settling in offers unique challenges. Some expats may find themselves ensconced miles away from the trendiest areas of the city, and those with families will likely be living in outer suburbs or in residential compounds. Our first apartment, provided by our employer, was an hour by car from downtown. We had hoped for glitzy urban life. We found something more subdued and more challenging, surrounded as we were by a semi-rural and suburban population that seemed to rarely appreciate the presence of foreign faces.

Underneath its sparkly couture, the reality is that this megacity is home to millions of average Chinese citizens, many of whom are migrants from rural areas and other Chinese provinces, seeking access to Shanghai's bustling job market. English is still not widely spoken or understood

Shanghai is a popular destination for domestic as well as international tourists.

in most of China, and in much of Shanghai. To make matters more complex, foreign visitors and long-term expats who lack language skills and cultural understanding can quickly find themselves faced with an impenetrable bureaucracy and confusing cultural norms. Navigating China's myriad bureaucratic quirks adds another layer of frustration and before long that dizzy feeling of dislocation, known commonly as culture shock, sets in.

I wrote this guidebook to help minimize the culture shock of arriving cold turkey in Shanghai. I've tried to include humorous and realistic descriptions of the culture shock my own family experienced, and I hope I've offered strategies for dealing with aspects of life in Shanghai which can frustrate and even infuriate new arrivals (Internet access, I'm talking about you). In general, I've approached this guide as a map to life in Shanghai, rather than as an introduction to broader Chinese culture.

Perhaps more importantly, China and the Chinese people are complex and far too diverse for a foreigner of a few years to ever fully elucidate. As with any large country, values and cultural practices vary widely from region to region, between rural and urban areas, and among social classes. China is home to more than 55 recognized minority groups, and many have unique customs and traditions. But Shanghai is its own city, and its atmosphere is wildly different in tone and context from cities like Beijing, Hangzhou, and Chengdu. Every inch of Shanghai is uniquely Shanghainese, and I've tried to highlight the spirit of the city that many foreigners may find both difficult to navigate and yet keenly exciting and attractive.

When I was living in China, I often relied on humor as the best way to approach curious or unexpected situations. When you are lost by a conversation in Mandarin, just smile. It's a universally recognized form of communication, although you may not find your smile is returned. When you are sent back and forth between offices—*you must have your passport to pay the bill; no, you must pay the bill before we return your passport*—find the humor in the situation (and practice pantomime). Be polite, even when you think the Chinese are not. Understand that when people use the phrase, East meets West, they really *are* referring to an entirely different way of understanding and experiencing the world. Learn the customs of the people. Recognize that you are a guest in the country and be thankful the officials have allowed you in! Try to take off your Western lenses and learn to see the world the way the Chinese do.

Relative to the Western world, China has remained somewhat removed. Chinese culture is conservative by nature, and it can feel introverted, especially compared to open Western cultures. Likewise, Shanghai has some of the characteristics of all big cities and can feel cold and distant to foreigners who arrive starry-eyed and naive. Not unlike your introverted friend or relative, once the Chinese know you and trust you, they will respond on the same human level as all people—with warmth (or not).

In Shanghai, my teenage daughter experienced the kindness of an old woman who offered to share an umbrella in a rainstorm. She has had Chinese men on the subway offer her their seat. Chinese citizens have helped direct my family when we were lost, and they've translated for us when we could not understand what the heck was happening. Our driver, Xiao Lin, was a lifesaver to my family, in more ways than one—quite literally, he once saved my husband's life during an attack of anaphylaxis. Chinese merchants, who love a regular customer, often picked out a better piece of fruit for my basket, rounded down my price, or showed me a quicker way to pay with WeChat. Complete strangers on the metro have regaled me with the universal language of baby photos, even without a more traditional dialogue.

In moments when I was frustrated by something in Shanghai or chastened by a local on the street for my foreign ways, I reminded myself of these deeply human interactions— all the times I've shared a joke without sharing the language. I cannot guarantee that you will never ask yourself, "What have I done by coming here?" But I can guarantee that if you choose adventure, you will find one in Shanghai.

MAP OF CHINA

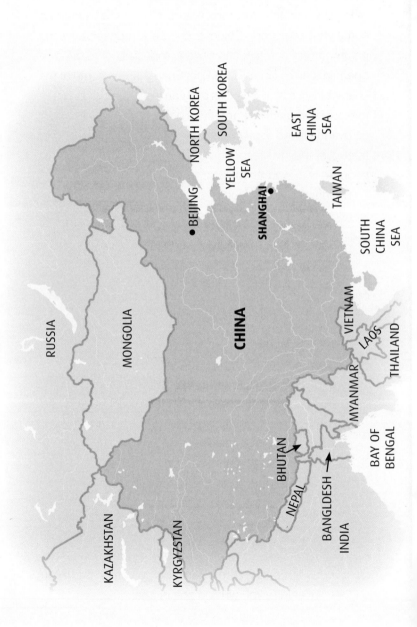

FIRST
IMPRESSIONS

If you live in a Chinese city, there's one feeling you never shake off: What a lot of people there are!

— Yu Hua, *China in Ten Words*

CITY OF CONTRASTS

Nearly everyone who experiences Shanghai for the very first time will say that the city feels irreconcilable. While China is generally a country of great contrast, in Shanghai, the juxtapositions feel more conspicuous. On the one hand, the city is decidedly futuristic—chock-full of modern skyscrapers, Michelin star restaurants, illuminated highways, bullet trains, and billionaires. On the other hand, many Shanghai streets are still packed with riders of rickshaws or rickety bicycle carts, hauling towers of cardboard and selling cabbages or flowers. Mobile payment technology is endemic, yet the sidewalks are still hand swept with brooms made of bamboo leaves.

Substantially more people live in Shanghai than in New York, or Paris, or Singapore, so the Chinese seem to physically occupy more of the surrounding space. No one, for example, steps aside when the sidewalk narrows. Certainly, your first impression might be of busy people, bustling streets, and rare or fleeting eye contact. Depending on your location in the city, you may experience conspicuous stares or be utterly ignored. I'm a naturally jovial person, and it took me a long time to acclimate to China, which can be a very serious place indeed. I've taken crowd photos on the Bund and on East Nanjing Road in which no one makes eye contact with anyone else. Expats can find themselves feeling very alone in the midst of these very big crowds.

Ancient and postmodern architecture coexist happily in Shanghai.

I remember one day in People's Square, a Chinese woman passed by me with her skirt hitched up into the top of her underwear, exposing her entire backside. I hurried over to her (with my too wide American smile) and reached out to help fix her skirt. She leapt away from me as if I were wielding a machete. When she realized my intent, she thanked me, but she also looked stunned that a stranger—and a foreigner at that—would make such a gesture. In my ignorance of Chinese culture, perhaps I did not realize that the concept of face would compel many Chinese to simply avoid calling attention to the situation.

My daughters like to point out that Westerners encounter a completely different sense of personal space in China. On the one hand, there is very little of it, which people accept. On the other, intruding into those small spaces in unfamiliar

Personal space takes on a new meaning in Shanghai where crowds can become overwhelming at times.

ways (especially if you are a stranger) can send shock waves through the recipient. Expats in Shanghai can behave in the same way. Since there are very few Westerners, you might expect a knowing nod every now and then. But I sometimes think expats who *live* in Shanghai show they *belong* in Shanghai by also avoiding eye contact with strangers. Some of this may just be a function of big city life. Traveling in China's rural provinces often revealed a completely different sense of space. People smiled more.

Although China is loath to admit it (and it is still a rare sight) homelessness does occur in Shanghai. Social division accounts for much of the incongruity of the city. The same class distinctions on display in San Francisco, Paris, or Bangkok are apparent in Shanghai too. Extreme wealth and dire poverty co-exist, even inside Communist China. In places

Crowds swarm through the Yu Garden Bazaar during the holiday season.

frequented by foreigners, beggars are more common than in Chinese residential areas. Sometimes disabled children or adults are placed conspicuously on sidewalks by family members. Immigration from rural provinces contributes further to the sense that Shanghai is a city where a traditional culture abuts the postmodern. So much of China's poverty is still agriculturally based and subsists in the rural provinces making up the bulk of China's Western geography. While social mobility has increased exponentially in recent years, it does not touch everyone. Social class, as well as a compelling sense of limited opportunity, drives much of the competition in current Chinese society.

While the well-heeled shuttle their children to school in BMWs, Chinese workers who pick up the daily litter (left behind in a culture that does not spurn littering) wear brightly colored uniforms that mark their place in the world like spike tape on a theater stage. Shanghai has an entire municipal workforce dedicated to a sole performance—hand sweeping

A more laid-back, charming side of the city lies behind all that jazz that foreigners usually see.

its sidewalks. The blue uniforms these employees wear serve very much as social markers. Those who sweep the streets for a living in Shanghai are likely to perform that singular job for a very long time. Crossing paths daily with these laborers are swanky corporate CEOs, managers of high-tech firms, and the many young Shanghainese who now fill offices in the city's high-rise buildings. Income inequality visits its vagaries on communist and capitalist alike.

There are days, visually, when Shanghai streets can feel like the streets of Paris, until you catch a glance at the people milling around. The city sometimes feels at odds with itself, and I have had wildly contrasting emotional experiences living there: entrapment and freedom, simplicity and complexity,

A man unloads his cabbages to prepare for business.

sublime and profane, and finally, the artful and the ordinary, which every city boasts. Decide for yourself what is what. Contrast—that is life in Shanghai.

FIRST NIGHT IN SHANGHAI

In the summer of 2014, much to our trepidation and surprise, my family of four was boarding a plane in Seattle, destined for Shanghai, China. Surely, we had some inkling that we were flying headlong into the greatest culture shock of our lives—but that didn't protect us from the effects. My husband and I had visited Shanghai for a scant three days the previous autumn for his executive interview at a large international school.

Like many potential executive hires in Shanghai, we were billeted in a fancy five-star hotel, chauffeured around by drivers, wined and dined at expensive restaurants, and shown townhouses and apartments in expat compounds. We were awed by the dazzling nighttime skyline of Pudong, and thrilled by the lights of its soaring towers, their tops obscured by low autumn clouds. In the whirlwind of the recruitment trip, everything felt like an adventure, but the brevity of the visit offered little time for us to imagine what family life in Shanghai would realistically entail.

At least we had some idea of what to expect. Our two teenage daughters, ages 13 and 16 at the time, did not. When my husband accepted the position, our transition, difficult as it was, was made easier with the knowledge that our daughters had a guaranteed spot in his school, where I would also teach English. For him, the move was a logical next step in a long educational career; for the girls and I, more like a leap of faith. I wish I could report that our adventure was an unflagging success at every turn, but that would be untrue. My youngest daughter told me later she had once considered running away! The People's Republic of China can be a challenging country for naive foreigners, doubly so for those with older children in tow.

I can still vividly recall that first sweltering July evening when we arrived in Shanghai. We were shuttled from the airport to a townhouse furnished with the bare essentials. We looked around our new home, hoisted our three bags of luggage apiece up an endless staircase, and breathed a sigh of exhaustion. Our daughters quickly retreated to their new bedrooms while my husband and I sat on the sofa somewhat stunned by our situation. Our personal belongings wouldn't arrive for another three months—the shipments of all foreigners will fall victim to the procedural red tape otherwise known as Chinese customs.

A heartbreaking basket of moldy dragon fruit and rotten nashi pears, along with a note that said "Welcome," sat front and center on the kitchen table. The air conditioning was broken. The appliances bore labels with indecipherable Chinese characters. We were without cell phone service or Internet access. We each had one blanket and one pillow, hard beds, and no idea where to buy food or how to stock the refrigerator. I'm not exaggerating when I say we wondered on that first night whether we'd made a terrible mistake.

Shortly after our arrival in Shanghai, one colleague, an international educator who had lived all over the world before moving to Shanghai, asked how we were faring with our transition. "Wow," was my one-word reply. He gave me a knowing smile. "China is one of the most challenging places I've ever lived. It's culturally so *different* from any place I've experienced," he said. It was not an understatement.

Foreigners, especially Westerners—with families or

without—frequently arrive in Shanghai unprepared to navigate China's restrictive Internet policies, impenetrable bureaucracy, and a transactional culture in which the concept of face determines how much or how little is communicated at any given moment. For all the talk of China's budding openness of the past thirty years, the PRC remains one of the most regulated and authoritarian countries in the world. To top things off, Mandarin, with its 50,000 unique characters and four tonal inflections, is ranked as one of the world's most difficult languages to learn.

One result of culture shock is that foreigners can become too easily ensconced in an "expat bubble," sidestepping the general hubbub and occasional chaos of life in Shanghai altogether. Avoid that path at all costs! Once you peek underneath the hood and beyond the surface frustrations, you'll find life in Shanghai offers a rich window into a five-thousand-year-old culture that is trying to shape the future at full throttle. Vexing as it sometimes feels, Shanghai is also a thrilling cosmopolitan city that offers a wealth of authentic cultural experiences for families and singletons alike.

About a month before we boarded that plane for Shanghai, a colleague in the States invited us to dinner to meet an old friend of hers—Shanghai's outgoing Consulate General, Robert Griffiths. The dinner provided us a rare opportunity to ask questions about life in the city, and our naivete must have seemed a bit humorous to him at the time. Every now and then, he tempered our impractical expectations with subtle hints of what kind of culture shock we should expect. Among his many comments now etched in my memory is one that still stands out: "Your thirteen-year-old is blonde?" he asked. "Oh, *she* will be an object of curiosity." We soon learned exactly what he meant.

The Chinese frequently make requests to take photographs with Westerners, who are still a relative novelty in present-day Shanghai.

WELCOME TO THE ZOO

"I feel like a zoo animal!"

Needless to say, our towheaded youngest daughter took some time to grow accustomed to the blatant stares, frequent requests to pose for photos with complete strangers, and once, while traveling in rural Yangshuo, multiple requests for her autograph. Those three incisive words we'd heard a few months earlier, "object of curiosity," weren't enough to fully prepare us for the disconcerting feeling that comes from such attention, even in a city as cosmopolitan as Shanghai. Indeed, staring is one of the more notable Chinese habits that turns off many foreigners.

Unlike Vietnam or Thailand, which have aggressively sought tourism and have had regular interactions with foreign travelers for many years, China still experiences the consequences of the Communist retreat after the Cultural Revolution. A surprising number of Chinese citizens have never seen a foreigner. Even in Shanghai—rebel city, Pearl of the Orient, trendy beacon of postmodernism—the foreign community remains enough of a novelty in some areas that you will find yourself stretched in remarkable ways. If you are of Caucasian or African descent, in particular, expect to be the object of intense scrutiny at times. Foreigners of Asian ancestry can expect the shock to begin once they start speaking English or Korean (or whatever their native language might be).

The question to ask isn't whether or not staring is rude in Chinese culture; there is no clear-cut answer to the question. Faces of Caucasian and African ancestry are still unusual for many Chinese, and the first time a Chinese person sees those faces, curiosity prevails. Unlike Western cultures, which attach a stigma of rudeness or malice to staring, Chinese culture sees through a different lens. By Western standards, such behavior is considered insensitive. It's imperative not to apply Western standards to everything in Shanghai. People in China also will stare at anything that seems interesting on the street, including public arguments, which often attract large crowds of onlookers. Allowing a Western lens to guide assumptions about social situations in China only leads to confusion. Enjoy your newfound rock star status for the cultural experience it is, instead of choosing to feel like an outsider.

During that first year, our daughters were stopped on the street to handle photo requests so often that after a while we barely registered the occurrence. Once, on the Bund, a young couple asked to pose individually with each of the girls, and a minute later another couple asked to pose with my daughters sandwiched between them. My kids have posed for photos while shopping for clothing, eating dinner, and strolling down the sidewalk. People in China will often take surreptitious photos of foreigners as well (and foreigners in China should take heed when they, too, take surreptitious photos of the Chinese). Don't be surprised to see cell phones pointed in your direction. For a young honeymooning couple from another province, a photo of you is the evidence they will show to their families that proves they experienced the worldly sophistication and openness of Shanghai.

The best approach to Chinese staring is humor. I've had young children stop and laugh when they see me, occasionally making circles over their eyes with their thumb and index finger (indicating a round eye). On the Bund and East Nanjing Road, which are popular tourist destinations for Chinese nationals, teachers frequently task groups of visiting school children with finding a foreigner with whom to practice their English. After the first two or three words, typically, "Where are you from," your conversation will likely end. Be generous. Pose for photos with school groups and make a V sign with your fingers for Victory (or peace)—it's a gesture commonly made by young people in China. Another good response is to ask kids to practice counting in English. Demonstrate by showing them that you can count in Mandarin. In short, the best way to react to all this new attention is to offer the universal symbol of friendship: smile and say, "Ni hao!"

THE ASIAN SQUAT

One of the most surprising culture-shock experiences for many Western visitors to China is the prevalence of public squat toilets, many of which lack stall walls and completely eschew privacy. Perhaps it's become less shocking in

the past few years as many of the most popular tourist destinations in the West have now installed squat toilets to accommodate the thousands of Chinese visitors who have been breaking their toilet seats by standing on them to squat. One summer, on a vacation at a National Park back in the U.S., my culturally aware daughter emerged from the public bathrooms and exclaimed, "Mom! There are squatty potties in here!" Yes, indeed, there certainly were.

Squat toilets are still the most common type of public restroom facility you will find in China, even in Shanghai. When you do find a Western-style toilet in Shanghai—in airports, restaurants, and hotels, it's often accompanied by hilarious instructions, or the international prohibition sign—a stick-man figure demonstrating how *not* to use the toilet seat (sit on it, don't *stand* on it). Finding footprints on Western-style toilet seats is common in China, and laugh as we may in the West, if you're Chinese, resting your naked rear on the same spot where other naked rears have perched is unfathomable.

There's a lot of discussion from purported experts who say that Asian squatting is the more *advantageous* toileting position. The Asian squat (a commonly used phrase), is not just a common position for relieving oneself in the bathroom. It is *the* common resting position found throughout Asia (and despite the misnomer, other parts of the world as well). People in China who are resting, hanging out, or helping young children, often do so in the squatting position. In a proper Asian squat the butt is almost to the ground, heels are flat, and legs are not too far apart. You'll know your legs are too far apart in a Shanghai public restroom because you won't be able to keep your feet on the narrow non-slip part of the porcelain toilet bowl. After practicing, and taking measure of my own vestigial hamstring flexibility, I eventually found myself exhibiting pride over my Asian squat. You might want to practice before you arrive.

The second aspect of Chinese bathroom culture that surprises many Westerners is the lack of toilet paper in public restrooms. Plan to bring it with you everywhere in China. This advice is offered in spite of the fact that the Chinese government, being no stranger to revolution, found a new one to get behind in 2015: The Toilet Revolution. As much as US$300 billion has been allocated in a Herculean effort to improve China's public facilities. The government recognizes what many already know: the toilet is the single most powerful symbol of social inequality in the world. As a result, it is now possible to *occasionally* find toilet paper in *some* restrooms. When you do find it, you may also see Chinglish signs telling you to *cherish* it. Unfortunately, "the revolution" has not always included improvements to old plumbing lines, which generally cannot accept the manifested toilet paper. As a result, most toilet paper in China must be discarded into waste baskets instead of flushed.

Not to belabor the point, but toilet paper is a more serious issue in China than many foreigners expect. The Communist impulse to control the allocation of resources applies even to this plebeian material. Though technological advances in China have not yet enabled the flushing of toilet paper, they have made it possible to monitor whether people are using *too much* of this valuable resource. A project that started in the Beijing Temple of Heaven restrooms in 2017 finally advanced to a few of Shanghai's public toilets by 2018. In order to access toilet paper in some heavily used public facilities, you will have to submit to facial recognition scanning. The scanner monitors a user's share of toilet paper. After allowing a facial scan, the machine will dispense 80 centimeters of toilet paper for your personal use. You will be required to wait nearly 10 minutes before you may scan your face for a second round, so to speak. In short, it's still wise to bring your own.

Toilet Revolution notwithstanding, don't be surprised to find men in the city relieving themselves in public gardens, next to trees, and in marginally discreet corners. Even women occasionally relieve themselves in gardens or parks when facilities are not convenient, and I once witnessed a young boy in the airplane aisle right next to me, relieving himself into a bottle held by his mother. The lack of cultural discomfort with this practice is no surprise given the absence of privacy in public bathrooms. Likewise, young children with slit bottomed pants may also be shuffled off to a bush. In lieu of diapers, many Chinese children, particularly in the outer suburbs, wear pants with a wide vertical slit across their bottoms. The bare bottom approach lets in the air and lets out the necessities. Diapers are more popular in Shanghai than in other areas of China, but open-air potty training is still a widespread practice.

THE SOUND AND THE FURY

With a population density of 2,059 people per square kilometer, it's not an understatement to say that Shanghai is crowded. Yet many Shanghai friends have told me the first thing they noticed when they arrived wasn't the number of people as much as the noise. For one thing, the city is constantly under construction. Old neighborhoods are razed and new buildings and roads seem to pop up overnight. The sound of jackhammers, power tools, and construction equipment accounts for a good bit of the city's noise pollution. The Shanghai Municipal Authority receives nearly as many annual complaints about noise as from other forms of environmental pollution, and in 2013, it finally drafted legislation to deal with the excessive noise problems during evening hours.

Construction isn't the only phenomenon accounting for what might be an overwhelming experience for foreigners unaccustomed to a Chinese city of this size. Many vendors hawk their wares by driving cars or rickshaws armed with mobile loudspeakers. Others, especially collectors of refuse and recycling, ride through the streets ringing loud bells to announce their presence. Although most scooter engines in Shanghai are electric, their horns are a constant nuisance. Traffic congestion is ubiquitous, and the added din of passing trucks and car horns is significant. Just in case all that is not enough, the city's vehicular street cleaners blare loud music (*It's a Small World* is a widespread, classic choice) as they hose and scrub down the streets.

The noise isn't only outside. Loud Chinese pop music blasts from loudspeakers inside many Chinese malls and large grocery stores. I have a clear memory of watching my oldest daughter, who is sensitive to loud noises, ride a conveyor belt to the second floor of Carrefour, a Western style grocery chain, looking completely shell-shocked by the decibel levels inside the store. Nor can evenings be counted on for silence. From 7:00 to 9:00 p.m. each evening, spring through autumn, small plazas, parks and sidewalks are used for dancing, accompanied by loud traditional Chinese music blaring over speakers. Parks and vacant entry ways are also used for musical activities during the day. Be prepared: it's rarely quiet in Shanghai.

Exercise and dancing in public parks happen at all hours of the day.

AIR QUALITY

When we told friends and family we were moving to China, the first question they asked was, "What about the air pollution?" The issue concerned us. At that time, dire images of China's air apocalypse events occupied much of the international news cycle. Generally speaking, however, weather and geography have benefited Shanghai, which sits on an alluvial plain next to the ocean, unlike Beijing, which is hemmed in by mountains. In 2008, the U.S embassy in Beijing began measuring local air quality with its own equipment as a way of advising American residents about the safety of outdoor activity. By 2012, the Shanghai consulate was releasing its own readings. Before long, the Chinese public became acutely aware of significant disparities between China's official AQI readings and those of the U.S., spurring accusations by China against the U.S. of illegal "interference" in Chinese affairs. Shortly afterward, access to cell phone apps and websites that reported U.S. air quality data were blocked, requiring use of a VPN.

Poor air quality contributed to many days of culture shock as we adjusted to life in Shanghai. After an introductory autumn of seriously hazy days, January hit like a sledgehammer. I still recall the pit in our stomachs when we saw multiple days of U.S. consulate readings over 300 AQI, followed by a few more days above 400 (hazardous). Many international schools, which also monitor local air quality for their communities, have put into place a variety of measures to keep indoor air quality healthy for students. General recommendations are to keep children indoors when the AQI readings are above 200. Air filters are a necessity in Shanghai and can be purchased in any of Shanghai's larger box stores. Most expats keep filters running in bedrooms and main living areas, and most businesses and schools operate with built-in air-filtering systems to keep indoor air quality at healthy levels.

In 2013, recognizing that frustration with air quality had reached unsustainable levels, the Chinese government pushed local municipalities to get serious about improving air quality. In Shanghai, municipal authorities unveiled a proposal known as The Shanghai Clean Air Action Plan, which put into place a goal of reducing PM 2.5 density by 20 percent in the year 2017. In the years since 2014, U.S. State Department data show some improvement in Shanghai's air quality. Anecdotal evidence, my own included, suggests the same. By early 2018, nearly everyone I know who has lived in China for more than three or four years agrees that the number and severity of bad air quality days has improved significantly.

While Shanghai's air quality has improved dramatically since 2014, expats will still contend with occasional "bad air" days.

WHAT IS AQI?

Air Quality indexes vary throughout the world. In the U.S. and China, the Air Quality Index (AQI) measures six criteria of air pollutants: fine and coarse particulate matter, sulfur dioxide, carbon monoxide, nitrogen dioxide, and ozone, often referred as PM2.5 (small particulate matter). Both indexes then convert the measured pollutant concentrations in a city's air to a scale of 0 to 500, with readings of 300+ defined as hazardous, however the conversions measured by China's Ministry of Environmental Protection vary slightly from U.S. conversions. By 2017, AQI readings released on mainland China have became more closely matched to international readings, but access to foreign readings is still limited. Expats can gain access to the U.S. Consulate AQI readings through a number of phone Apps that should be downloaded before arrival in China. In addition, the U.S. State Department maintains a website that monitors air quality for several Chinese cities, including Shanghai, at: http://www.stateair.net/web/post/1/4.html.

The stacked highways of Shanghai's East/West Yan'an Elevated are an engineering marvel.

LIFE ELEVATED

One appreciable irony about Shanghai is that despite being a sea level, alluvial city, (and sometimes it is actually *below* sea level, since much of the city has been sinking under its own weight), Shanghai is, at the same time, a city *elevated*. Shanghai is home to two of the world's eleven tallest buildings, and its skyscrapers place it at number five on the list of tallest cities in the world (based on the number of buildings over 150 meters tall). Shanghai also has an immense number of *generally* tall buildings—at this writing, 1,400 are over 100 meters tall, second only to Hong Kong's 2,700. In Shanghai, you will spend a lot of time looking down from high places. Most apartment complexes are lofty, and if you reside downtown, you likely will be living high.

A glance down from the airplane when flying into Pudong International Airport in the daytime will reveal a stark line that looks like a crease in the ocean or a sudden rift from deep blue to cowhide brown—like the hem of an unseen giant's shirt meeting the elephantine top of his blue jeans. This demarcation is where the alluvial sediment from the Yangtze River meets the deep blue ocean. When you look up, you'll often see buildings poking through a wave in the air that's typically a matching brown hue.

Once on the ground, you won't be finished dealing with elevation in Shanghai. The main east-west dividing highway that travels from the Huangpu River across Puxi is the aptly named Yan'an Elevated, built directly above Yan'an road. The highway bisects Shanghai's Puxi section, running from suburban Minhang to the Huangpu River where it takes the form of the Yan'an River Tunnel.

The Elevated, as it's commonly known, is one of many raised expressways in Shanghai that wrap around and over one another in a colossal game of concrete Twister. Driving through the city, you'll be struck by elevated sections of freeway stacked like pancakes–freeways on top of freeways, double, triple, and quadruple-decker roads captured in famous photos, memorable images from above. The whole of the city now requires elevated driving as well as elevated living. In Pudong, with its newer, wider, sprawling mass of raised highways, elevated footbridges provide safe havens for pedestrians. The enormous, circular Lujiazui Pedestrian Bridge, reminiscent of the floating promenades in *The Jetsons*, meanders above crowds, among shopping malls, restaurants, tourist attractions, and skyscrapers.

A humble bicycle turned into a mobile flower market.

THE MOST DANGEROUS GAME

One of the first sights capturing the attention of new arrivals, especially Westerners, in Shanghai is the presence of innumerable rickshaws, bicycles, tuk tuks, and scooters of every imaginable variety. Shanghai may be a 21st century city, but evidence of its history can be found everywhere. Enjoy the commotion. The riders will amaze you as they whizz by with their precariously balanced cargo—massive towers of cardboard, sprays of flowers, fish tanks, bamboo, plastic bottles, car engines, and carts filled with trinkets. Often, you'll see passengers riding atop huge piles of cargo.

Motorized rickshaws and rusty, forlorn bicycles weave precipitously between buses, cars, and people. Modernization has begat a startling number of motorized electric scooters which add to the congestion. According to China's Ministry of Industry and Information Technology, there are as many as 200 million electric bikes registered in China, with 30 million

A bicycle cart laden with precariously balanced cargo.

Chairs pulled along a busy street on a rickshaw cart.

more added to the roads every year. Bi-pedals in any form are still workhorses in this modern city.

Also noticeable is the apparent lack of enforceable laws regarding a safe number of passengers on rickshaws and scooters. Helmet laws are nonexistent in China. Motorized scooters overflow not just with cargo, but with people—adults, children, pets, and occasionally babies are often riding in multiples. Standing or sitting, all hang on for dear life. Even the sidewalks are hazardous, since scooters and motorbikes regularly drive on them to beat the traffic.

Depending where you live and how adventurous you are, you will almost certainly enjoy having a bicycle or a scooter. Be forewarned. A shiny new bike is likely to be stolen in short order. When we first arrived, my husband was thrilled by his expensive, bright red bike, which he rode for only three days before someone lifted the bike off the streets with its chain and lock intact, and hauled it away while he picked up his take-out order at a nearby restaurant.

Most local RT Marts (a generic Chinese Walmart) will sell cheap Chinese bikes that are unlikely to attract criminal attention. Dingy and dinged-up bikes are always the better choice. If you live in the Shanghai suburbs, you'll use bicycles for everything: grocery shopping, visiting friends, riding to work and to restaurants. There was (and still is) a fair amount of intoxicated bike riding in Shanghai, and that goes for expats as well as locals. However, if you live downtown with easy metro access and close to a grocery store or wet market, a bicycle will be less of a necessity.

Expatriates learn fairly quickly to accept their fate when it comes to riding bicycles and scooters. In contrast to Westerners, Chinese bicycle riding is not about fancy hardware and spandex. China is about functionality, and many expats follow the local example, welcoming the risk that comes with the freedom of having their own transport. Riding home on bicycles one night with my two teenage daughters, my youngest casually observed, "This is the most dangerous thing we do in China." She was right. We were zooming along without lights or helmets, on dark streets, dodging scooters (many without headlights) that blasted like bullets out of the bad-air fog. I can't claim the experience as an optimal moment of responsible parenting, but the ride certainly was an adventure. I like to believe we were practicing cultural competence.

Put in historical context, the number of bicyclists cruising the streets of Shanghai today is relatively low. In the decades preceding the 1990s, the bicycle or rickshaw (or some variation of bipedal transportation) was so primary to the way residents moved through cities that China earned the nickname "The Bicycle Kingdom," a play on China's historical moniker, "The Middle Kingdom." Unheard of in those years, the motor vehicle congestion clogging highways today now accounts for a fair amount of China's air pollution.

Bicycles form an integral part of life in Shanghai.

As cars became more popular, and affluence more prevalent, reliance on bicycle transportation began to plummet in the late 1990s. According to China's transportation commission, bicycles accounted for almost 63 per cent of all journeys in the 1980s but only 17.8 per cent by 2014. But in 2015, bike-sharing programs emerged in Shanghai, enabled by mobile pay phone apps like WeChat and Alipay, and bicycles are once again in plentiful supply downtown. Rows of orange and yellow shared bikes park on (and block) sidewalks throughout the city.

Driving in Shanghai presents serious challenges for expats, although I do know of a few folks who braved the Chinese driving test, which they claim has very little to do with practical driving knowledge. In 2016, The World Health Organization in China estimated that nearly 260,000 traffic fatalities occurred in China.

BIKE GRAVEYARDS

In 2017, Shanghai had over 1.5 million undocked bike share bicycles, often cluttering passageways and blocking driveways, since residents could simply drop off borrowed bikes anyplace they pleased. What started as a good idea ended in disaster. Rampant private speculation produced more than 60 bike sharing startup companies, many of which overproduced bikes and then quickly declared bankruptcy. Soon vacant lots and landfills across Shanghai turned into bicycle graveyards, brimming with broken and discarded bikes. Type "China's bike graveyards" into your search engine for an interesting glimpse into the photographic art created by catastrophic bicycle waste.

BAMBOO

In Shanghai, as in much of China, bamboo is a crucial artifact of daily life. The most traditional example of the continuing importance of bamboo in Shanghai is the copious bamboo scaffolding that fronts many buildings. Bamboo scaffolding is still widely in use for Chinese construction projects, although the legal safety limit on such structures is now six stories. The scaffolding is often held together, alarmingly, by pieces of hand tied wire. A short walk around the city reveals many other common shapes and forms of bamboo: brooms with bamboo shafts and bristles of bamboo leaves, pole saws, hanging rods, fences, platforms, ladders, pipes, flutes, floors, blinds, steamer baskets, floor mats, gardens, and, of course, bamboo shoots cooked and eaten!

The Chinese place a high value on many plants for their medicinal, aesthetic, and culinary properties, and the bamboo plant holds a special place of distinction in Chinese culture. Because it is tough and it grows upright, it is symbolic of a strong spine. Bamboo is also featured in ancient Chinese stories and poems and is a famed subject of art and calligraphy. If you've ever grown bamboo varieties in a humid climate, you'll know the plant exhibits a sense of place (and a

Bamboo scaffolding is still used for construction in Shanghai.

commitment to proliferation) that defies constraint. Perhaps most notable, bamboo has an associative link to China's chosen diplomatic gift to the world: Pandas. The ubiquity of bamboo is one of the truly delightful sights in this modern city.

EMBRACE YOUR INNER LAOWAI

Laowai, one of a couple Chinese words for foreigner, is one of the most common words expats will hear in Shanghai. Although it originally had a pejorative connotation to it, it has now transformed into a fairly neutral term out of common use. Westerners in the expat community commonly refer to one

Bamboo poles lay piled on a Shanghai sidewalk.

another as *laowai*, as in, "You only see laowai populating that restaurant." Almost every aspect of life in China will remind you that you are *laowai*, from stares and catcalls on the street, to the daily struggles with language or those ever-present photo requests. Rather than taking offense, relax and enjoy your unique position, which, if you're of African descent or if you're a blue-eyed blonde, will give you celebrity ranking. Your standing as a *laowai* may be the very heart of the culture shock that comes with a move to Shanghai, but it can also be one of the best ways to experience the city.

CHAPTER 2

GEOGRAPHY AND HISTORY

What's past is prologue.

— William Shakespeare,
The Tempest

WHAT'S IN A NAME?

One of the first things that comes to mind when foreigners hear the word Shanghai is its popular usage as an English idiom. If a person has been "shanghaied," he's been carried away against his will. Kidnapped. Forced via artifice or ruse into an unexpected position or place. The usage originated during a time when laborers, drifters, drunks, and peasants were tricked into working on undermanned ships, a common practice in many port cities around the world between the sixteenth and nineteenth centuries. There is, in fact, a Chinese word for "shanghai' that also means "to ruin someone" (*shang hai*), but the term is unrelated to the city of Shanghai and uses a different Mandarin character (傷害). In Mandarin, the word Shanghai is actually a compound word: *shang*, meaning "above," and *hai*, meaning "sea." The name of the city quite literally means "upon-the-sea," or "above the sea," which is apropos if you happen to be looking down from the top of a Pudong skyscraper.

The name is an obvious reference to Shanghai's location at the far southeastern edge of the Yangtze River Delta. Scholars have identified the first appearance of a town named Shanghai (上海) in the 11th century Northern Song Dynasty and believe the word originated with the name of the nearby Shanghaipu, a tributary of the Wusong River, also known as Suzhou Creek, which today runs through the center of Shanghai's Puxi.

Historically speaking, Shanghai has been known by a number of other names as well. Two of the earliest, often used as abbreviations, reference the Warring States period (475-225 BC). The first, Shen, originated with the name of the Lord of the Chu State, Chunsen, who led an excavation that created the Huangpu River which currently bisects downtown Shanghai. A second nickname, also relating to the river, is Hu, after a tool used by Chinese fishermen. These days, it's not uncommon to hear expats refer to the city just as "The Hai," a nickname widely considered among Westerners to be a term of endearment.

BRING A RAINCOAT (AND A FAN)

Shanghai has a humid, subtropical climate similar to the southeastern states of the U.S. The weather is often brutally hot and humid in the summer and can be damp and chilly in the winter, with occasional light snowfall and sub-freezing temperatures. The city's four distinct seasons lean toward

Umbrellas are a necessity whether riding or walking in Shanghai.

rainy, and an umbrella will be necessary year long. Upwards of 45 inches of precipitation can fall each year, mostly during the rainy autumn. June and July rains are sometimes referred to as the "plum rain season" for obvious reasons: These months are plum season in the region.

Typhoon season follows the same pattern as much of Southeast Asia, lasting from early summer through late autumn. Spring is the best time to visit the city. April is dry and sunny with a greater chance of seeing blue sky days with spring breezes. An umbrella and a raincoat are essential tools for residents of Shanghai, and air conditioning is a must for surviving the summer, although small establishments, such as local groceries or noodle shops, will not have it. When the weather is hot, Chinese men frequently roll their shirts right up to their necks, something expats refer to as "the Shanghai bikini." On a day when the air quality is clear, the blue-sky and shady lanes can make a day in Shanghai as lovely as a day in Paris.

Air conditioning units get a workout during Shanghai's hot, humid summers.

BRIDGES TO EVERYWHERE

Centrally positioned along China's eastern coast, Shanghai enjoys an auspicious geographical location, equidistant between the megacities of Hong Kong and Beijing. Politically, Shanghai is an independently administered municipality—essentially its own province—reporting directly to the central government in Beijing. The city has been an important port for centuries and in 2010, surpassed the Port of Singapore to become the world's largest and busiest container port by shipping volume.

Shanghai is a sea-level city in every sense of the word. Its highest point, Dajianshan Peak, a mere 300 feet above sea level, isn't even part of the mainland but makes up most of a small offshore island. Not surprising, given Shanghai's coastal location, the city sits atop thousands of years of silt and clay sediment, deposits that form the base of an alluvial plain. Unfortunately, Shanghai is also located in the seismically active zone of the Pacific Ocean known as the Ring of Fire. Its silt base makes it a candidate for earthquake liquefaction should the city experience a severe magnitude earthquake. The fact that little to no bedrock undergirds Shanghai makes architectural walking tours about the engineering of its Pudong skyscrapers well worth your time and effort, but you might avoid thinking about it during a visit to the top of the city's many tall buildings.

To that point, much has been written in recent years about the fact that Shanghai is currently sinking at a surprising rate—it has dropped more than 2.5 meters in the last century, 1.8 meters of that subsidence (nearly 6 feet) having occurred since 1960. One report by the Shanghai Geological Research Institute revealed that the weight of the city's skyscrapers accounts for nearly 30 per cent of the city's downward movement. Add to that the effects of global warming—intense heavy downpours— and the makings of a large-scale disaster sit like a dark cloud, hovering in the background over Shanghai's bright future. Over four years in Shanghai, we twice encountered dramatic city flooding after heavy rains. One such flood in 2015 buried much of Hongqiao Airport's concrete runways under a virtual lake of water.

The city itself is surrounded by water on three sides and bordered by sprawling flood plains. The tumescent Yangtze River—whose muddy waters carry millions of tons of lithogenous sediment from inland—hugs Shanghai's northern and eastern edges, emptying into the East China Sea and ultimately into the Pacific Ocean. Hangzhou Bay lies to Shanghai's south. The Huangpu River, a major tributary of the Yangtze, bisects Shanghai, separating it into its halves—Puxi and Pudong. A bird's eye view of Shanghai reveals a large web of smaller tributaries, creeks, and canals winding their way between the ocean and the furthest reaches of Shanghai's suburbs. To navigate across and around its many water obstacles, the city has developed an extensive network of bridges and tunnels.

Three alluvial islands lie in the northeast estuaries of the Yangtze River—Chongming, Changxing, and Hengsha, all of which are administered by Shanghai. Of the three, Chongming is the largest, with an area of approximately 1,400 kilometers and a burgeoning population of three quarters of a million people. The island, China's third largest, is currently the site of a number of newly developed organic farms, and contains the Chongming Dongtan National Nature Reserve, a sizable wetland habitat for a wide variety of overwintering endangered species of waterfowl. (See Chapter 7 for details about visiting Dongtang reserve.) While most of Chongming

Island is administered under the municipality of Shanghai, the northern portion of the island is administered by neighboring Jiangsu Province. The island's economy is dedicated primarily to the maritime industries and agriculture. In addition to the nature reserve, the Chongming Confucian Temple is one of the oldest in the area, having been rebuilt during the Ming Dynasty. While Chongming Island currently feels as if it occupies the far outer reaches of Shanghai, plans are underway to extend the Shanghai Metro system to the island, turning it into another soon-to-be suburb.

Perhaps the most interesting feature of Chongming Island is the way it connects to Pudong—via the 25.5-kilometer Yangtze River Tunnel and Bridge, completed in 2009 at a cost of more than US$1.8 billion. Crossing the bridge by car is awe inspiring. Although it is an impressive feat of engineering, the bridge plays second fiddle to Shanghai's Donghai Bridge, one of the longest sea-crossing bridges in the world. More than 20 miles in length (32.5 kilometers), the Donghai connects Pudong with the Yangshan Deep Water Port in Zhejiang Province to the south.

Shanghai's second major river, the Huangpu, is the last major eastern tributary of the Yangtze. The most famous photos of this river are typically taken from the top of one of Shanghai's three famous skyscrapers—the Shanghai Tower,

The Yangtze River Tunnel and Bridge, viewed from above through Shanghai's haze, connects Shanghai to nearby Chongming Island.

the Jin Mao Tower, and the World Financial Center. From these vantage points, the Huangpu can be seen snaking in a half-circle loop around the jutting Lujiazui peninsula, home of the new Pudong financial district and Shanghai's most famous cityscape.

With the Huangpu dividing the city, Shanghai has become, by necessity, a metropolis of tunnels and bridges. Four major suspension bridges and one arch bridge cross the Huangpu River to convey daily travelers between the Puxi and Pudong sides of the city. The newer Nanpu Suspension Bridge mirrors the architecture of its sister bridge the Yangpu. Every evening, the Lupu Bridge, the world's first steel arch bridge and one of Shanghai's most prominent architectural sights, glows in spectacular greens, blues, yellows, and purples. The bridge is equipped with a 100-metre high observation platform that offers sightseers a spectacular view of the Huangpu and the Shanghai Expo Center, built in 2010. Underground, a complex series of auto tunnels connects the two halves of the city, along with a number of tunnels that accommodate Shanghai's many metro lines. And of course, don't miss the Bund Sightseeing Tunnel, which hosts a nightly psychedelic light show for the enjoyment of tourists.

PUXI AND PUDONG

Shanghai is a city divided quite neatly into halves, Puxi and Pudong, by the mighty Huangpu river. Expats spend a fair amount of time debating which side of the city is superior. Puxi is the elder statesman of the two and remains the cultural heart of Shanghai—home to The Shanghai Culture Center, the Shanghai Opera, Symphony, Theater, The National Museum, Jing'An Temple, Jade Buddha Temple, Fudan University and Shanghai Jiao Tong University, two of

The Nanpu Bridge serves as a primary connector between Puxi and Pudong.

China's most prestigious institutions of higher learning. Puxi also claims the famed pedestrian shopping areas, such as East Nanjing Road and Hua Hai Road, as well as the Bund and many of its best clubs, five-star restaurants, bars, ethnic restaurants and older Chinese neighborhoods, including The Concessions and most of the foreign consulates.

In the eyes of some, Puxi is considered the better place to experience true Chinese character, though the millions of Chinese who live and work in Pudong might beg to differ. Nevertheless, Puxi is old, and the city's history is centered there. Many sections of Puxi are made up of narrow lanes and *hutong*-like villages—small self-contained settlements tucked behind the street-side shops between blocks. Puxi is also home to most of Shanghai's remaining *shikumen*-style buildings, referred to by locals as lane houses. The Former French Concession is one of the best areas to see the *shikumen* as well as the city's remaining *longtangs*, long, narrow buildings similar in architectural style to the *hutongs* of Beijing. The roads are tree-lined, winding and narrow, but increasingly Shanghai city officials are razing Puxi's older villages and residential districts to make way for newer apartment towers and business complexes. Puxi contains most of the city's history, and for that reason, its proponents have a slight edge in their favor.

It seems impossible to imagine, if you're standing on the Bund at night gazing at Pudong's world famous skyline, but back in 1980, Pudong was mostly marshy, rural farmland with few buildings and no skyscrapers. One of the best places in the city to get a sense of Pudong's rapid visual transformation is on the ground floor of the Shanghai Tower where you can see the Pudong financial district gradually appear before your eyes in an exhibition that features 30 years of time-lapse photography. Pudong is now home to some of the world's tallest buildings, as well as art galleries, enormous shopping complexes and, of course, the financial district. The heart and soul of Pudong is the Shanghai Stock Exchange, located in

Puxi's narrow streets and older lanes make it a favorite spot to experience daily Chinese life.

the Shanghai Securities Exchange Building, the world's third largest stock exchange. As a result, many expat businesses are also located in Pudong. If you see a recognizable photo of Shanghai, it will be an image of the Pudong skyline, rather than the staid row of British built buildings on the western side of the Huangpu River. Shanghai has committed to developing the Pudong waterfront into as exciting an area as the Bund.

Many expats enjoy living in Pudong, especially in the Jinqiao area, because it replicates the spacious feel of Western-style suburbs. The streets are newer, wider and generally less congested, and the expat compounds play host to a variety of Western shopping choices and a number of large, Western international schools. If your goal is to replicate life outside of China, then Pudong might just fit the bill.

THE PAST AS PROLOGUE

If you've ever wondered whether history repeats itself, you have only to look back to Shanghai's place in the 19th century world to find your answer. Americans, who occasionally take an ahistorical approach to problems, tend to view their 21st century trade deficits with China as solely an economic problem. But the Chinese, who officially lay claim to a 5,000 year-old continuous history, see the issue of trade surpluses and deficits in a more historical context. A trade surplus with Great Britain in the early 1800s triggered China's two Opium Wars with Western alliances, leaving the Chinese dispossessed of influence in Shanghai for decades.

Compared to China as a whole, the history of the city of Shanghai is relatively modern. Prior to the Qing dynasty (1644–1911), Shanghai was a marshy, moderate-sized residential area with fishing, agriculture, and textiles shaping its economic core. The city's proximity to the Yangtze River and the East China Sea made it an excellent port location and by the late 1700s, Shanghai was firmly established as a center for the maritime trade in cotton cloth.

The arrival of Western imperialism in the early nineteenth century changed the face of the city forever. The British, Americans, and French set their sights on the city in a quest to expand international trade. At that time, the Chinese were producing goods—tea, silk and porcelain—that the West craved. Unfortunately for the imperialist Brits, China's appetite for Western goods did not equal the voracious consumer demand coming from the British Empire. To further exacerbate matters, China refused to open its market to British wares. Sound familiar? The result was a startling trade surplus for China and a corresponding deficit for the merchant companies of the Empire of Great Britain.

In an effort to maintain control of trade inside China, successive Qing emperors had for nearly a century tightly regulated the flow of goods and silver into China through the single, southern port of Canton (currently Guangzhou), creating a system of trade known as the Canton System. The powers of the British Empire, in the form of the East India Trading Company, searched for a way around these trade barriers in order to rebalance their enormous trade deficit. The East India Company, whose imperial tentacles were already deeply embedded in India, found its solution in Indian opium. In short order, the company, under the auspices of the British government, would soon become one of the world's largest drug cartels. The importation of opium allowed British merchants to bypass the Canton System as they swapped silver for Indian opium and used the opium as a bartering chip in China.

Tea leaves are left to dry in the sun on wood-framed screens.

The demand for opium in China swelled, creating an unfathomable addiction that many scholars argue was indirectly responsible for much of China's long history of economic misfortune. In 1842, after the British trade deficit was resolved, Chinese officials who worried about the effects of the opium trade attempted to halt the influx of drugs by confiscating large quantities of opium and shutting off the spigot of foreign trade through Canton. What followed was the beginning of a decades-long clash between East and West.

THE OPIUM WARS (1839–1860)

If the Opium Wars marked the beginning of wider China's modern historical period, then they also marked the beginning of Shanghai's transformation from an agricultural port city into a decadent and licentious Western-style city known as the "Paris of the East" or more pejoratively, "The Whore of the Orient."

In retaliation for China's confiscation of opium, the British government resorted to military action. The defeat of China's Qing Dynasty rulers put a temporary end to the opium dispute in what is known as the First Opium War. The defeat also forced the Qing rulers into the Treaty of Nanking (Nanjing), which granted Britain exemption from local rule, established a series of Chinese ports for foreign trade (including Shanghai), and surrendered Hong Kong to British authority.

The opium trade resumed and by the mid-1840s, the British and Americans, followed by the French in 1847, had divided Shanghai into local, independently governed settlements known as Concessions—the areas of the city China conceded at the end of the war. By the end of the century, Jews escaping persecution in Russia had formed their own community in Shanghai as well. Tours of Shanghai's Jewish settlements are still offered to foreign visitors today.

Tensions between China and the foreign Imperial Powers remained high for a decade, ultimately resulting in the Second Opium War, which broke out in 1856 during an attack by Anglo-French forces in Canton. The war lasted four years and ranged across coastal China from Hong Kong to Beijing, ending with a clash that still sits harshly with many Chinese people. After Chinese forces tortured and killed captive British military and civilian personnel, Western forces in Beijing retaliated by looting and burning the spectacular Qing Dynasty Yuanmingyuan Summer Palace (the Garden of Perfect Brightness). This cultural injury still burns hot in the hearts of contemporary Chinese, fanned further by China's patriotic education programs. For the next half-century, American and European powers would shape Shanghai into a thoroughly Western city.

China still refers to its defeat in the Opium Wars as the beginning of a "Century of Humiliation"—a good thing to keep in mind when interacting with the Chinese.

FEMALE PIRACY

The golden age for Chinese piracy along China's southern coastline extended from the 16th to the early 19th century. What initially began as merchant piracy (raiding merchant ships) evolved into rebel piracy followed by commoner piracy, when the outlaw seafaring life offered an opportunity for many people to escape poor job prospects. According to the International Institute for Asian Studies, "significant numbers of women" were involved in piracy in China, which distinguished this part of the world from Western countries where female pirates had to disguise themselves as men.

Piracy offered women an opportunity to break away from the constraints placed on them by Chinese society.

Piracy played such a big role in China's history that it's impossible to live in China without someone mentioning the fact that the most prosperous pirate in history was a 19th century Qing dynasty woman named Chin Shih. After a stint as a prostitute, Chin Shih married her pirate husband. When he died, she took over his role and built an empire in which she commanded an estimated 1,800 junks with between 70,000 and 80,000 pirates under her management. One of her notorious rules was that female captives should not be raped—under penalty of death, of course. She was a pirate after all.

THE CONCESSIONS

By the mid to late 1800s, the foreign concessions had become firmly established communities that portioned the city of Shanghai into culturally distinct areas. The British developed their enclave along what is now known as the Bund, eventually combining with the Americans and other European enclaves to form the Shanghai International Settlement. The British constructed buildings in their own image. The popular Romanesque and Neoclassical architecture of the time—originally grand banks and trading houses, now mostly hotels, restaurants, and financial buildings—is still one of the essential tourist attractions along the Bund. Building heights remain restricted in this area to preserve its historical integrity.

Likewise, the French settlement, constructed to the southwest of the international enclave, reflected the popular Western European architectural styles of the time. This area of the city housed a diverse European population, and

The European-style architecture of the Bund as viewed from Pudong.

many of the concession's spectacular homes were built by the well-established Jewish merchant families who resided in Shanghai in the early twentieth century. Each of these settlements was an autonomously governed region of the city with its own school systems, police forces, hospitals and clubs.

The shady tree-lined streets of the Former French Concession make it one of the most attractive areas of Shanghai.

Poverty was rife throughout China during this time, and many Chinese were relegated to living in a walled off section of Shanghai that is still referred to as the Old City. However, large numbers of Chinese residents also lived inside the concessions and the International Settlement and, in fact, they greatly outnumbered foreigners. These included many well-to-do Chinese families who ran businesses. The Chinese author Adeline Yen Mah, in her memoir, *Falling Leaves*, documents her aunt's success as a banker in Shanghai through the early stages of the Japanese occupation and later during the onset of the Communist Revolution. Like many wealthy Chinese families during this time, Mah's family escaped to Hong Kong.

Today, the Former French Concession remains an architectural hotspot and one of the most popular places to view Art Deco architecture from the 1920s and 1930s. The area is one of the most attractive residential and commercial parts of the city. In addition to its stunning architecture, myriad gardens, and European-style homes, another defining characteristic of the Former French Concession is its winding avenues and narrow roads which are lined with deciduous London plane trees, a relative of the majestic American sycamore. The trees provide a necessary shady respite during

THE CHINESE REVOLUTION OF 1911

Although foreigners continued to extract economic value from Shanghai into the early twentieth century, China was dealing with political discontent over its long history of imperial rule. The 1911 Chinese Revolution ended in the overthrow of the Qing dynasty. After 268 years of Qing emperors, China was declared a Republic, Nanjing was designated as its capital, and Dr Sun Yat-Sen was installed as the provisional president. However, the new government was unable to unify the country, leaving much of China controlled by factional warlords and vulnerable to foreign invasion and civil war in the mid-20th century when the Communist Party emerged victorious.

A Shanghai apartment building in the popular Art Deco style of the 1930s.

Shanghai's long, hot summers and add much of the charm to the shopping districts and residential neighborhoods.

THE WHORE OF THE ORIENT (1850s–1942)

The importation of opium had devastating effects on China. Some historians estimate the country's addiction rate at between 30-40 million, despite efforts of China's Qing Dynasty rulers to suppress the opium trade. By the early 20th century, the Chinese were growing enough domestic opium to supplant imports, and the Chinese government found itself opposed not by the British, but by Chinese farmers, who found opium cheap and easy to cultivate. The entire economy of China was now wedded to the taxes and income provided by opium production.

The port city of Shanghai became ground zero for the vice and corruption that rode in on the shirt tails of the opium trade. Prostitution was rampant and the French Concession became Shanghai's best-known red-light district. Brothels, casinos, jazz clubs and opium dens provided a haven for drug addicts, gunrunners and gangsters. The city was rife with corrupt police forces and crime. Western missionaries and members of the British parliament railed against the corruption that the opium trade, via British influence, had inflicted upon the city.

Despite its reputation for vice, however, Shanghai was also a significant center for art, business, architecture, theater, and finance. In 1917, The Great World, an entertainment arcade housing showrooms, casinos, vaudeville theaters, freak shows, Chinese opera, and Western music halls, was built on what is now Shanghai's famous Yan'an Road. After suffering a calamitous shelling incident during the war and falling into disrepair, the building was renovated and is now a popular tourist attraction for Chinese visitors to Shanghai. By the early 20th century, Shanghai had overcome many of the most profound historical and political obstacles on its way to becoming one of the leading financial centers in the world.

THE JAPANESE OCCUPATION (1942–1945)

World War II and the Japanese incursion into Shanghai in 1937 brought a conclusion to 80 years of economic dominance and social decadence, ending Shanghai's century-long tenure as a treaty port. After years of skirmishes between the two countries, a full-scale conflict, the Battle of Shanghai, raged over three months in the central city. At one point in the battle, the Republic of China Air Force, tremendously outnumbered by the Japanese Air Force, accidentally bombed the International Settlement as well as the Great World complex, killing and injuring thousands. Eventually, suffering from fatigue and outmatched by Japanese weaponry, the Chinese retreated from Shanghai, paving the way for the brutal Japanese march to capture China's then capital city, Nanking.

THE GREAT LEAP FORWARD AND FAMINE (1949–1963)

The year 1949 marks not only the ouster of the Japanese from Shanghai, but also the victory of the Communist Party over Chinese nationalists known as the Kuomintang, in a civil war that had been raging since the late 1920s. This period marks the official formation of The People's Republic of China. For ten years, the Communist Party oversaw China, although political factions and infighting continued

THE NANKING MASSACRE

The atrocities committed against the Chinese at the hands of the Japanese Imperial Army in Nanking are viewed by China as the equivalent of a holocaust. The events are not as widely understood in the West as the German Holocaust of World War II, but the Nanking Massacre carries similar historical weight for many Chinese. The Japanese army engaged in widespread looting, mass rape, and mass murder of Chinese civilians over a period of six weeks. Chinese historians have estimated that over 300,000 Chinese were murdered by Japanese soldiers while the army marched from Shanghai to Nanking and during its occupation of Nanking, China's former capital. (See Chapter 7 for information on taking a day trip to Nanjing to visit the Nanjing Memorial Museum, a moving testimony to the horrors of the Sino-Japanese war and the atrocities committed in that city.)

While the event is too comprehensive to cover in a guidebook, Iris Chang's landmark book, *The Rape of Nanking*, details the nature of the crimes committed during the Nanjing Massacre. Although the book has received some criticism from academics and historians (mostly for diving too loosely into the psychology of the Japanese army), it's worth reading for those interested in learning more about modern Chinese history and understanding more thoroughly the continuing rift in the Sino-Japanese relationship. The book, and the 2007 documentary *Nanking*, based on Chang's work and directed by Bill Guttentag, are the two most accessible contemporary depictions of the Nanking Massacre.

After communist revolutionaries liberated Shanghai from the Japanese in 1949, the city disappeared from international importance for nearly 40 years. The government of Mao Zedong is generally credited with putting an end to the widespread use of opium by meting out harsh punishments (the death penalty for thousands of drug dealers) and by forcing millions of Chinese into drug rehabilitation centers. Although the government is also credited with destroying most of the opium crop, some historians have suggested that the Communist government also grew opium to fund projects and raise money.

to plague the country, especially inside the city of Shanghai. By 1958, Mao Zedong had launched China's disastrous Great Leap Forward. While technically The Great Leap Forward refers primarily to the three-year period of brutal famine that occurred between 1958-1961, in which tens of millions of Chinese died, the failed farming and economic policies enacted in the preceding ten years by the Maoist government are largely blamed for the catastrophe.

In an effort to move China "forward," the Mao government curtailed the traditional agrarian practices of rural Chinese farmers, forcing some into new farming collectives and others into the mass production of steel. Private farms were deemed "illegal" and new, ineffectual models of farming were forced on farming collectives, resulting in low crop yields and dismal levels of food output. Worse, the steel generated by unskilled farm laborers was largely of low quality and unusable.

Despite plummeting grain production, the Party exported massive amounts of the existing grain yield that *was* produced, exacerbating the situation. Local officials, who feared reprisals for reporting low yields, often over-reported production or hid the fact of declining yields. When natural disaster in the form of floods and drought struck China, the ingredients of widespread famine were already in place. The entire economic project was one of Mao's greatest failures.

SHANGHAI DURING THE CULTURAL REVOLUTION (1966–1976)

Shanghai played a pivotal role in Chinese politics during this era. As a nerve center of political unrest, the city was chosen by Mao as the place to institute a "seizure of power by proletarian revolutionaries." This path led directly to the Cultural Revolution.

By 1966, scores of anti-authoritarian and socialist political factions, based mostly in labor and student organizations, had mobilized in Shanghai. Some factions, including elements inside the Red Guard, pledged loyalty to the Communist Party on the surface, yet resisted its efforts in practice, creating additional strife on the ground. Frustrations with the Mao government in Beijing were simmering along with rebellion against the bureaucratic Shanghai political class. Political upheaval was widespread throughout the city.

By August of 1966, an alliance of political organizers had formed the Headquarters of the Revolutionary Revolt of Shanghai Workers. Unrest continued. In January 1967, during what is now known as the January Storm, revolutionary groups ousted Shanghai's political leadership and formed a short-lived government called the Shanghai People's Commune, using as their template the radical Paris Commune. Eventually, Mao saw that these types of alliances, called "revolutionary committees," could form the basis for a wider form of government. The Shanghai Commune was disbanded, and the Revolutionary Committee of the Municipality of Shanghai was created as a way to reduce the political infighting in the city.

By this time the Cultural Revolution was in full swing, and Shanghai was at ground zero. The Red Guards, a student led paramilitary movement, formed independently of the Mao government, but Mao quickly realized that he could use their propaganda and their fervor to achieve his own political ends. Eventually, the Central Committee of the Communist Party called for the eradication of the "Four Olds," (traditional ways of thinking), to make way for progress. These concepts were the very building blocks of civil society: Culture, Custom (tradition), Habits and Ideas. What followed was the violent and wholesale destruction of Chinese cultural and historical artifacts, art, literature, and religious iconography in an attempt to purge all remnants of pre-communist China. A 10-year period of chaos and violence ensued.

RICHARD NIXON AND THE SHANGHAI COMMUNIQUÉ (1972)

By 1972, still in the grip of the Cultural Revolution, Shanghai was one of three cities to host the American president, Richard Nixon, during his venture to normalize relations between the two countries after a 25-year break in diplomacy. While in China, Nixon signed the Shanghai Communiqué, a diplomatic agreement that pledged cooperation between China and the U.S. in the interest of all nations and pushed to expand the two countries' cultural interaction. The trip is widely credited as the impetus for China's push toward economic reform and increased openness to the world. Within two decades, China would institute economic market reforms that included more openness toward foreign investment and turned China into the economic powerhouse we know today.

The contemporary Western observer tends to see China's focus on "harmony" and the current government's insistence on control as a dangerous Orwellian landscape. But this view often fails to consider the chaos of civil war, colonialism, and factional infighting that has shaped China's world and political views well into the late 20th century. The political and social upheaval of the Cultural Revolution, and the violence it fomented, exists in recent memory for the Chinese—many people are alive now who lived through its terrors. The Cultural Revolution, the history of Japanese aggression, and the devastation of colonial rule shape China's concern about political instability. The current government, authoritarian as it may be, has also overseen a period of relative openness and a mere three decades of stability, safety, and prosperity in contemporary China. It is a government, despite its flaws, that heeds the lessons of Chinese history: Economic prosperity is the key to political stability.

- Estimates of Shanghai's population in 2019 range between 24 and 25 million.
- As part of a government master plan, the city has set a maximum population limit of 25 million by 2035, a goal few experts even in China believe is attainable.
- Shanghai has the world's largest rapid transit system as measured by route length.
- The Shanghai Maglev train, which runs from Pudong International Airport, is the world's fastest high speed commercial electric train (maglev trains levitate over a magnetized track).
- As of 2017, Shanghai had the fifth largest stock exchange in the world with a market capitalization of nearly $4 trillion (USD).
- Shanghai has a professional baseball team called the Shanghai Golden Eagles.
- Shanghai secondary school students are famous for having the highest international test scores in the world in the subjects of reading, math, and science.

CULTURE AND NATIONAL PRIDE

In her book, *The Girl at the Baggage Claim*, the Chinese-American writer Gish Jen, who has spent over 30 years traveling back and forth between China and the U.S., has acknowledged the difficulty of identifying specific aspects of cultural thinking that truly clash between East and West: "What can we really say about culture when it's so hard to say what we even mean by the word "East," exactly, or for that matter, "West"; whatever they are, they have intermixed from time immemorial."

Jen's point is a fine one. Culture and culture shock sometimes take on an ineffable quality that makes them difficult to define. Chinese culture is inextricably intertwined with Western culture, via history, via the interchange of people and ideas, and now more than ever, via economics. The Chinese are acutely aware of this. But even in 2020, and

Many of Shanghai's long-time residents have lived through tremendous social changes.

despite the reemergence of Chinese mega cities, China is still, in many ways, a poor country. The epic sense of renewal, and the growing international regard that comes from China's emergence as a new world power, despite its challenges, is an important source of pride for the Chinese people. Chinese history is also a source of national pride. When new expats are able to show their Chinese acquaintances and colleagues that they've taken the time to learn about the country's past, an important step toward building relationships and acceptance naturally follows.

BETTY BARR AND GEORGE WANG

Among long term expat communities in Shanghai, George Wang and Betty Barr are well known. Betty, a British citizen, was born in Shanghai in 1933 to missionary parents. Her husband George, a native Shanghainese, was born in 1927. In their fascinating memoir, *Shanghai Boy*, *Shanghai Girl*, George and Betty chronicle their lives growing up during the 1940s in antithetical worlds inside the same city. Betty, like many expats of the time, lived within the International Settlement and her brother went to school with J.G. Ballard.

George, like many Chinese residents of the city in the 1920s, did not experience Shanghai as The Pearl of the Orient. His family, suffering from the extreme poverty that was common for Chinese citizens during that time, was forced to sell his younger sister as a child bride at the age of 8. Another sister died shortly after birth. George's father was tricked by the Japanese, "shipped secretly to Japan" and died shortly afterward in a labor camp.

In this interview, they talk about living through some of the most extraordinary times in world history.

SG: *How has Shanghai changed, not only in appearance but in character and attitude?*

George: The leadership of the country has changed, and the social system has changed. There are now no powerful gangsters such as there were when I was a child. For example, I recently saw a street cleaner arguing with a policeman. He would not have dared to do that before 1949.

SG: *You were in high school when the Communists finally defeated the Nationalist Kuomintang. What was the energy and feeling in Shanghai at that time?*

Betty: The key word for foreigners in Shanghai at that time was uncertainty. Many of my SAS classmates left during the year 1948-1949. The new Communist government immediately dealt with the severe inflation. Since then, the standard of living has risen immeasurably, but I think most Westerners do not realize how low the base was. China has always been short of food because it is short of cultivable land and fresh water. When I married George in 1984, food was still rationed. For my family, there was a strong feeling of uncertainty, both during the war—how long would it last? What would happen to us internees—and before 1949, rather than chaos.

George: Under the leadership of the Communist Party, the first priority in 1949 was to get rid of the underground (KMT) enemies. At the same time, they tried to control inflation so that the people could live happily. My sister became a different person almost overnight. You can read her story in our book, Between Two Worlds.

SG: What was it like growing up in this city in the 1940s?

Betty: My parents went to movie theaters and took me to concerts by the Shanghai Symphony Orchestra in Jessfield Park (Zhongshan Park). They both came to China because they wanted to help a country in need, especially with education. My father taught in Medhurst College, which is celebrating its 120th anniversary this year. My mother came with the International Y.W.C.A. and was involved in social work in Shanghai. My parents had many Chinese friends, perhaps because they were involved in education and social work rather than business. I am still in touch with the second generation of two of those families.

SG: You were in Shanghai during some of the Cultural Revolution. Was there a precipitating event that made your family leave?

George: I left Shanghai in the spring of 1950 to go to college in the USA. As during WWII, my parents wanted to stay in China as long as they could be helpful to their Chinese colleagues. When it became apparent that this was no longer possible, they applied for exit visas. Just before they left, they were given a traditional farewell banquet at which, my mother liked to relate, a large winter melon containing soup was set in front of her. Traditionally, a dragon would be carved into the melon, but in front of her were the Chinese words "Down with the American imperialists!"

SG: What aspects of Chinese culture do you feel foreigners today misunderstand the most?

Betty: Many Western visitors are surprised by the modernity in China. I think they expect it to be like it was during the Cultural Revolution with everyone wearing blue cotton jackets. Both George and I agree that many Westerners do not fully understand the ways [the Communist Revolution] came about. We have a serious lack of knowledge of Chinese history, both ancient and modern. How many Westerners know about the Opium Wars? George says that when he was young, he heard the saying that China was like a piece of fat pork: Any dog could come and bite it. The Chinese admire Western countries, particularly the USA. At the same time, I have yet to come across a Chinese person who is not proud of his or her country's five thousand years of history.

CHAPTER 3

PEOPLE AND VALUES

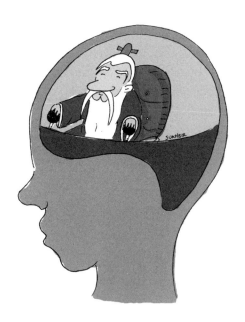

> ❛Where woods grow deep,
> you find many kinds of birds.❜
>
> — Chinese saying

DIVERSITY

There's always a risk of oversimplifying people and places when trying to pin down the cultural values that define a city like Shanghai. Nationally, China is far more diverse than many Western visitors expect. Although Han Chinese are the dominant ethnicity throughout China—accounting for over ninety percent of the national population—even Han from a far western city like Kangding will have a profoundly dissimilar cultural background from someone in Beijing. It is still fairly uncommon to experience regional diversity playing out within a local geographical area, since much of China's diversity is regional. But business opportunities are rife in Shanghai, which uniquely situates it to attract not only the largest expat population in China, but also a diverse Chinese migrant population from other provinces.

Despite the fact that many Chinese citizens do not generally have unlimited freedom to pick up and move to their city of choice, Shanghai still finds itself filled with residents who have traveled from nearly every corner of the country. You may find yourself buying street food from a Uyghur vendor, talking to a shopkeeper from Shaanxi, meeting with a coworker of Mongolian heritage, or lying on a table under the care of a masseuse from Sichuan. Add to that a dabbling of Europeans, Americans, Japanese, Koreans and even some Vietnamese influence from Guangxi province, and you have the ingredients of a truly diverse city. Yet, while its diversity makes it an outlier inside China, Shanghai remains a very central part of the Chinese nation. As a visitor, you'll find a number of uniquely Chinese circumstances that shape the way things work.

SECULARISM IN CHINA

Few subjects have attracted more attention in the West than China's stalwart commitment to atheism. The 10-year duration of the Cultural Revolution, which by some estimates left nearly half of the nation's temples and iconic religious structures damaged or destroyed, looms large in the minds of foreigners and often shapes perceptions about Chinese religious tolerance more than it should. Many foreigners arrive in Shanghai with the notion that China prohibits peoples' religious practice entirely, which isn't exactly the case. What is true is that the Communist Party is dedicated to promoting a somewhat paradoxical concept called "dialectical materialism," which insists on a wholly secular government. China's constitution spells out a strict separation between church and state. On a more personal level, the government requires that the more than 90 million individual members of the Communist Party have no religious affiliation whatsoever. Yet, Article 26 of the Chinese Constitution contains a clause clearly protecting religious freedom.

When trying to understand Chinese values, secularism is a somewhat easier concept to grasp than religion. The sheer complexity of China's religious history (and the diversity of its population) make generalizing about religious practice impossible. The history of secularism in China did not begin with the Cultural Revolution as many foreigners assume. Historical tensions between religious and atheistic philosophies have existed for millennia in China. During a long stretch of intellectual engagement known as the Spring and Autumn Period (770–221 BCE), competing intellectual, moral, religious, and secular philosophies gave rise to the Hundred Schools of Thought, also known as a golden age of ideas.

Yet even during this period of scholarship, disputes between adherents of some religious and secular philosophies bubbled up, especially as a counterpoint to feudal and imperial power. China's imperial system, which ended in the early 20th century, functioned much like Western monarchies—kings, usually members of dynastic families, were believed to have been ordained by God or some other supreme being. Unsurprisingly, the word for emperor (*shangdi*) was often translated as "supreme deity." Among the many philosophies that flourished during the Hundred Schools era, Confucianism and Taoism, along with Buddhism, which migrated from India, have remained influential in contemporary China. Confucianism, in particular, is widely considered the pervasive force shaping Chinese values and social relationships.

Today, the PRC officially recognizes five religions: Buddhism, Taoism, Islam, Catholicism, and Protestantism. A number of contemporary watchers have noted a revival of religious practice in China over the past 20 years. In his 2017 book, *The Souls of China*, the Pulitzer Prize-winning journalist Ian Johnson argues that China is "undergoing a spiritual revival similar to the Great Awakening in the United States in the nineteenth century." The actual number of adherents to religious teaching is difficult to pin down, since many Chinese do not consider themselves overtly religious, yet maintain some spiritual practices (especially Buddhism) or adhere to some precepts of Chinese folklore or ancestor worship.

Like many historical churches in China, the domed mosque in the background is now a government-owned facility.

At best, the government is inconsistent in its approach to religion in China, but it does exert significant control over the influx and practice of organized belief. Since 1999, the government has waged an aggressive campaign against a contemporary spiritual philosophy called Falun Gong—a *qi gong* martial art and meditative practice with an emphasis on moral improvement, something analogous to Yoga. In 2018, the PRC government also banned the sale of the Bible for online retailers like Taobao, China's version of Amazon.

Most expats soon come to understand that there is more widespread religious practice on the ground in China than expected. Visit any Buddhist Temple and you will find people freely burning incense and praying without interference. Some in the Chinese diaspora who have since returned, have brought Western religious practice back with them. Chinese adherents of some religions like Latter Day Saints often hold church meetings in private homes, and there is a surprising number of stately Christian and Catholic churches scattered throughout Shanghai. Buddhist monks live and work in active Buddhist temples as well. Though not exactly known for its religiosity or its temples, Shanghai is home to three Buddhist temples worth visiting—Jing'An Temple, Jade Buddha Temple, and Longhua Temple—as well as a Daoist temple and a truly beautiful Confucian temple (see Chapter 7). Thousands of years of war and social change mean that most of Shanghai's temples have been restored, sometimes as recently as decades ago.

CONFUCIUS SAYS

Confucianism, sometimes referred to as *rujia* (scholarly tradition), has been experiencing a popular resurgence in China since the 1990s. Some would argue it never truly

Old world meets new world at a Buddhist Temple in the heart of Shanghai.

disappeared. If you're looking for a lens through which to view Chinese attitudes and social relationships, Confucianism is the best you will find. Just as Western values are rooted in Greek philosophy, Confucianism is considered the cornerstone of Chinese values. The Chinese-American journalist and Shanghai expat, Lenora Chu, has referred to Confucius as "a little man who resides inside the head of every Chinese man and woman whether they know it or not. He governs how they find their mates, what they look for in jobs, how they treat their parents and how they educate their children."

Not quite religion, not quite philosophy, Confucianism is a system for moral guidance that emphasizes harmony in human relationships. Confucius, or Kong Qui, Master Kong (Kongzi), born in the 6th century BCE (551-479), was technically not a religious leader, yet he did have a large group of disciples, many of whom are known for writing down his aphorisms after he died. His influence was spread mostly by the Han Dynasty over the course of 2,000 years. In the Confucian model, people, not nature, are fundamentally at the center of life. Many of Confucius' teachings—aphorisms about how to live a moral life—were collected in a classic work known as the *Analects*. A few scholars have raised eyebrows with claims that Confucius was actually not the scholar/philosopher he has been characterized as, but it's now widely assumed he was not the sole author of all of the works attributed to him.

Confucian teachings venerate family loyalty, humane authority, virtue (*ren*, meaning "goodness"), loyalty to superiors, hard work, reverence for ancestors, and social order—the same concepts that still inform contemporary Chinese culture. The Confucian emphasis on education, authority, and respect plays out in contemporary Chinese social, business and family relationships, as well as in the acceptance of a one-party political system. The Chinese wield a fair amount of parental authority with their children, but parents also will go to great lengths to ensure their children's educational futures. Even the PRC government, which officially eschews spiritualist values, views Confucian ideals as a cultural cornerstone. The Ministry of Education has opened hundreds of Confucius Institutes on university campuses throughout the world as a means of promoting Chinese values, culture and language.

The resurgence of academic and spiritual interest in Confucianism by average Chinese citizens, by which I mean the dominant Han culture of Shanghai, isn't surprising given how much Confucian thinking already permeates daily life. Even the government-sponsored public service announcements that arrive regularly on Chinese cell phones have a Confucian bent. "Everyone participates in disaster prevention and reduction to create a harmonious and safe life," is a fairly common example of a message from the Civil Affairs Bureau. Another text, from the Shanghai Safety Authority might say something like, "Focus on fire to give peace to you and me." Time and again, you will notice messages from the government that promote "harmony" for the greater good of all. It is just another example of how Chinese values remain Confucian at heart.

Two of the Four Heavenly Kings in the Jade Buddha Temple.

SOCIALISM WITH CHINESE CHARACTERISTICS

If you plan to work or study for any length of time in Shanghai, it helps to be moderately knowledgeable about the Chinese view of their 21st century position in the world. Of course, no one can claim to find a unified view among the Chinese. Yet Shanghai is a city that views itself as the sophisticated center of the Middle Kingdom, and many Chinese harbor a profound belief In the superiority of Chinese history and culture as well as in China's destiny as a global force. Myriad European, Australian, and American news organizations produce top-notch reporting about China's current economic and political direction, and they are well worth reading if you plan to live in China for any length of time. Within China, *China Daily* and *Xinhua News*, both state-run and Communist Party approved news agencies, provide English language reporting that offers expats a healthy comparison.

In general, Chinese people are wary about discussing politics with foreigners, just as they can be reticent to say anything that might be misconstrued as unsupportive of the government. And with good reason. After a period of rapid, somewhat unrestrained openness in the 1990s and early 2000s, PRC leaders in 2013 began to take a more authoritarian turn. In a four-year period from 2014-2018, the use of our personal VPNs (See Chapter 5), once a very functional workaround to China's Internet restrictions, gradually turned into a cumbersome game of one-upmanship. Additionally, government oversight of foreign businesses and international schools has grown more intrusive since 2015. While you may be curious to learn Chinese opinions on local politics, it's better to avoid asking the Chinese about Communist policies. Instead, seek safer opinions about other countries or ask about China's formidable goals for the future. The Chinese are often curious about the politics of Western countries and have strong opinions on the topic that they may be more inclined to share.

The ideological concept most deeply embedded in China's vision of itself is Socialism with Chinese Characteristics. Beginning in the 1980s with economic and market reforms, China began defining (and redefining) the ideology behind its new policies. Economic reforms were recast as a type of socialism that is uniquely Chinese. The phrase itself refers mainly to the country's economic, political, and social policies, which the government claims must always be viewed within the specific historical contexts in which such policies are sanctioned. In essence, Socialism with Chinese Characteristics has been understood until fairly recently as an expression of traditional Communist ideology with the unique addition of capitalist market reforms. A cursory view of the consumer culture in Shanghai might have you questioning such a definition, but we will leave it to scholars to argue that point.

Deng Xiaoping Theory, the first bona fide incarnation of Socialism with Chinese Characteristics, originated with the country's eponymous leader from 1978 until 1989, and largely justified moving to a semi-private market economy, which Deng was known for encouraging. A more recent incarnation of Socialism with Chinese Characteristics, Xi Jinping Thought, is an updated theoretical framework for China's political future and its greater economic role in the world. Developed by China's president and Communist Party General Secretary, Xi Jinping, the doctrine, officially titled, Xi Jinping Thought on Socialism with Chinese Characteristics for a New Era, was formally ratified in China's Constitution during the 19th National Party Congress in October, 2017, during which time our own Western television coverage of the event was routinely blacked out (yet another thing to keep in mind).

In addition to ratification, presidential term limits that would have restricted Xi's time in office to two terms were abolished, leaving an opening for Xi to remain in office beyond the end of his second term in 2023, which he is widely expected to do. This development was viewed, both inside and outside China, as a unique change that cemented Xi's status as the third most important political and historical leader of China after Mao Zedong and Deng Xiaoping.

THE 14 TENETS OF XI JINPING THOUGHT RATIFIED IN 2017

1. The supremacy of Communist Party leadership over the public and private workforce
2. A people-centric approach in which government serves the public interest
3. Expanded socialist reform
4. Scientific development and openness to new ideas
5. Adherence to the principles of Socialism with Chinese Characteristics
6. Adherence to and reform of the "rule of law"
7. Practicing the values of Marxism, communism and socialism
8. Role of government is to improve the well being of the people and promote social harmony
9. Coexistence with nature; instituting conservation policies
10. Improve and strengthen national security
11. Communist Party as sole head of the People's Liberation Army
12. Reaffirmation of one country-two systems policy with a stated goal of future reunification of Hong Kong, Macau, and Taiwan under "one China"
13. Promote a peaceful and stable international order between China and other countries
14. Zero tolerance of Party corruption

Nothing frustrates a people more than government paralysis, and despite common complaints by Chinese nationals about government bureaucracy, paralysis is not something China has experienced at the national level. China is a competitive country, but it is also a country filled with dreamers. Since his arrival to power, Xi Jinping often extolls China's "great rejuvenation" and refers to the delayed dreams of the Chinese people. The Chinese are proud of their enormous advances and technological accomplishments over the past 30 years. The sting of China's "Century of Humiliation" recedes with every passing achievement.

To this end, the People's Republic has implemented some impressive projects to ensure a strong future for China both domestically and internationally. Shanghai has been only one of many cities in China benefiting from rapid infrastructure expansion. A visitor to Shanghai for as little as six months

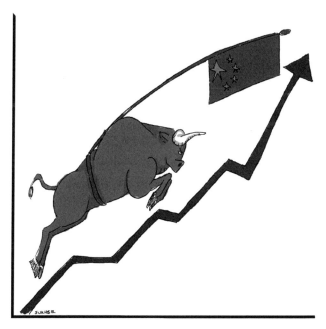

Shanghai's ever-present construction cranes are seen as a sign of the country's auspicious future.

will witness the stupefying speed of construction. Xi Jinping Thought is the central force propelling China to reach these new goals. Two long-term programs in particular will continue to dominate headlines in China and the world: the One Belt, One Road initiative and the Made in China 2025 program, unveiled in 2013 and 2015 respectively.

Both programs layout ambitious goals. One Belt, One Road is the largest infrastructure development program in human history. The project delineates China's economic and infrastructure investments not only at home, but also in neighboring countries throughout Asia as well as distant Africa. According to *The Atlantic* magazine, as of 2017, China was the largest export/import trade partner of 92 foreign countries, dwarfing the U.S. which had only 52 such partners. The People's Republic has strategically invested in infrastructure in African and Asian countries that are rich in natural resources. The investment is as much about China as it is about establishing geopolitical influence. Made in China 2025 outlines similarly lofty and expensive goals and is the second government-sponsored program you will hear Chinese nationals discuss on a fairly regular basis. Under this initiative, China envisions becoming mostly self-sufficient in areas of technological development. Industries ranging from pharmaceuticals to artificial intelligence to green energy, along with research and development, will receive astonishing levels of government support to achieve domestic independence. These two plans, together with China's dazzling world record book of highest, tallest, longest structures, give average Chinese citizens a glimpse into a future in which China dominates the economic and political world order. As a foreigner in China, it's difficult not to be awed by China's grand plans and breathtaking accomplishments.

China's One Belt One Road Initiative lays out the most ambitious infrastructure program in human history.

TABOOS AND SUPERSTITIONS

Chinese culture has an impossibly long list of superstitions about luck, chance, and destiny. Animism, numerology and folkloric belief in things such as ancestral ghosts are fairly common, even in a modern city like Shanghai filled with wealth and privilege. Every occasion, every holiday, every part of daily life, from pregnancy to gift giving, could potentially be sabotaged by a foreigner who is innocently unaware of cultural taboos. Nearly everything is subject to good or bad luck. Foreign marketing executives arriving in China face a complexity of folk beliefs and superstitions that can be difficult to navigate. It is always safest to ask a Chinese citizen specifically how *yuanfen* (fate or luck), might determine Chinese views about a particular concept, lest you end up like one international school with a logo of a bird in the "falling" (diving) position, a very unfortunate symbol indeed. Rising objects, which indicate increased value, are always auspicious. Falling objects, portents of decline, should be avoided. Most animals have overwhelmingly positive symbolic traits. When in doubt about color, always choose lucky red.

Many of these beliefs have been combined over centuries from different aspects of Chinese culture. Superstitions about ghosts and animals are often connected to ancestor worship, the Chinese zodiac, and Chinese folklore. Others are versions of Confucian and Taoist ideas, and still others relate to the phonetic qualities of the language itself. Don't be surprised to find someone extolling the benefits of herbal remedies for a ligament tear or discussing the unlucky circumstances of a birth on the fourth day of the month. A good rule of thumb is to think figuratively about objects. Sharp objects (like knives or scissors) are never auspicious gifts because they can symbolize the cutting off of a relationship. Clocks, unfortunately, suggest the passage of time, a gift that might put you on a path toward your inevitable death.

Numerology is especially prevalent. The number four (*si*) is so widely considered unlucky—the sound is similar to the Chinese word for death—that many tall apartment buildings in China have elevators missing a fourth floor. On the other hand, the number 8 (*ba*) is auspicious since it's phonetically

similar to the Chinese word for wealth (*fa*). These common beliefs play out in important ways in daily life and can affect how you do business or how you are viewed by those with whom you interact. If budget is an issue in housing, consider carefully your choice of an apartment building floor or you could find yourself paying more (like we did) to live on the lucky 8th floor. Unlike in the West where dragons have long been a metaphorical creature of evil, in most of Asia dragons represent good fortune, and the rising dragon, best of both worlds, is an expression of national pride that many local Chinese use to refer to their upwardly mobile country.

SYMBOLS OF GOOD AND BAD LUCK

Good luck	Bad Luck
Dragons	Sweeping during the lunar new year
Cabbages	The color white (for funerals)
The color red	Black clothing
Rising things	Falling things
Eat dumplings	Crying
The number 8	The number 4
Tortoises	Leaving laundry out at night
Bamboo	Crows
Fish	Mirrors near a door or bed

CHINESE NEW YEAR

Chinese New Year (Spring Festival) is the longest and most important national holiday in China. In terms of significance, the holiday is analogous to both Christmas and New Year in the West. The holiday's origins are often disputed, but one common myth involves folk tales about a monster, Nian, that terrorized villages until it was appeased with food and gifts or frightened off with brightly colored ornaments. It is the most widely anticipated national celebration of cultural tradition in China. The celebration always involves copious gift giving, fireworks, and home-cooked family dinners. Streets and homes are decorated with the traditional red lanterns. *Chun lian*, traditional red banners adorned with poetry, hang from the doorways as offerings to various gods, and calamondin or kumquat trees (laden with small, tart oranges) are displayed as symbols of wealth and good luck. Each month of the Chinese lunar year is represented by a different animal corresponding to birth years and personal traits. Because the lunar year is shorter than the Western solar year, the date

Red lanterns adorn an Old City street during Chinese New Year.

of Chinese New Year differs from year to year in an effort to play catch up.

Family reunion is the heart and soul of Spring Festival, and workers in China expect a week or more off during the two-week celebration. Chinese citizens from cities like Shanghai often travel to visit family who live in more rural or suburban areas. As a result, small shops, street food vendors, restaurants, and local businesses are almost universally closed during the entire period of New Year festivities. On the other hand, tourist attractions are packed to the gills, and fireworks are abundant. Foreigners living in China typically leave the country during the holiday as traveling anywhere inside China, by train or plane, is prohibitive.

The conventions and folk customs that align with the festival are some of the most important traditions to master for foreigners living or working in China. Traditional gift giving is integral during the two weeks of the festival, and the gift of *hongbao* or "red envelope" is an expectation among family members and between employers and employees. The red envelope itself is where the exchange or a wish of good luck lies. Since red is the luckiest color, the envelope itself is nearly as important as the cash it contains. Drivers, *ayis*, and other personal employees or other people you daily rely upon will appreciate a red envelope gift—think of it as an annual bonus. To ensure that the circle of luck is complete, red envelopes should never contain an uneven number of bills.

Cleaning is also an important task during the Spring Festival, and many Chinese will spend days "spring cleaning" their homes before the celebration. The very act of sweeping is a symbolic gesture in China—Tomb Sweeping Day is yet another national holiday—and the Chinese generally avoid cleaning or sweeping on the first day of the lunar new year in fear of symbolically sweeping away the year's good fortune.

Orange trees are placed near doorways during Chinese New Year as a symbol of abundance and good fortune.

COMPETITION AND HARD WORK

In her book *Little Soldiers*, Chinese-American expat Lenora Chu describes a discomfiting scene of cheating at her American son's Chinese elementary school. During a day of outdoor games in which the elementary school classes compete against one another, Chu witnesses her son's teachers cheating (and enabling their students' cheating) in order to win the games. Chu describes the moment as shocking to her Western sensibilities. On the other hand, she recognizes that the act is indicative of some essential element of Chinese culture. There is concurrently a focus on both hard work and cutting corners. If competition is the heart and soul of capitalism, it is just as essentially the bread and butter of China. To many foreigners, this pairing of communism and competition seems paradoxical given the culture's Confucian emphasis on harmony, but that is the crux of Socialism with Chinese Characteristics. This irony has been a frequent topic of discussion in my own family, and we sometimes humorously refer to China's economic strategy as the inverse:

Capitalism with Chinese Characteristics. Much about Chinese culture can be deeply, irrepressibly competitive.

A quick peek into the tutoring and test prep industry in China's cities reveals both how competitive Chinese culture can be, but also how committed the Chinese are to hard work. Since the late 1990s academic cheating scandals have rocked China and the U.S. standardized testing industry. The headlines about widespread cheating both in education (the U.S. College Board has cancelled its SAT exams numerous times) and business and industry are difficult to avoid. At the same time, Chinese students are among the hardest working students in the world, putting in long hours of after-school tutoring and test preparation for the notoriously difficult *gaokao*, the Chinese national exam that shapes the future of more than 10 million Chinese high school students each year. Economic inequality throughout China drives much of the culture around China's education industry and fuels the nation's competitive drive. Everyone wants the best for his or her children.

The Chinese aren't just competitive about education. The country's historical obsession with size goes back centuries. The Great Wall of China, a UNESCO World Heritage site, is still the world's longest wall and has been the subject of centuries of myth making (no, it cannot be seen from the moon). The Leshan Grand Buddha, carved into a Sichuan cliff, is now the world's largest Buddha as well as the world's largest pre-modern statue. China also has the world's tallest Buddha, a statue completed in 2002 in Henan. It makes sense for a country that has the world's largest population and the world's most widely spoken language to take pride in building the biggest things. There is even a Chinese expression, "four big things," (*sì dà jiàn*) used among Chinese to denote artifacts

The Shanghai Tower, right, has the world's highest observation deck and the world's fastest elevators.

of affluence and success. This competitive tendency to build the biggest, longest, tallest, fastest things (including companies) is why a wealthy Shanghai businessman told my husband that he thought he was witnessing the end of Western dominance. "How is America going to compete with us?" he asked. Good question!

CHINA'S RECORDS

- China has the four highest airports in the world
- China will complete the world's' largest airport in Beijing in 2019
- China built the world's largest supercomputer
- China is home to the world's largest floating solar farm
- China has the world's longest bridge
- China has two of the world's tallest buildings
- China has 17 of the world's 19 highest bridges, including the top five
- China has the world's longest and highest glass bridge
- China has the world's fastest trains
- China owns the world's largest money market funds
- Inside the Shanghai Tower are the world's fastest elevators
- China has the world's largest radio telescope signal receiver (looking for alien life)
- China's Alibaba Group holds the record for the world's highest single day sales ($25 billion)

MODESTY

A strong element of conservatism still runs through Chinese culture, manifesting as a commitment to modesty, especially among older generations. Whether it's modest clothing for a particular occasion (the Chinese tend to be formal dressers), or how much personal information you divulge during a conversation, it's best to err on the conservative side. As with most cultural practices in China, the emphasis on modesty is rooted in the country's Confucian, Taoist, and Buddhist traditions. All three philosophies emphasize the virtues of personal humility and moderation and shun boasting of any sort. Cultural emphasis on modesty in China is almost exclusively about public behavior, linking it intimately with the concept of face as well. However, among younger and wealthier generations with more international exposure, the traditional values of modesty are beginning to wane somewhat.

HOMOSEXUALITY

In addition to its philosophical emphasis on modesty, China is also a politically conservative country. Although homosexuality was legalized in 1997, it can best be described as tolerated, more so among expats and youthful Chinese than among older generations. Traditionally, the Chinese place a heavy emphasis on marriage and children, and these are still paramount in the world of Chinese parental expectation. Party officials appear mostly indifferent to the issue, neither supporting nor denying the rights of the LGBTQ community, but there is still tension between a broader push for traditional gender roles and an emerging and increasingly visible LGBTQ community. It will be interesting to see if current demographic obstacles play a role in the future of LGBTQ rights, at least for men, since China's one child policy has left 1 in 4 men without access to a traditional, female marriage partner.

Western culture has had some influence on attitudes toward homosexuality in China, especially in Shanghai, which retains its status as China's most Westernized city. There is a gay community, as well as a gay expat community, to explore. But be realistic with expectations. Many Shanghai based websites report a "sizable" turnout of 500 people at an LGBTQ event or party, which in a city of 24 million gives an uneasy sense of the scale and scope of open homosexuality.

Yet, there are signs of compromise. In 2018, Weibo, a popular Twitter-like social media outlet announced a preemptive ban on gay content and was met by fierce online resistance, which also garnered editorial support in *People's Daily*, the official media mouthpiece of the Party. Weibo quickly reversed the ban. As for LGBTQ venues, that's a different story. Bars and dance clubs are given a certain latitude, but it's not uncommon for them to be suddenly shut down by the police, only to "pop up" in a different location a year later. However, it's worth noting that this happens to popular expat bars and clubs as well.

For what it's worth, the gay community in Shanghai is an active and close-knit group. With LGBTQ clubs rather sparse, events are often hosted at changing venues throughout the city. Snap! and Heaven Party are popular hosts, but organizational names can quickly change in Shanghai, as groups play a game of cat and mouse with municipal authorities who are less friendly to the gay community. The Shanghai LGBTQ community also hosts a popular Pride marathon, charity events, film and art festivals. If you're a foreigner arriving long term with a same sex partner, be aware that China does not, at this writing, recognize married same sex partners as legitimate spouses, and getting a dependent visa for your partner is unlikely. It's common practice for businesses and international schools in China who hire one member of a same sex couple from overseas, to make discrete or specialized arrangements to get partners abroad too. This often takes the form of hiring the partner individually or encouraging and assisting the partner in finding employment.

Views among expats on gay nightlife in Shanghai are almost always a matter of perspective. If you're moving to

China from a city like San Francisco or New York, you might find yourself a bit traumatized by the dearth of clubs and community in Shanghai. On the other hand, an Indonesian friend of mine, who moved to Shanghai from Jakarta, has not been remotely afflicted by disappointment. "Gay nightlife in Shanghai is great," he claims. "People create themed parties all the time. There's a young spirit and fresh ideas; that's one thing about the gay scene in the city! I feel much safer here than I do in Jakarta. [Chinese] people just stare at us and awkwardly laugh or smile. [They] are never rude or aggressive toward gay people in Shanghai. The younger generation is totally open minded." Measure the length of your relative experience and move forward from that point.

CHAPTER 4

SOCIALIZING
AND FITTING IN

So much of what mystifies us about the East need not mystify us.

— **Gish Jen,** *Girl at the Baggage Claim*

XENOPHOBIA

As I mentioned earlier, the Chinese are not shy about staring at foreigners—especially at people of Western or African ancestry. A well-known Shanghai comedy troupe called Mamahuhu, a collaborative group of Chinese and Western humorists, produces delightful videos about staring encounters in China. Regardless of the country's links to the global community, a surprising number of Chinese in Shanghai still find racial differences fascinating. Many residents who have arrived in the city from other provinces view expats with amusement and see them as something of an oddity. An undercurrent of xenophobia also still exists among the older generation and can pop up at unexpected times. Social class and context also influence people's responses in Shanghai, and whether or not the local Chinese population wants social interaction with you can be a bit unpredictable.

China's openness over the past thirty years is still relative when considered against the broad context of the rest of the world. Unfortunately, some Western expats feel insulted when the Chinese remain aloof, but the country is still coming to terms with global participation, while many of its Asian neighbors are not. Foreigners will almost never find themselves the object of personal or nationalistic animosity, at least in a public context. This doesn't mean that they won't be an object of generalized animosity, but the feeling often has little to do with nationality or politics and more to do with xenophobia and the presumed cultural ineptitude of *laowai* (especially with the language). For many working-class Chinese—taxi drivers and street cleaners—expats are viewed as an annoyance that mars an otherwise lovely day. Don't be surprised if your presence in a taxi or Didi occasionally irritates the driver.

On the other hand, many Chinese, especially those studying English, find expats interesting and will enjoy the opportunity to practice their English skills with you. Near tourist areas and at hotels, expats represent an opportunity to make money and will be generally be well treated, even if reactions on the street range from insulting to heartwarming. While I have certainly experienced shouts of *laowai* (foreigner) or *bairen* (white person) hurled from a passing scooter during a walkabout, I've also experienced my share of the friendly "hello" shouted out by strangers in English.

Younger generations are very open to foreigners. A strong inclination among wealthier Chinese to have their children study abroad has created a climate in China that sometimes makes expats rock-star popular, particularly when they hail from well-known Western universities like Oxford or Yale, which bestows instant respect in educationally minded Shanghai. Highly educated Chinese will want to know not where you hail from, but which university you attended, in the event you find some connection to friends and family abroad.

In short, you'll experience a wide variety of reactions to your presence at any particular moment and knowing exactly what to expect can be difficult. The bottom line is simple: Shanghai is the most open city in China, and you will find acceptance.

MAKING FRIENDS

Living, working, or studying in Shanghai offers *laowai* many opportunities to make friends and experience the unique rewards of Chinese culture. Making friends often takes a conscious effort in Shanghai, and for better or worse, many new friendships will naturally occur between expats. The expat community tends to be close knit, aided by a healthy cluster of expat organizations, most notably the Shanghai Expatriate Association. One consequence of the difficulty of penetrating local Chinese culture is the growth of expat hubs in certain areas of the city like Minhang, Jinqiao, and Hongqiao. Though not nearly as defined and isolated as the history of the International Concessions, these foreign enclaves are popular residential areas that can help expats navigate through the overwhelming culture shock of an initial move. While living in an expat hub can help prevent social isolation, it can also reduce opportunities to experience "real" Chinese life on the streets.

The language barrier remains a universal divider separating foreigners and locals in China and too often it limits interactions between expats and area residents. Despite the fact that all Chinese educated in Shanghai's secondary schools are required to take English, it is still not widely

BUILDING FRIENDSHIPS

Building local friendships with Chinese is most likely to occur through employment. Chinese and Westerners are often found socializing over lunch or dinner in the business districts and Former French Concession. Once you're outside of the work environment you might feel a greater divide between the local Chinese and the foreign community. English is still not widely spoken in China as it is in other countries, but the two language communities often operate in tandem in the executive and educational worlds.

spoken. Learning some basic phrases will help expats navigate daily life. Those who plan to spend a significant number of years in Shanghai will do well to learn Mandarin, mostly by taking local classes. Even a working knowledge of the language will leave you with a bevy of highly impressed Chinese acquaintances and make it more likely that you will form some enduring friendships with the Chinese.

In the tourist areas, especially along ast Nanjing Road and in the fake markets, you'll experience a barrage of English, all of it oriented toward getting you to buy counterfeit products such as watches, handbags, or sneakers. "Hey lady, hey lady" (or "mister, mister") is a near constant refrain in these areas. The amount of English these hawkers know is typically minimal. Your best response is a curt "*bu yao*" (I don't want).

SOCIALIZING

Much of Shanghai is walkable or accessible via metro, and a host of dynamic bars and restaurants throughout the city

provide no shortage of opportunities for expats and visitors to socialize, party, or interact. Getting out to experience the glamorous side of Shanghai's nightlife is an important part of what makes foreigners feel at home in the city. More often than not, foreigners tend to patronize establishments (especially clubs and lounges) that quickly fill up with more and more foreigners and fewer and fewer locals. When local establishments begin to garner a reputation as hotspots for raucous foreigners, the Shanghai municipal government has a tendency to shut the venues down (almost always under the guise of "licensing" issues). Learning upon arrival at your favorite establishment that the place you've frequented for months has suddenly disappeared or relocated is a somewhat unexceptional Shanghai social experience.

In recent years an increasing number of clubs (jazz, beat, and rock) as well as cultural outlets (museums, concerts, and theaters) have assumed a prominent role in city life, and these venues continue to inform the social lives of the expat community. The Chinese government appears to support the idea of Shanghai becoming the cultural center of China. When it comes to promoting artistic endeavors, officials have cities like New York, Berlin, or Paris firmly stationed in their sights. The promotion of contemporary art and culture is a rather new phenomenon in China, and it still occurs under the limits of Party guidelines. Cultural pushback against the government is not something that fits neatly into the traditional Chinese view of harmony and respect for authority, like it does in the West. That said, socializing in Shanghai often revolves around the large number of Western theater productions, art festivals, concerts, opera (Chinese and Western), and a stunning collection of museums (see Chapter 7 for specific details about Shanghai's cultural scene).

As in other countries, the foreign expat community in Shanghai tends to be transient. Most expat posts last an average of two to three years—sometimes cut short by an inability to overcome cultural barriers, pollution issues, and commonly cited problems with Internet accessibility. Despite it all, friendships made under such circumstances, for both adults and children, tend to be enduring.

Depending on your level of commitment and your language skills, you may find your closest relationships with Chinese locals to be with your *ayi*, your driver, shopkeepers, and employees at the lunch counters you frequent. I've found that Chinese merchants appreciate a returning customer, and friendly relationships can be built from basic words and a good game of charades. When working with Chinese colleagues where language is not a barrier, you may find you're your friendships are still somewhat limited, unless you are interacting with Chinese who have a connection, through school or work, to the international world.

MAKING THE TRANSITION

As with any transition to a new city, personal circumstances will dictate the ease or difficulty of the adjustment. For those who arrive in Shanghai with children, life revolves around school. Adults can quickly find a close community among other expat parents, and children will find a community with other international students. For those living in a residential expat compound, the social support system is built into the housing arrangement. Many families with young children absolutely love life in Shanghai since housing is frequently part of expat packages, and child care, cleaning, and cooking services are eminently affordable and abundant. Although salaries may seem low by Western standards, employment as

Shanghai's many green parks can make the urban transition easier.

an *ayi* (household help) for a foreign family is an excellent job with more than satisfactory compensation for many women in Shanghai. Young children who live in expat compounds often roam freely between residences with groups of friends. Compound amenities such as swimming pools, gyms, and health clinics add to the quality of life and can help reduce the general feeling of culture shock.

For single women, Shanghai might be one of the most exciting places in the world to live. Not only is the city one of the safest in the world, but thanks to an overly effective one-child policy and a longstanding preference for boys, the ratio of men to women runs firmly in women's favor. I know one American woman who moved to China, and after finding herself in the midst of an unexpected divorce, learned Mandarin and started a travel guide business. Before long she also had a boyfriend (who later became her husband) through one of the many available Chinese dating apps. Likewise, many single expat men enjoy the social scene in Shanghai, thanks to the city's youthful population and general vibrancy. Whether you arrive alone or with a family in tow, approaching life in Shanghai with confidence—and assuming a positive outlook about the future—can help overcome any cultural challenges. There truly is something for everyone in Shanghai.

GUANXI

One of the more complicated cultural concepts expats grapple with when living and working in Shanghai is *guanxi*. Literally translated, *guanxi* quite simply means "relationship." But in reality, there is no simple definition for *guanxi*. Broadly speaking, the term aligns closely with the concept of "social influence," and it functions like type of professional currency for the Chinese. Status, social connections, and hierarchical relationships are extraordinarily important in Chinese culture, as in many interdependent societies, and attaining, respecting, and managing one's *guanxi* is an essential part of professional and social life in Shanghai. Unlike their Western counterparts, the Chinese rarely compartmentalize relationships, so an individual's *guanxi* is really an abstract measure of his or her level of influence across all social networks. In some sense, *guanxi* is very much a byproduct of Confucianism and Communism: Both promote egalitarian principles but have yet to produce truly meritocratic societies. What has emerged instead is relational *guanxi*.

On the face of things, *guanxi* may not seem like a very unique concept. In Western cultures, the common expression "it's not what you know, but who you know that matters," sums up a somewhat parallel notion. In this sense, *guanxi* can be viewed as a Chinese version of "social networking" on steroids. A person's *guanxi* may play a role in the type of job he finds, the effectiveness of his communications, his management style, and even how easily he gets help in a time of need. The concept underlies many, if not most, social interactions in the workplace. (Chapter 9 contains an explanation of *guanxi* in the workplace).

The significance of *guanxi* in Chinese culture accounts for much of the preoccupation with Western "prestige schools" like Cambridge, Harvard, or Oxford, much to the frustration of international schools which try to emphasize the concept of "best fit" only to find themselves faced with blank stares. Many international educators protest against the ubiquitous desire among Chinese students to attend elite institutions. Yet the desire is less about educational aspirations than it is about the *guanxi* gained by attendance. Unlike Western countries which couch similar aspirations in somewhat disingenuous narratives about meritocracy, the pragmatic Chinese can completely dispense with such narratives. They have *guanxi*.

For the Chinese, the essence of *guanxi* moves beyond prestige or influence. In addition to professional connections, family connections and a wide circle of friends and acquaintances play a role in establishing a person's *guanxi*. For instance, a well-connected individual who is said to "have a lot of *guanxi*" may not necessarily also be a wealthy individual. He or she may simply be in a position to

> Unlike Western countries which couch similar aspirations in somewhat disingenuous narratives about meritocracy, the pragmatic Chinese can completely dispense with such narratives. They have *guanxi*.

know many people. Even mid-level government employees in China can gain a lot of *guanxi* if they play their cards correctly. There can be a humorous, cyclical quality to earning *guanxi* in China. Once people earn enough *guanxi*, they will gain influence over time. The more they can influence people, the more *guanxi* they will receive in return. My husband defines *guanxi* in the workplace as a way to establish win-win situations. Two important people gain influence together by inflating or enhancing the importance of one another. In this sense, *guanxi* is deeply intertwined with the concept of face (see next section).

Some Westerners complain that emphasis on *guanxi* makes interactions with the Chinese feel inauthentic—expats sometimes find themselves asking whether every interaction is merely a way to establish a future benefit. While it's true *guanxi is* about reciprocity—it is deeply transactional—the concept is so embedded in Chinese culture that most Chinese do not view *guanxi* as transactional at all. Indeed, when I asked a Chinese friend about "the transactional nature of Chinese culture," her response was: "But we don't have a transactional culture!"

Anyone planning to do business in Shanghai will have to establish *guanxi* with their Chinese counterparts and likely with government officials. Achieving it allows one to transcend boundaries and influence decision making beyond traditional parameters. In many cases, foreigners, especially Westerners, mistakenly equate the application of *guanxi* with corruption, as when a government official weighs in to change a rule on your behalf. Given the vastness of Chinese bureaucracy, it's not hard to see how *guanxi* can help people get things accomplished. A person with a lot of *guanxi* can support people outside the confines of Chinese bureaucracy (and tradition), and from that point of view, obtaining a lot of *guanxi* can help one rise above bureaucratic or hierarchical hurdles. A degree from Harvard gives you one kind of *guanxi*. Having family members working in the government or for an airline might offer a different kind of *guanxi*. And among family, helping and supporting one another offers yet a third kind of *guanxi*.

FACE

Perhaps no other aspect of Chinese culture captures as much attention or is as difficult for foreigners to understand, as *mianzi*, or face. At first glance, the concept appears obvious. After all, "saving face" is a broadly human principle, hardly unique to Chinese culture. We all think we know what it means to "save face" (avoid humiliation), and on the surface at least, that is indirectly true! Yet, in Chinese culture, face is far more nuanced than refusing to own up to an embarrassing mistake. It is part of an important and meaningful social transaction, and it plays out in complicated ways, especially in business and social relationships. In China, face holds the power to cement (or destroy) a deal, to shape friendships, to secure prestige, and to confer good standing upon whoever is given face. Face can be exchanged (given and taken away) like a commodity. It's a concept that is eminently confusing and frustrating to foreigners.

Saving face is rooted in the historical and structural framework of Chinese culture: It is intimately tied to a person's public role, and its expression is built upon the primacy of personal reputation and shame. To "have" or "save" face in a situation has to do with lending proper authority and influence to a public persona. One can support a friend or business associate in gaining *guanxi* by also helping that friend save face. Face is especially relevant in times of challenge, where a person may need affirmation or social investment, and in this sense it's a product of a profoundly communal environment. If one fails to help one's colleagues or friends during a time of challenge, one has embarrassed those friends instead of supporting their need. Giving someone the favor of face, in a public way, simultaneously builds their *guanxi*. Since face is so intimately connected to *guanxi*, the more status one has, the greater care needed when saving face.

Expats who have Chinese friends or colleagues will have to pay careful attention to this concept. They will find that many things in China—especially difficult things—do not get communicated directly. The most complicated aspect of face for foreigners is that it sometimes has little to do with preventing humiliation or avoiding confrontation. There are many ways in which the Chinese do not struggle with confrontation. Instead, cultural indicators play a significant role in which *types* of confrontation are acceptable. Ultimately, face is deeply contextual which, again, is what makes it so confusing for foreigners.

One of the best examples I've seen of *mianzi* and *guanxi* in action came about when my husband, an international school head, faced off with the local government. He was publicly dressed down by a Shanghai government official over a sensitive situation. By allowing himself to be chastised, and by respectfully agreeing that he was at fault, (although both parties *knew* he was *not* at fault), he allowed the official to save face. The man got to publicly establish his authority and demonstrate that he was doing his job by being an authority.

In return for this face-saving gesture, my husband built his own *guanxi* (respect), something that he knew would protect the school from burdensome restrictions, sanctions, reports, and inspections. Reciprocity was at the heart of this unspoken transaction. The meeting ended with the official explaining how much the local government respected the school's standing and reaffirming its value to the community. The same official then affirmed my husband's value and helped him save face. Face allows important people to support the importance of one another.

SOCIAL MEDIA

The Chinese rely on social media networks to a surprising degree. Living successfully in China as an expat will likely require some basic knowledge of how social media works inside the country. All influential news sites, social media sites, and private texting apps from outside mainland China, including Twitter, Facebook, Instagram, YouTube and WhatsApp, are blocked by China's Great Firewall. Foreign expats can access personal social media accounts with a VPN (see Chapter 5), but depending on the situation, access can be spotty. Despite this, most Chinese citizens who travel abroad, especially wealthier ones in cities like Shanghai, are knowledgeable about Western social media. Many even have accounts themselves.

Cell Phone Addiction

Communicating and socializing in Shanghai is impossible without a China-based cell phone and a few necessary social media accounts. The Chinese have gained a worldwide reputation for their intense cell phone addiction, and it often seems as if everyone in Shanghai is walking while texting or talking on their phones. It's not unusual to see couples or even entire groups sitting at restaurant tables without speaking, heads pointed down toward their tiny screens. Don't be surprised if you find that the wait staff of local restaurants are also tucked away in corners scanning their phones rather than bringing your food to the table.

Worldwide trends involving cell phone addiction have hit China with just as much force as the West. Many Chinese parents find themselves concerned about teenagers who are addicted to social media and online gaming. Not only do Shanghai drivers routinely text on their cell phones, people (without helmets) routinely ride scooters and bicycles while looking at their phones. Voice messaging functions are extremely popular in China, so it is now a common sight to see Chinese walking and talking with their phones balanced out in front of their faces. In fact, the problem of walking with cell phones has become so extreme in China that the city of Xian has created colorful pedestrian walking lanes designated especially for the cell phone-addicted. The practice was so popular that cell phone lanes are now being constructed in other Chinese cities. As of 2019, cell phone walking lanes have not yet come to Shanghai, but the trend speaks volumes about the centrality of cell phones in the daily lives of the Chinese. While there are stories in Western countries of distracted people dying while on their phones, the sheer volume of such stories coming out of China is shocking.

Expats in China may find that they are slightly less dependent on cell phones for news and information, since unpredictable VPN access makes accessing Western news difficult (see Chapter 5). On the other hand, even foreigners will have to use a cell phone for nearly every financial transaction from shopping at local markets and street food stalls to buying dinner at restaurants, paying for gym memberships, and ordering take-out. While some expats prefer to use an international plan through their home country's phone service, signing up for a Chinese phone number and SIM card better assists expats in navigating the increasingly electronic world of the city. Having a Chinese phone number makes it easier for local businesses like food delivery services to contact you, and better yet, keeps expats abreast of information provided through the city government's automated text messaging system.

Weibo and WeChat

That said, Western social media will not be the best way for expats to communicate within China and with their Chinese colleagues. The Chinese government has encouraged Chinese corporations to develop a "mirror" Internet. Nearly every existing social media site found outside mainland China has a corresponding Chinese version inside the country. This includes popular dating apps like TanTan and Momo, (often called Chinese Tinder) to Meituan (a Chinese version of Yelp), and QQ, Tencent's private messaging app. While the list of popular Chinese social media sites is a long one, two social connection sites dominate the field: Sina Weibo (usually referred to just as Weibo) and WeChat.

It's not an exaggeration to say that nearly everyone inside mainland China communicates via text or voice message through WeChat. With over *one billion users* (and growing), the social media platform maintains a totalitarian-like dominance over the social lives of the entire nation. The app has become so popular that many Westerners regularly use WeChat as a texting platform outside of China. As of 2019, WeChat had more than one billion active users. WeChat users are assigned a QR Code and a WeChat ID and can form groups for planning activities, hosting meetings, or sharing photos and itineraries. The app offers nearly limitless

functionality (including mobile payment), making it China's one-stop spot serving nearly everyone's needs.

Weibo, a somewhat less ubiquitous but still very popular social media platform, functions as a combination of Twitter, Facebook and Instagram, allowing users to share comments, videos, and post photos. All of China's social media sites are censured and monitored by the government, so political discussion tends to be limited and personal sharing more popular. In its continuing efforts to control social media conversations, the Chinese government has instituted rules that make WeChat group administrators responsible for the posted content of all group members.

China's Social Credit System

When using Chinese social media, be aware that Chinese citizens are increasingly subject to a broad and punitive social credit monitoring system in which they receive or lose points toward a national "social credit rating." The new mandatory system is widely expected to be implemented nationwide by 2020. Under the rating system, Chinese citizens will receive scores based on both social behavior (jaywalking, bad driving, helping their fellows) as well as online behavior. Those with poor social credit scores risk losing access to many privileges including financing and

QR Codes

WeChat, along with other mobile networks in China, work by assigning users a unique QR code (quick response code). An individual's QR, a newer generation of the old linear barcodes, is as unique as a fingerprint or a retina. Friends and acquaintances add one another to contact lists—or pay for products in the supermarket—by scanning QR codes with cell phones. Although QRs have been around for years, they have had little relevance to daily life in the West, having been traditionally used for encoding manufacturing information on packaging. Thanks to China's success with QRs, things are rapidly changing in the rest of the world.

In Shanghai, the QR code is approaching omnipotence. One of the first things many visitors to Shanghai notice are the large-form QR codes plastered across city walls, inside subways, on buses, and on billboards. Thanks to QR codes, China is well on its way to becoming the world's first cashless society.

traveling abroad. Expats should always remember to abide by Chinese law on social media.

Study the Great Nation App

Introduced in late 2018, Study the Great Nation is a popular cell phone app dedicated to supporting Xi Jinping and the Communist Party. Most of the app's 100 million users are Party members who were required to download the app when it was first released. Increasingly, Chinese business and schools are requiring students and employees to download the app as way of currying favor with the government. The app awards its users points based on their knowledge of Chinese history, culture, and Party current events.

WEDDINGS AND MARRIAGE

The importance of marriage in China is rooted in the central roles that family and ancestry play in Chinese culture. Social status is often a predictor of how elaborate a wedding celebration will be. The importance of social status is emphasized in marriages in ways that connect to a family's

CYBER AWARENESS

All social media communication via WeChat and Weibo, China's second most popular social media website, are monitored (and censored, if necessary) by the Chinese government. It's common practice to establish group chats on WeChat, but in 2017, strict laws were enacted that made group administrators responsible for all communications of individual group members. This is a clear attempt to prevent subversive groups from communicating and gathering new members, and it is designed (like China's new social credit system) to encourage repression of "dangerous" political dialogue via peer pressure. Some writers and expats have experimented with Chinese censorship on WeChat by sending sensitive but innocuous texts to Chinese counterparts. The typical result is that communications simply never appear in their message streams, despite showing in the sender's app as sent. As with all communication in China expats should always assume that they are being monitored and should communicate accordingly.

maintenance of both face and *guanxi*. Even in modern cities like Shanghai, many marriages are sometimes still viewed as partnerships between families, and familial pressure on young people to marry and start families of their own can be considerable.

Along with family expectations that children marry come other social expectations: the ability to achieve financially, build social status and own property, for example, all of which require a certain level of education. Young adults looking for a life partner must typically prove they can provide some financial and social benefit that will offer long-term security. That holds true as much for rural Chinese youth as it does for the high-powered professionals in urban Shanghai. Since China is still a predominantly patriarchal culture, the groom's family has been the one traditionally viewed as having the most to lose over a bad match.

Chinese weddings tend to be well-planned, time-consuming celebrations. One Chinese acquaintance of mine has referred to them as "the most important party of your life." If you are lucky enough to attend a wedding in Shanghai, expect to find an interesting mix of traditional and modern practices (cultural superstitions will certainly play a role), but on the whole, weddings in Shanghai have become heavily influenced by Western styles. In most large, modern Chinese cities, unless the wedding involves a traditional theme, the bride will usually wear white, the groom a tuxedo, and the celebration will be accompanied by fancy limousines and other familiar accouterments. Photography is something of a Chinese preoccupation. During spring and summer weekends in Shanghai, brides and grooms can often be found snapping wedding photos in popular locations such as the Bund or Yu Garden.

Yet, despite its worldly sophistication and capitulation to international influence, Shanghai is also the perfect place to find evidence of more traditional marriage customs as well. The most notable of these is the famous Shanghai "Marriage Market," a captivating and regular weekend fixture in The People's Park.

The Shanghai Marriage Market

China is currently experiencing a dramatic marriage crisis. Decades of a disastrous one-child policy combined with a historical preference for boys has created a gender imbalance that is now playing out among twenty- and thirty-somethings across the country. As I write these words, there are now 33 million more available marriageable men in China than there are available women to marry them. For millions of Chinese men—rural men in particular—the possibility of finding a heterosexual mate is now zero. Like trends in most countries, Chinese youth typically choose partners from a similar social class or cultural background, and in China, social standing is important. While this fact somewhat reduces the pressure of the gender imbalance among the wealthier and more urban areas, Shanghai is also a city of migrants.

Although it is more common for urban Chinese marriages to occur between partners of choice, the Shanghai Marriage Market is still a surprisingly crowded venue. Each weekend in People's Park, elders such as grandparents and parents gather to advertise the marriageability of their single, unmatched children, many of whom range in age from their early 20s to late 30s. In what appears to be a kind of generational clash, some of these parents are seeking marriage prospects without their children's knowledge! The prospective partners in question are almost never present; the marriage market is for parents.

Handwritten signs are typically affixed to personal objects or on nearby fences and benches. The event draws such large crowds that park pathways are transformed by a sea of open umbrellas with paper advertisements pinned to the canopies encircling the entire park. These advertisements include a description (and sometimes a photograph) of the candidate's age, height, education, employment, and property ownership. The event itself feels more like a social outing for aging parents than a match-matching or dating event for the younger generation. The concept of a marriage market is so foreign to Westerners that the event has become a well-known tourist attraction. Many Chinese who are advertising in the park will balk at having photos taken of their

signs. As odd as the concept of parental matchmaking is for Westerners, the weekly event offers some insight into the importance of marriage and family in Chinese society.

CHINESE ETIQUETTE

In addition to its conservative bent, Chinese culture also leans toward formality. Physical appearances are nearly as important as social

Family members browse advertisements for marriage partners at the Shanghai Marriage Market.

ones, and you should expect to see Chinese people dressed quite formally and fashionably for business and social events, even at events a typical Westerner would deem informal. Business attire is not quite as uniform as it is in Japan, where it is more common to see large groups of employees, male and female, wearing exactly the same suits, but the expectation that work requires formal dress is quite common. Most professionals in Shanghai wear dark suits with light shirts and women often wear straight skirts or formal pants in a business setting. Foreigners have more flexibility in the city and often stand out for their more creative attire.

Two men discussing a prospective match at the Shanghai Marriage Market.

Chinese and English Names

It's common practice in Shanghai for Chinese and Westerners to use two names: an English name and a Chinese name. Your Chinese counterparts (especially those who frequently interact with foreigners) will often choose an English first name for themselves, sometimes choosing them from a wide variety of Western sources, not the least of which are Hollywood films. Names like Simba and Ha Ha may seem odd to expats, but they are not all that uncommon. That said, the majority of English names used by the Chinese are perfectly common ones like as Ricky or Maria.

As a matter of respect, many companies and international schools likewise provide Chinese names for their foreign employees. Since Chinese is a logographic language, Westerners tend to make out quite well, typically receiving Chinese names with characters that correspond to a concept, object, or idea that seems meaningful.

When learning Chinese names, remember that Chinese surnames are always placed before given names, not after, as in the Western tradition. When greeting people while using their Chinese names, it is important to be as formal as possible. This means using their surname as well as their first name, unless they have already given you permission to use only their first name. Physical touching in conversation suggests a high level of familiarity and is never a good idea. The Chinese smile far more than they are given credit for, but during new introductions, smiling too much can be viewed as an informal gesture. If you are unsure how to proceed in a situation, it's safest to keep things as formal as possible.

The Manners Gap (Littering and Spitting)

The flip side of all this formality and focus on appearances is a startling acceptance of certain behaviors that many Westerners consider rude. Public spitting is routine despite the government's best efforts to halt the practice out of fear of spreading viruses and disease. Not only do many Chinese, male and female, spit in public, but there is a strong tendency to clear the lungs by scraping up everything inside the thoracic cavity before actually leaving the saliva on the sidewalk. Only slightly more shocking for many expats is learning that the practice of public spitting is not limited to men. You are just as likely to see young and older women leaving impressive puddles of sputum on the ground as you are young men.

Littering is also a routine practice in Shanghai. Expats are often shocked when they encounter instances of people casually dropping empty drink containers or wrappers on the ground. Research on China's littering problem has found that between 65 and 90 percent of Chinese drivers throw trash from their vehicles. It's rare for the garbage to pile up, however, since Shanghai has an enormous, mostly migrant, workforce dedicated to keeping the streets clean and picking up the large amount of daily trash that finds its way to the curbs.

TO QUEUE, OR NOT TO QUEUE

"An Englishman, even if he is alone, forms an orderly queue of one," said British writer George Mikes. Queues, or the utter lack of them, are another area in which Westerners may struggle to understand the Chinese rules of etiquette. In short, there really aren't any rules. Sometimes there is a line. Often there is not. If you do find yourself in a queue,

Many street sweepers in Shanghai are migrants from other areas of China.

especially in airports or at large public events like concerts, it's always good to prepare for the line to break down rather quickly into a mass of pushing and shoving. Every time we disembarked from the plane in Shanghai, my family liked to say: "It's time to get our China on." Most expats learn to adjust to the necessity of fighting their way through a door or onto an airplane with a well-placed elbow and an aggressive push forward. I still remember one time, as I left a crowded transport bus at the airport, seeing a Western mother with two young children exiting the bus. The mother kept repeating to the children, "push-push-push-push, keep going, keep going, keep going," like a cheerleader encouraging her little linebackers to muscle their way off the crowded bus.

ETIQUETTE SUGGESTIONS

- Carry business cards with you at all times. Share them and show you value them
- Accept or offer your credit cards with both hands
- Take your shoes off when entering a home
- There is no need to tip for delivery and service
- Respect personal space
- Don't ask questions that are too personal
- Respect elders. Elders are seated first and greeted first
- Avoid too much direct eye contact, which might be viewed as rude. Eye contact between strangers in public is unusual

CHAPTER 5

SETTLING IN

First say to yourself what you would be, and then do what you have to do.

— Epictetus

One of the most invigorating aspects of living and working overseas is the realization that a fresh beginning awaits: a new culture, new friends, new food, a new life. The sensation of being on the periphery of a culture—observing the world from a different perspective—doesn't only produce culture shock, it opens up an opportunity to remake oneself. Reinvention can be intoxicating, and maybe even a little addictive. But just as your feet start to leave the ground, the details of finding a home, getting a visa, and acquiring a residence permit will bring you back to earth.

OBTAINING A VISA

Once you've made the decision to move to Shanghai, the details of getting there will take on a life of their own. Obtaining the necessary permits and visas can sometimes produce headaches or confusion and often involves a certain level of redundancy. China's Great Firewall isn't only technological; the government bureaucracy involved in processing paperwork before and after your arrival is no small feat. The best-case scenario is that your new employer will handle much of the paperwork for you and walk you through the process. Most respectable international schools and established businesses will have Human Resource Departments staffed with employees dedicated to helping overseas hires and their families process paperwork, show up at the proper offices, and secure residence permits. Many companies even reimburse for the cost of these.

If your future employer can't provide specific parameters for your arrival, or isn't willing to help navigate the details, you might want to reconsider your prospects. Employers in Shanghai must provide extensive documentation to the government about their employees. If a company doesn't seem aware of this, something is wrong. A number of fly-by-night schools and organizations have popped up in Shanghai in recent years, often advertising for English teachers or other English-speaking employees. A fair number of enthusiastic foreigners have arrived in China only to realize too late that these institutions are not reputable or financially stable and cannot follow through on the salary, visa, and housing promises that were offered. Reputable companies that hire expats almost always provide new employees with some transition support and very often with residences or housing stipends.

China's Ministry of Foreign Affairs handles international visas, but most entry visas will be provided by a Chinese consular office or embassy in your home country. In some cases, extensive travel to designated Chinese consulates

EMPLOYMENT SCHEMES

There is a growing number of schemes in which foreigners are enticed to China with the promise of a job only to be caught up in scams in which they are reported by people as illegals inside the country in return for payments. In 2018, a group of South African teachers was lured to China with incorrect student visas, under the auspices of obtaining working visas and teaching jobs after their arrival. The students were detained for nearly six weeks by Chinese authorities for breaking the country's immigration laws. If you're heading to China to teach English, do your homework about the school's reputation. Although it's not always possible, visit your new employer and verify your living situation before deciding to move or talk to other employees who work with the institution.

Check with a Chinese consulate in your home country to verify Visa regulations.

in your home country may be necessary. Prepare all your documents ahead of time: passports (they cannot be within six months of expiration), official birth certificates (of all traveling family members), marriage licenses, and letters of invitation from an employer. Some of these documents may likewise need to be notarized in your home country prior to presenting them to Chinese officials. If you've already been offered employment in China, your employer must write a letter showing that you are filling a role that cannot be filled by a Chinese national.

All non-PRC citizens who wish to work in China require a temporary Z visa to enter the country, which will be converted to a permanent Z visa after settling. Students can obtain a number of different X visas, depending on their length of study. Visa types vary quite extensively for long and short-term business travel and tourism. Visa details will depend on your employer and your specific situation or country of origin. Regulations pertaining to visas and the prerequisites for each type of visa change so frequently that it's best to check with a Chinese consulate and your employer to verify current regulations.

In addition to your visa, you must be issued a Chinese residence permit. The People's Republic generally only issues one-year, renewable residence permits to foreigners. Z visas also require annual renewal, which can be another lengthy process. However, many executive hires and high-salaried expats and their families are granted 5-year Z visas and residence permits. Keep in mind that reputable schools and businesses often use their own personnel or Chinese liaisons to execute the renewal process since they are often audited by municipal commissions. Completing the paperwork for a residence permit will take anywhere from several weeks to several months, and you will not be in possession of your passport during that time. Consequently, you will be unable to travel outside of China until the process is finalized.

POLICE REGISTRATION

China is diligent about keeping track of foreigners within its borders. Foreign visitors and residents are required to register with the local police within 24 hours of their arrival. Hotels complete the process for guests. Otherwise, you or your employer will be required to complete the registration. Many large apartment complexes and compounds that cater to expats will have a concierge or managerial staff who will assist expats in completing their police registration. If you choose to live in smaller accommodations without concierge services, you will have to register with the police on your own. Your home country consulate can provide you with the appropriate information. Bring multiple photocopies of your passport and at least six passport-sized photos of yourself. Be aware that you could be fined if you aren't prompt in registering. Also know that when family or friends from abroad plan a visit, you will need to provide a letter of invitation for them, and they will likewise need to register with the police when they arrive.

FINDING A HOME

As in many modern cities, the styles and prices of homes in Shanghai can vary widely depending on their location. The choices are myriad, dictated only by budget, imagination, and lifestyle preferences. Housing prices in the city, especially in the trendy central locations, have risen precipitously for more than a decade, and Shanghai regularly occupies a top-ten spot on lists of the most expensive cities in the world for expats. On the other hand, China's major cities have experienced an epidemic of real-estate speculation. Estimates are that China has more than 50 million empty homes or apartments. Many of Shanghai's local residents

Most apartment buildings in Shanghai are tall enough to offer spectacular views of the city.

are priced out of apartments and villas in the city. Even a moderate expat budget often exceeds the annual income of the average Shanghainese. As a result, you should have a wide selection of vacancies to choose from, and occasionally there are deals to be found. If you are house hunting on your own and find a landlord with multiple vacancies, he/she may be flexible on price.

Deciding *how* you want to live before you embark on a housing search will go a long way toward smoothing out the process. Whether you are looking to maintain a lifestyle similar to your home country, or to experience the adventure of authentic Chinese life, you should have no trouble finding the right fit. For expats with children, living in proximity to schools often drives the decision-making process. It's helpful to make a list of necessities, amenities, and experiences you desire. Do you have children who need space to ride bikes away from congested city streets? Will you need to live close to their schools, or are you comfortable with a commute? Do you want easy access to nightlife, bars, and fabulous international restaurants? Are you energized by the din of Chinese life? Will you have a driver, or do you want access to the metro? These questions and more should define the parameters of your search.

Perhaps the most compelling choice is the one between life in the suburbs or life in central Shanghai. Housing choices in the suburbs range from gated communities called "compounds" that resemble sprawling American neighborhoods, to modern high-rise apartments with expansive views, to cozy lane houses (*longtang* or *shikumen)* tucked in hideaway *lilong* (city villages). *Most* expats are given one of two choices by employers as part of a contract—an allowance that gives the freedom to find independent housing, or a compound apartment provided by your employer. If you must use a real estate agent and your new

Many apartments in Shanghai come fully or partially furnished. With unfurnished housing, it's worth inquiring whether essentials such as beds or tables can be provided, especially in serviced apartment complexes, which often keep such items in storage. In China, everything is negotiable.

employer cannot refer you to an English speaking one, they are easily located through the many real estate websites that cater to foreigners. Many apartments in Shanghai come fully or partially furnished. With unfurnished housing, it's worth inquiring whether essentials such as beds or tables can be provided, especially in serviced apartment complexes, which often keep such items in storage. In China, everything is negotiable.

PUXI OR PUDONG

Choosing your home, especially from a distant continent, can be daunting. However, once you have settled on a lifestyle, focusing your search on the residential areas of Shanghai that meet your needs will be easier. There are endless debates among expats about whether it's better to live in Puxi or Pudong. These two very different "sides" of Shanghai, which are separated by the long stretch of the Huangpu River, offer quite different living experiences. Such arguments usually involve which "half" of Shanghai feels more authentically Chinese. The fact is, they are both Chinese. Thirty years ago, Pudong barely existed. As a result, its streets are wider and its buildings newer, but many foreigners argue that Pudong lacks the rambling character and energy of the older, Puxi side of the city. In the end, which area of the city you choose to live in will more likely depend on the location of schools and employment.

Central Shanghai (including both Puxi and Pudong) is divided into business, financial, industrial, and residential districts. Highways and smaller arteries usually define the borders of residential areas. The Yan'an Elevated Highway cuts an east-west path through Shanghai, dividing the city into northern and southern regions. The Inner Ring Elevated highway forms a wide loop, dividing Puxi's downtown region from outer suburban sprawl. The following list of expat friendly residential areas is comprehensive without being absolute. These popular locations are home to many of Shanghai's best international schools, shopping, transportation, and healthcare services. My own family has lived in both the Former French Concession—bustling and densely packed in central Shanghai—as well as the suburban "outer ring" district of Huacao Town (Minhang District). Polar opposites, to be sure, but each area offers advantages and disadvantages.

Xuhui (Former French Concession)

The most culturally and internationally diverse residential area of Shanghai, the Former French Concession ranks highest in desirability for many expats. The area is full of funky shops, cafes, groceries, wet markets, bars, restaurants, and street food vendors, making it one of the liveliest areas in the city. The French Concession is also known for having an energetic nightlife. Some of the best housing options in Shanghai are here, and the area's eclectic mix of colonial and Art Deco architecture make it one of the most aesthetically appealing places to live. Leafy tree-lined streets are so prevalent it's easy to forget how tall the high-rise apartment buildings can be.

Housing in the French Concession varies, but mostly consists of high-rise apartments with spectacular city views, or what many refer to as "lane houses" or *longtang*. Prices in the apartment complexes can range considerably. Many foreign teachers are able to afford very nice, renovated apartments in reasonably-priced buildings that cater to Chinese citizens rather than to expats. Luxury high rises with fully-serviced apartments are popular among expat executives with more generous budgets.

Chinese lane houses, typically of older construction, tend to be attached, single-family residences located inside small *lilong*, or "villages," which occupy the space between city blocks and are often hidden behind walls along quieter residential streets. Lane houses have a rather posh reputation among expats and securing a refurbished one is considered a coup. Such a find will also require a generous housing budget. There are still some *shikumen*-style homes inside the *lilong*, which function like small, contained communities, sometimes with their own wet markets and sidewalk shops, making them attractive to people wanting a more Chinese experience. But as with apartment living, life in a lane house can feel somewhat close. Finding a good lane house or even a swanky apartment in the French Concession will require the use of a bilingual real-estate professional, something that is not difficult to find in this international area.

Longtang or lane houses are highly sought after residences.

Good healthcare is easily accessible from nearly all locations in the Xuhui District, but there are few international schools here, so children may have to commute. There are a sizable number of highly sought-after Chinese kindergartens (elementary schools), and it's not uncommon for expats to place their children in a Chinese school in the primary years. Admission to these schools requires some effort, and fluency in Mandarin is usually necessary, but there's no better way for young children to learn the language than by being fully immersed in it all day long. Access to the metro is excellent from most residential areas.

Xintiandi/Tianzifang

Technically speaking, Xintiandi, one of Shanghai's trendiest residential locations, is still a part of the Former French Concession. As such, it boasts interesting architecture and amazing nightlife options. But it's also a favorite spot for tourists, so its reputation suffers among long term expats for being a bit less authentic. Life in Xintiandi mirrors that in the rest of the French Concession, with good access to restaurants and the metro, attractive tree-lined streets and access to both Chinese and Western markets.

Tianzifang is a touristy curiosity market tucked away in the lanes and alleys of old *shikumen* buildings. The architecture is interesting, but most buildings have been remodeled into a tight cluster of shops, restaurants, and trinket markets. Many of the surrounding neighborhoods are truly Chinese residential areas and can offer a sense of life quite different from other residential areas in Xuhui. This area is within just two or three metro stops of some of Shanghai's most interesting markets, including the bird and flower market, the cricket market (with cricket fights and all the paraphernalia

Xiantiandi is popular among expats for its trendy restaurants and bars.

related to "raising" crickets), and the fabric market. Xintiandi also offers easy access to other tourist destinations such as the Yu Yuan Garden.

Jing'an/People's Square
Replete with luxury hotels and smack in the heart of Puxi, Jing'an offers easy access to everything downtown, including the Bund, the French Concession, as well as more touristy areas such as the Yu Yuan Garden and People's Square. The area is vibrant, and densely populated, and quite literally teems with luxury shopping and extremely active traffic patterns. Jing'an exudes urban sophistication, which is what accounts for its pricey real estate.

If Jing'an tops your lifestyle list, you'll need a fat wallet or a generous company package. High-rise, serviced apartments dominate the living options, although there are smaller lane houses and older more traditional apartments in the adjacent areas and side streets. Unlike the roads in the Former French Concession, which stretches along the area's southern border, Jing'an roads are wider and more spacious, the better to accommodate the crazy number of people and cars.

Living in Jing'an likely means you enjoy a modern, urban lifestyle. Some of Shanghai's best luxury shopping runs along East Nanjing Road. The Shanghai Exhibition Center, the National Museum of Shanghai, and the Natural History Museum are all within easy walking distance. Central to the area is the eponymous Jing'an Temple, a touristy but functioning Buddhist Temple, and one of Shanghai's must-see tourist attractions. For a more authentic Chinese scene, a daily walk through the adjacent Jing'an Park yields a constant stream of elderly dancers and outdoor tai chi classes.

Most of the benefits and drawbacks of Jing'an are similar to those of the French Concession. The area lacks proximity to international schools, but that is offset by access to good healthcare, nightlife, and general fun.

Changning/Hongqiao/Gubei

Not quite the suburbs and not quite city center, Hongqiao is nestled on the western side of Shanghai and offers convenient metro access to downtown with a slightly less crowded feel than the residential areas in central Puxi. Expats who live here choose the location for its wide variety of housing options, wide streets, access to healthcare, and shopping convenience. Apartment complexes dominate the eastern sections of Changning District, while expat compounds, complete with spacious single-family houses and townhomes, are plentiful throughout. Hongqiao is especially attractive to expats who find Huacao Town simply too isolated from the metro system, yet still want access to its great schools. Within Hongqiao proper, The Shanghai Community International School (SCIS) is one of the city's largest and best international schools.

Hongqiao is loaded with restaurants, including international and Western chains. *Laowai Jie* (foreigner street) offers every kind of international food option, despite suffering constant rumors of closure by the government. It operates near one of Shanghai's most popular fake markets, The Hongqiao Pearl Market. Gubei has some of the best Western-style grocery shopping in the city, including Metro, City Shop, and Carrefour, all within easy access of residential compounds. The Hongqiao Airport, best for domestic flights in China, along with Hongqiao Railway Station, one of Asia's largest train stations, are both located here, making it extremely attractive to expats who travel frequently to other major cities in China. Hongqiao's primary medical facility is the Shanghai United Family Hospital, whose emergency room my own family has beta tested more than once. The care is first rate.

Gubei has a reputation for being the area of choice for east Asians, and it is home to thousands of expat Koreans, Japanese, and Taiwanese. The area also has a sizable population of Western expats as well. Koreatown and Little Tokyo are located here, and they are popular destinations for those seeking a little variety from everything Chinese. If easy access to international schools and a balance of Chinese and Western living ranks high on your lifestyle list, then Hongqiao may be the place for you.

Huacao Town/Minhang

Minhang District is the epitome of the Western expat "bubble," thanks to the presence of three of Shanghai's largest international schools. Home life in this suburban area can sometimes resemble life in an American or European suburb, and most of the residential facilities here hunker behind walls inside gated compounds. In China, the term *villa*—a European holdover—typically refers to a single-family house. Central Shanghai is far too densely populated to offer the luxury of Western-style space. As a result, most expat compounds that contain Western-style villas— complete with prodigious lawns and fountains—are located in the outer suburbs of Minhang, Hongqiao or in Pudong.

Many of the apartments in Huacao Town are owned by businesses and schools and are used to house employees rent free. If your budget is top notch, the Forest Manor, or Rancho Santa Fe compounds, have tree-lined streets, large yards, and huge single-family homes with impressive amenities. Take a glance at the real-estate listings in this area and you'd never know you were in China.

The downside of choosing to live in Minhang is that access to downtown can be challenging. Some compounds, as well as the international schools, offer shuttle service to and from downtown for residents and employees. Taxis often line up outside compounds to pick up residents, but taxi drivers downtown will sometimes refuse to drive out as far as Minhang for a return trip. For these reasons, hiring a driver from any of the local driving agencies is a popular option for expats who live in this area. Since 2017, the Shanghai Municipal Transportation Commission has had its eye on better connecting Minhang to the city at large, and metro access is expected to stretch out to Huacao Town.

The newest metro line (the southern extension of Minhang Line 5), opened in December of 2018. By late 2020, new metro stops are expected in Minhang, connecting it directly to airports and central Shanghai.

One of the more popular expat gated compounds in Huacao is the Shanghai Racquet Club, a full-service community of apartments, villas, and penthouses with access to club facilities, including a swimming pool, community center, and tennis courts. Compound life tends to benefit families with young children by providing an instant community of friends and schoolmates, as well as a place where even very young children can easily ride bikes or walk to nearby homes of their friends. Compounds can also provide a much-needed support network for trailing spouses who have given up jobs to follow their mates overseas. Our younger daughter enjoyed living in Minhang more than in downtown, since our residence was convenient to her school (she could walk or ride her bike) and most importantly, to her friends.

A man walks his camel down a Minhang street. Anything is possible in Shanghai.

While Huacao is often criticized for being an inauthentic cultural experience, there is still Chinese life to be found there, especially if you walk to the neighboring Zhudi Town, a small Chinese section of the city that offers glimpses of more authentic Chinese life. Both Huacao and Zhudi have large, quite excellent wet markets. The residential population of Zhudi tends to hail from rural areas of China, so intense staring at Westerners (and exhibiting annoyance at their presence) is sometimes more common in this outer area than in downtown Shanghai.

Jinqiao/Kangqiao

A running joke among expats, usually those living in Puxi, is that Jinqiao or Kangqiao, the primary residential expat areas in Pudong, feels a bit like living in New Jersey. The fact that New York University established a satellite campus in Jinqiao only reinforces the observation. Jinqiao is the Pudong twin of Huacao Town. It is completely and unapologetically suburban and is known as a Western expat "bubble." That said, expats with families love these areas as they offer wide, safe roadways for biking and all of the comforts of a mostly Western lifestyle. Like Huacao, metro access to Jinqiao is not superb, but newer lines are in the works and things have begun to change as Shanghai's ever-expanding metro line makes its way to the outer reaches of the city.

Living in Jinqiao is all about compound life. The apartment complexes and villa homes are sprawling and the streets are wide. The Green Court Complex, one of the most popular compounds for Western expats, offers shady tree-lined boulevards and a convenient location near international schools and shopping. Some expats complain of a dorm-like feel to the compound campuses, but others love the built-in communities that come with compound living. While much of the outer areas of Jinqiao and Kangqiao are crowded with Chinese apartment buildings, (and much of the staff in those buildings work in the expat area), it's possible to live here and see mostly Westerners most of the time. For those working in the financial district, Jinqiao and Kangqio offer commutes that are unimpeded by bridge and tunnel crossings.

WHAT TO BRING

Shipping your household belongings to China is not for the faint hearted. Most corporate relocation packages cover the cost of shipping furniture and personal belongings to your new home. Expats without corporate packages often choose to avoid the exorbitant costs of shipping and leave most of their belongings in storage or in homes that they maintain outside China. The prospect of moving far away for an extended time and having to leave most of your personal belongings in storage is enough to give anyone pause. Rest assured household goods at affordable prices are available in Shanghai. Decorating with a few Chinese 'fake' antiques is part of the fun. Nevertheless, there are some small items that many people find more convenient to bring with them.

Feminine Hygiene Products

These products are available in Shanghai, but not always at a moment's notice. In addition to being expensive, many Western women find the Chinese style of pads (thinner, with less reliable adhesive) to be quite uncomfortable and less absorbent than other brands. Tampons can be quite difficult to come by as there are lingering cultural taboos in China against using them. Most women bring a healthy stockpile of feminine hygiene products with them from their home country.

Prescriptions and Over-the-Counter Pharmaceuticals

General over-the-counter medications such as aspirin, ibuprofen, flu relief, and laxatives can be difficult to obtain in China and sometimes require a prescription. Most foreigners choose to bring a small personal pharmacy with them. Those who suffer from severe allergies should bring a supply of anti-allergen medications from their home country. EpiPens, in particular, are quite difficult to find in China.

Medications such as antidepressants and antibiotics are widely available by prescription in Shanghai, but they also tend to be very expensive. When health insurance allows, you'd be wise to fill all your medical prescriptions in your home country and bring a supply with you. Many international health insurance plans actually prefer members to fill prescriptions outside of China and provide better coverage for doing so. When you are feeling under the weather in Shanghai, local Chinese will tell you incessantly to use *Chinese medicine*, typically a mixture of brewed herbs and teas. While there is much to be said for the benefits of traditional Chinese medicine, it sometimes isn't quite enough for foreigners who are reliant on pharmaceuticals.

Books and Magazines

Foreign language books are available in Shanghai at a number of small local bookstores downtown. For those living in the outer ring areas, finding English language books is a non-starter. Since foreign language books are imported, they often cost up to twice as much in China, and the selection of titles is thin. The largest English language library in China is actually contained at the Shanghai American School, Puxi campus. Of course, illegal pdf copies of Western books are widely available from WeChat poachers, if your ethics permit. With an internet connection, downloading e-books on an e-reader like the Kindle or on an app like Apple Books works fairly well, but it's possible you'll need a VPN and the download can take a long time. Also, it may be impossible to download any e-book on a banned book list in China. Most foreigners choose to bring at least a temporary supply of reading material with them.

Videos and DVDs

The advent of Internet streaming has made DVDs nearly obsolete in many Western countries, yet pirated DVDs remain immensely popular in China since Chinese Internet censorship makes streaming illegal foreign movies difficult. Pirated DVDs seem to bypass the long arm of government

紀录片
Documentary Film

卡通电影
Cartoon Movie

Buying pirated DVDs is easy in Shanghai's numerous DVD stores.

censorship which willingly turns a blind eye to these very healthy businesses.

Bringing DVDs from your home country is not advisable. If they are not confiscated in customs, they will not likely work in any Chinese DVD player that you purchase in Shanghai. Chinese DVD players are designed to play pirated Chinese DVDs. You can't buck the system. DVD stores with pirated DVDs populate all the residential neighborhoods and fake markets in Shanghai, so you will not suffer from a lack of choice.

Voltage and Outlet Adaptors

Americans and Canadians will need to bring outlet adapters in order to use appliances (including computer power cords) from their home countries. It's easier to buy small appliances such as hair dryers and kitchen appliances in China to avoid overloading outlets. Cell phone power chargers often work without an adapter.

Shoes and Clothing

Large-sized shoes, bras, and underwear can be nearly impossible to find in China. If you are a towering Scandinavian or an average-sized American, shopping for these items will be challenging. That said, one of the great benefits of living in Shanghai is that clothing can be made to order, and many expats enjoy having copies of their favorite dresses, shirts and pants duplicated. Men's suits and women's winter coats are specialty items that are easily tailored and made to order at the fabric market.

Identification and Documents

There are never-ending requests for legal documents in

China. Expats who live in China on an annual visa must be prepared to have paperwork handy at all times. Legal documents often need to be notarized as well. Home country consulates in Shanghai will likely provide notary services, or you can make use of a notary before arriving in Shanghai. Most expats will need some sort of identification with them at all times. It's advisable to make photocopies of birth certificates, marriage licenses, educational diplomas, driver's licenses, and passports and leave them with a family member in your home country. Do not pack identification in checked luggage.

SHOPPING FOR THE BASICS

Western-style grocery stores tend to cluster in expat areas and near compounds. Residents of Jinqiao and Hongqiao will have a wide range of shopping options. Metro is a German multinational wholesale market with locations throughout Shanghai. This store is convenient for large families and carries both Western and Chinese items that are available to purchase in less expensive bulk sizes. A membership

SNACKS

Certain snacks unique to your country of origin may be difficult to find, and if you do find them, they will be quite expensive. Even basic items such as oatmeal and dark chocolate, both of which are available in Shanghai, cost a small fortune. Here's a list of items you may consider checking in your luggage or sending with your shipment. Most dry goods can be checked inside luggage on a flight, but produce, meats, cheeses, alcohol, or live plants cannot be brought into the country.

- Oatmeal and cereals
- Canned meats
- Graham crackers
- Snack biscuits
- Dark chocolate bars

card is required at Metro, and it is easily obtainable at the service desk without any advanced Chinese language skills. Hauling home your bounty requires the use of a hired driver. In the fall of 2019, the U.S. wholesale market Costco opened its first location in Shanghai's Huacao Town, receiving over 90,000 membership requests on the first day. Like Metro, Costco requires membership and some planning to carry your purchases home.

Western-style big box stores are located in expat areas of the city.

The former French Concession lacks the space of other residential areas, but still has an adequate supply of small corner markets that stock basic Western goods. A large Western-style underground market is hidden at the Jing'an metro stop and City Shop is located in the Shanghai Centre.

The Chinese, including your *ayi*, will likely shop in local wet markets, the open-air produce markets that crop up almost everywhere. Many expat guides suggest avoiding wet markets in favor of buying imported produce, since there is no way to know what type of water has been used to irrigate wet market vegetables. That said, many expats who are interested in learning about Chinese culture tend to shop in local wet markets or at produce stalls. These stalls contain a large variety of produce for Chinese cooking that cannot be found in Western markets. I always shopped in wet markets for our produce and found it to be one of the most enjoyable experiences I had in Shanghai.

Shanghai is home to three different IKEA stores. Shopping at a Shanghai IKEA is considered a unique cultural experience, since many Chinese consumers use the store furniture for napping and the tables for picnicking, which Westerners find delightful. Some lonely, elderly Chinese citizens have been known to use IKEA as a dating venue. There is an abundance of very good furniture vendors aside from IKEA, as well as stores offering imported rugs and high-end design consulting. A number of Chinese-style "antique" furniture stores are popular among expats as well. When shopping for Chinese antiques, remember that "antique" is more of a stylistic description than a factual one.

Online Grocery Delivery

Without a driver, grocery shopping for a family can be a challenge in Shanghai, since there is only so much that can be carried at once. Add to that urban congestion and long hours at work, and many foreigners find they rarely have time to sleep let alone shop. As a result, online grocery delivery is booming. Fields and Kate and Kimi are by far the most popular online grocery delivery services among expats, and they stock a large supply of imported products such as meat, milk, and produce from Australia as well locally sourced organic food. Western imports are usually presumed safe, and many expats who are worried about China's food scandals use these delivery services.

Taobao

Taobao is China's most popular online marketplace. Increasingly, expats have found their way around the popular shopping website looking for hard-to-find items, despite the fact that the site offers only moderately effective English language translations and apps. However, the company is gaining an international reputation and it likely won't be long before the website is fully functional in English. Taobao sells both used and new items and allows individuals to sell their own goods directly to consumers. If something exists, it can be purchased on Taobao—from footwear to furniture to live fish. Most Chinese users will tell you that buying on Taobao is far more inexpensive than purchasing in a physical store. But be wise about false claims on the site since it is also one of the world's largest fake markets. With over 600 million monthly users, you'll have to take your chances. To register for a Taobao account, you'll need a Chinese cell phone number and a well-funded Alipay account to pay for your purchases.

HIRING AN AYI

Ayi culture is integral to life in Shanghai, and hiring a good *ayi* (literally, an auntie) can be integral to expat survival. In many Western cultures, hiring domestic help is strictly the purview of the rich and famous. In China, not only do many middle-class Chinese households hire *ayis*, most expats, even teachers, or single men and women, often have at least one *ayi* to help with cleaning, cooking, or childcare. Domestic help is quite affordable in China, and many expat families with young children hire two *ayis*, since *ayis* view cleaning as a separate function from nannying. *Ayis* rarely live with the families they work for. Hiring a full-time *ayi* is not necessary, and many *ayis* only work part-time two or three days a week for specific tasks. Most part-time ayis will also be working part-time for at least one other family as well, so you will have to lock in to specific days and times.

Hiring an *ayi* is not a requirement. Expats who live in

serviced apartments rarely need *ayis* to handle the cleaning, for example. But employment as an *ayi*, especially for a foreign family, is considered a very good job prospect for many women in Shanghai. As a result, there is something of an expectation that you will provide the opportunity.

There are benefits to hiring an *ayi* that go beyond cooking and cleaning. A good *ayi* can make navigating daily chores like paying utility bills, arranging for home repairs, and ordering drinking water, smoother and easier. *Ayis* are also frequently the ones to handle house repairman and deal with Chinese-speaking apartment managers when need be. Part of the culture shock of arriving in China is the realization that all your household appliances are covered with Chinese characters. Deciphering the difference between hot and cold cycles on a washing machine, or figuring out how to operate a microwave, can cause a severe bout of culture shock. Your *ayi* can help you navigate such things (or avoid them entirely)!

Due to its considerable international population, Shanghai has a large number of agencies and hiring services that expats use to hire *ayis*. The process typically involves filling out paperwork and giving extensive interviews. You should prepare a list of questions for your potential hire, and offer a list of your expectations, especially if childcare is on the table. This will make finding a good match more likely. Since most *ayis* do not speak English, plan to have a translator present for the interview. Once you've hired someone, the translation app on your cell phone will make daily communication with your *ayi* less challenging. Although Google is banned in China, the Google Translate app is not, and it is a popular choice for Western expats.

Although it may not always be feasible, the best way to find a dependable *ayi* is through word of mouth rather than agencies. Especially if you are moving into an expat compound, or into a school or business community where foreigners are frequently coming and going, it's not uncommon for one family who is leaving to pass along their *ayi* to an arriving family. Ask your employer if they are aware of any families leaving the country who may have an *ayi* who needs a new job. Question the outgoing family about their experiences. More likely than not, they will want to find an excellent placement for an *auntie*, whom they will miss very much. This is how we found our *ayi*, an amazing cook, and one of the most hardworking women I've ever known. She took wonderful care of my family and made our lives significantly better during a year of tremendous transition.

Even after you've hired an *ayi*, you will have to be clear about what specific chores you want her to manage, and what rules you have for your children. Depending on her comfort level with foreigners, some *ayis* will not hesitate to criticize your child-rearing skills, while others will take no initiative without your direction. One of the greatest benefits of hiring an *ayi* to help care for young children is watching the child's rapid language acquisition. Young children with Chinese *ayis* are soon translating for their parents in the grocery store.

Most expats with young children will need to tell an *ayi* to refrain from using "Chinese medicine" (usually herbals) with children, and make sure she knows the location of the nearest Western medical clinic. You'll undoubtedly hear some *ayi* horror stories floating in the ether among expat families. One friend of mine, for example, learned her *ayi* was sedating her baby during the day, which resulted in long sleepless nights for the parents, but such problems are the exception, not the rule. Nanny cams are becoming a popular option for those who feel something isn't quite right (like my friend), but due diligence during the hiring process, along with good references, will help avoid such problems.

Ayis who work in expat communities frequently discuss (and compare) compensation amongst themselves. You should ask other families about the going rate for an *ayi* and try to stay within the general bounds that others are paying. In our first year, an *ayi* "revolt" (an ironic occurrence in current day China to be sure), occurred in one compound over disparities in compensation offered by expat families. While the pay may seem very low, or even unfair to you, by typical Chinese working-class standards, it is not. As with most employees in China, you should provide a red envelope with a 13-month payment (*hongbao*) at the beginning of Chinese New Year.

If you would like your *ayi* to cook meals in the style of your home country, provide recipes for her in Chinese. If you're looking for an *ayi* to cook *Chinese* meals—and this is one of the great benefits of finding an *ayi* who is a good cook—make clear your expectations about diet. Chinese cuisine is wonderful, but it can also be somewhat lively. Many *ayis* cook in the local style which sometimes includes very bony dishes. You should come to a prior agreement about how much of the chicken will show up on your plate. If you do not enjoy eating the feet, for example, let your *ayi* know ahead of time.

Finding an *ayi* who has worked previously for an international family will make the smoothest transition. Once you become accustomed to having someone in your house, you will be pleasantly surprised at how much easier life is with an *ayi*. Leaving money along with a grocery list (translated, of course), and coming home to warm Chinese dumplings and a clean house, or opening a drawer full of neatly folded underwear, are extravagances in most Western countries. In China, it's just part of daily life. If you and your *ayi* are a good match and can build a trusting relationship, she will become a new member of your family.

GETTING AROUND TOWN

Pedestrian bridges, crosswalks, sidewalks, and skywalks traverse most of Shanghai's major highways and intersections making it an extremely walkable city. I know a few brave expat souls who ventured into the world of driving cars on Shanghai's crowded and chaotic highways, but most find that public transportation, bicycles, taxis, scooters, or hired drivers provide the best means of getting around.

Cars and scooters don't always stay on the roads in Shanghai.

Scooters

The quintessential mode of transportation in China is no longer the bicycle or the rickshaw; it's the electric scooter. By far the most popular method of transit for many expats in China, scooters are affordable and do not require a driver's license. Anyone can scoot! A good quality rechargeable scooter will cost about ¥4500 (US$654) new and can range in price up to ¥7,500 (US$1,090). Used scooters can cost from ¥1,200–4,000 (US$174–581) and are easy to purchase through English language second-hand exchanges. Be careful. The quality of used scooters varies considerably.

Scooting is its own culture in Shanghai. Helmets are not required, and scooter operators rarely obey traffic laws, including red lights. Shanghai scooters know no boundaries, regularly zipping along on the sidewalks to avoid traffic congestion. One of the more interesting sights in Shanghai will

Scooters are the quintessential mode of transportation in Shanghai.

be the wide variety of items residents carry on their scooters, including entire families. Scooters must be registered with the local police. Once purchased, a *fapiao* (an official Chinese receipt) must be presented to the local police along with proof of residency and a passport. The police will then provide an official form that must be returned to the seller (whether a store or an individual). Once this process is completed, you will receive a license plate.

Cars

Very few foreigners have the courage to apply for a Chinese driver's license, and China will not accept international ones. Even if your language skills are not an impediment to understanding the awkward translations of the extensive written exam, you will need nerves of steel to navigate Shanghai's congested highways and dizzying traffic patterns. Car culture in China is still relatively novel compared to the rest of the world. That said, a few Westerners do brave the concrete jungle for reasons that are utterly incomprehensible to most.

Drivers

Similar to *ayi* culture, hiring a personal driver is an accepted practice and an extremely common part of daily life. In some sections of the city, hired drivers are ubiquitous. In certain residential areas, lines of drivers can be seen standing around outside apartment buildings, shopping centers, and villas, smoking cigarettes, scrolling through their cell phones, or napping in one of the universal gray vans while waiting for their charges. You should set clear boundaries with your driver and provide him (or her) with a list of rules—for example, no smoking in the car, and seat belts always on the children.

Many professionals with families (both Chinese and foreign) hire personal drivers, who remain on call nearly all the time, shuttling children to and from school activities or taking parents to dinner across town. Companies often provide personal drivers (with vehicles) as part of relocation packages. If that's the case, you'll have very little to do with the process. As with taxi drivers, using a translation or destination app can be helpful when communicating locations to your driver. Foreigners who lack a personal driver can hire through agencies for single occasions.

Similar to an *ayi*, your driver will be someone with whom you spend a lot of time. Driving is a very respectable service-industry job in Shanghai, and a driver's duties often include much more than driving. Drivers will often be responsible for carrying groceries or luggage, helping you navigate *fapiaos*, smoothing over communication issues, even paying bills. As with *ayis*, drivers will expect a red envelope with a 13-month payment (*hongbao*) during the Chinese New Year holiday.

Metro/Maglev

Shanghai's world-class metro system, the longest mass transit rail system in the world, has been a flagship venture in the city's twenty-year infrastructure frenzy. The system seems to spread much like a bamboo forest—swiftly, and relentlessly. With at least five lines under construction as of this writing, new stops open with astonishing regularity. The multicolor map illustrating its 16 lines and more than 400 operating stations might seem daunting. It's really not. Station names use pinyin (Roman letters) as well as Chinese characters. Traveling by metro is the easiest and most efficient way to move through Shanghai.

Metro lines connect with Shanghai's four major railway stations as well as both airports. From Pudong, riders can take the celebrated Maglev (magnetic levitation) train, the fastest electric train in the world. In true Chinese fashion, the Maglev doesn't really go anywhere—it connects to metro Line 2 at Longyang station in Pudong, where riders can transfer. The Shanghai Metro System has one of the most expansive strategic plans in the world, and most areas of Shanghai that have been underserved by metro access, including expat suburban hubs like Huacao and Jinqiao, will soon have metro stations.

A metro ticket costs between ¥3–12 (US$0.44–1.74), which makes riding the metro just one step above free. The metro is clean, safe, and modern. Rush hour in Shanghai is overwhelming, whether one is driving or using public transit. Squeezing into a jam-packed metro car in the morning is one of the defining experiences of working in the city. Anyone who has mastered it is immediately a verifiable resident.

Tickets, which are available at automated machines inside metro stations, have enough English options that deciphering a purchase isn't difficult. If you stand around long enough looking confused, a kind-hearted Chinese soul will almost always pity you and help. If you plan to use the metro regularly, purchasing a reloadable magnetic card from an information booth in one of the larger stations is an option. The metro system is quickly catching up to the mobile payment craze. In some (not all) stations, you can now use WeChat or Alipay instead of purchasing a ticket. The Shanghai metro is not a late night-operation, perhaps its only downside. Traveling across the city after 10:00 pm when the stations close requires a different mode of transportation.

Taxis

Shanghai is flush with taxis and nearly all Westerners in China have a story to tell about riding in them. From mercurial drivers that make fun of foreign speech to stories of dropping foreigners at not-quite-there locations, Chinese cab rides can be a bit unpredictable. It takes some practice (and occasionally nerves of steel) to get a taxi to stop for you in Shanghai, and it's been cited as one of the more frustrating activities for foreigners who are not visibly Asian. The first rule of success is to find the right street corner, one busy enough that taxis drive by but not so busy that they will not stop to pick you up.

It's not uncommon for taxi drivers, whether motivated by xenophobia or general indifference, to switch off their rooftop "available" lights as they approach a signaling foreigner. Don't count on drivers speaking English. Instead, use a taxi

Using the Didi app will make getting a tax easier for expats.

card app—there are a number of very good apps that will translate addresses into Mandarin, and provide a destination "taxi card" for your driver. Smart Shanghai, a do-everything app for English speaking expats, also has a convenient taxi-card function.

In general, taxi drivers in Shanghai are far more open to picking up foreigners than in Beijing, where one friend of mine once jumped into the car of a random Chinese family and begged for a ride after being stranded and unable to find a taxi to pick her up. Finding a ride in Shanghai's outer rings, beyond the city center, is more challenging than in center city where foreigners are quite common. Taxis are numerous outside the expat residential compounds and finding one there is nearly effortless. Hotel taxi queues are always a good bet too, and they are easily accessible to foreigners who are not patrons.

Ride Hailing/Didi Chuxing

Ridesharing made a bumpy arrival in in China in 2016 when Didi acquired Uber China, quickly becoming the country's most popular ride hailing app. By mid 2017, Didi Chuxing was listed as the third most valuable startup company in the world and had expanded its ride sharing functions to bicycles, private cars, and taxis. The arrival that same year of an English language version of its popular app offered foreigners a reliable way to circumvent the problems of drivers not wanting to pick them up. Using the Didi app to hail a ride (sometimes a taxi) means that a driver does not know who the rider is until he arrives at the pickup point.

Ridesharing has become enormously popular in Shanghai. The Didi app functions much like Uber. Riders can track their rides or taxis as they approach and ensure, via a map function, that they are heading in the right direction. Didi accounts can be directly linked to WeChat payment accounts or to bank cards. Many official taxis in Shanghai are members of the Didi network, so don't be surprised if your ride turns out to be an official cab.

HEALTH INCIDENTALS

State Medical Exam

Foreigners are required to provide evidence that they do not harbor communicable diseases including HIV and Hepatitis. Before leaving your home country, you'll need to gather the appropriate medical paperwork from your doctor. If your employer does not ask for these forms, bring your test results anyway along with a letter from your doctor certifying your health status.

One of the most talked about new experiences among expat arrivals is the completion of the state medical exam.

I've had the benefit of completing the medical exam twice, for two separate residential entries into China. The entire process is a paragon of Chinese efficiency. The state facility that performs these medical exams is typically bustling with other foreigners who are also feeling slightly dazed, so you'll be in good company. After filling out forms and receiving a personalized collection of numbered barcode stickers, you will be shown to a changing room and provided with a locker. Be prepared to make some of your first expat acquaintances while wearing a hospital gown.

From the changing room, you will be shuffled through six to eight different exam rooms, each of which is for a single medical test, including, but not limited to a blood draw, an abdominal ultrasound, temperature check, blood pressure, a chest x-ray, and an EKG. A few weeks later you will receive a mailed copy (in Mandarin, with little English) of your medical report. A quick chat with other expat friends and you'll soon see that an inordinately high number of foreigners are diagnosed with "fatty liver." Don't be alarmed if that's your diagnoses, too.

Excellent medical care is available in Shanghai in both Chinese and Western staffed hospitals. English is the still the international language of choice in hospitals, but there are services available in other languages as well. Most hospitals that cater to the international population have both European and Asian staff who are themselves expats. It will not be difficult to find someone with whom you can communicate. The glossary at the end of this book provides a list of hospitals and medical clinics that cater to expats.

Medical Emergencies
That said, medical emergencies are no laughing matter in

China. Although the worldwide 112 emergency number used in the E.U. and other countries theoretically works in China, do not bother testing this theory. Summoning an ambulance in Shanghai is the least efficient way to get to a hospital during an emergency. Rarely will you see an ambulance zipping through the streets with efficiency. Nor does there seem to be any expectation for traffic to move out of the way. Even if you did manage to get an ambulance, it is unlikely the personnel on board will be medically trained.

Having a plan in place for a medical emergency is good practice when travelling, and it will provide you with some sense of security while living in a foreign country. The best emergency advice given to us when we arrived was to hail a cab. My family has thoroughly tested Shanghai's emergency medical establishments—with stomach issues, kidney infection, Dengue Fever, and anaphylactic shock, and we've lived to tell the tales. Two friends have had emergency appendectomies in Shanghai, and they were both impressed with the medical expertise and care they received. Rest assured, you can survive an emergency in Shanghai. If you become seriously ill and are wondering how long to wait before heading to the hospital—play it safe and go.

Most expats travel extensively throughout Asia during a stint in China. If you do travel, remember that Chinese officials will quarantine any foreigners who contract communicable diseases abroad. Medical professionals in hospitals are required to report communicable diseases when they encounter patients with them. When my daughter returned to Shanghai from Vietnam with Dengue Fever, we spent a restless few nights worrying that she might be quarantined in a hotel with a population of people who were far sicker than she. In the end, quarantine for Dengue means staying inside the home until fever passes.

Wise emergency planning includes preparing an emergency kit for home that contains all of your critical documents—birth certificates, passports and visas, prescription medicines, vaccination records for children and pets, cash (both your home currency and local currency), credit cards, a first aid kit, and a backup power bank for cell phones and/or medical devices. Foreign prescriptions are not valid in China, so if you need refills, you will have to find a doctor inside the country. Most expats stock up with medicine before they arrive.

Make an emergency plan and make sure your family understands the plan. Having an accessible list of emergency numbers—including your home country consulate and the customer service number of your insurance carrier—on quick dial is always a good idea. Be sure to include your local hospital's Chinese address on an emergency card (written in Chinese characters) to hand to a cab driver in the event of having to take a cab in an emergency.

Hospitals

Shanghai has two basic types of hospitals: public hospitals and international hospitals. Price and quality of the service can differ dramatically. While fees at public hospitals are quite low, lines and wait times can be long and exasperating; personal privacy less or nonexistent, and interactions with staff more impersonal. Some public hospitals have VIP departments, which are more costly and come closer to the levels of care offered at the international hospitals. Be aware that many public hospitals lack pediatric care. Others have age limits.

Shanghai United Family Healthcare Group is the most commonly used hospital by expats with international health insurance packages. This group of hospitals charges Western prices, but also accepts most international health care plans offered to expats and foreigners inside China. Shanghai United has hospitals in both Puxi and Pudong, and both hire Western and Chinese doctors and medical staff who can, for the most part, speak English. In Minhang, Shanghai United maintains the Fengshang medical clinic that caters to local expats and their families. Located on Yunle Lu, the clinic serves this area's large expat population and can make referrals to the group's hospitals. For a general sample of hospital costs, see the United Family Healthcare website, which publishes their outpatient prices online.

Another popular hospital and clinic system with expats is Parkway Health, which has six clinics located around Shanghai all of which have English-speaking staff. For a list of locations, see the resource guide. Parkway offers medical and dental services and an onsite pharmacy. As with other premier hospitals that cater to Westerners, costs are higher. Most international hospital providers enable direct billing for medical services, (excluding pharmacy charges), to the insurance companies they recognize, which saves you from having to settle your bill at time of visit. Co-payments and excluded services are paid up front.

Last, but certainly not least, St. Michael Hospital in Changning is also popular with expats. A member of the Asia Pacific Medical Group, St. Michael provides medical services in Chinese, English, Russian, Hindi, Japanese, Tagalog (Filipino), Korean, Urdu (Pakistani), Polish and Russian. All these hospital groups maintain a long list of specialists, including cardiology, dentistry, family medicine, gynecology, internal medicine, maternity, neurology, oncology, orthopedics, pediatrics, sports medicine and pain management, and surgery.

Choosing a hospital means taking into account a number of factors beyond language. Do they have emergency room services and pediatric services for your children? If so, are there age limits? Will they accept your insurer? If you're lucky, the hospital nearest you will meet all your requirements. However, you may have to settle on a hospital that is not as close as you'd like and/or that charges higher fees. Once you determine your hospital, you will need to register with them. You can contact English speaking hospitals by phone and make an appointment to come in and register or wait until you need their services and register then.

Insurance

Most hospitals in Shanghai will accept insurance, although you may have to pay first and wait to be reimbursed. Before signing up with a hospital, check whether they accept your provider, information that may be available on their website. If your home health insurance policy does not cover you outside of the country, you will need to buy an International Health Plan that covers hospitalization. Depending on your situation, the length of your stay, where you plan to travel and what activities you're planning to engage in, you may want to add coverage for emergency evacuation and repatriation (within and out of China). Supplementary evacuation/repatriation policies are available from International SOS, which has clinics in several major cities in China.

Pharmacies

When it comes to medical care, prescription drugs, and over the counter medications, China's regulations are in constant flux as its leaders work to upgrade their medical system to Western standards. Antibiotics can be purchased over the counter in most Asian countries, but widespread antibiotic resistance forced China to require prescriptions in 2012. Looser standards often apply in rural areas. Chinese Traditional Medicine (CTM) is still favored in many places including Shanghai, and CTM products can occupy more space than Western medicines on pharmacy shelves.

If you have to renew a prescription medicine in China, you'll need a doctor's prescription written in Mandarin, unless you use a pharmacy connected with an expat hospital. The only place to purchase common over-the-counter items such as aspirin, rubbing alcohol, or laxatives is through local pharmacies which can be identified by the green cross in their window. It's wise to bring a supply of over-the-counter medicine (ibuprofen and allergy medicine) with you from your home country as finding these common items can take a considerable amount of time in Shanghai.

International SOS

Some international health insurance companies provide automatic membership to covered individuals in International SOS (ISOS). Expats who do not get guaranteed membership can buy membership packages for families, students and individuals. ISOS has created a global medical infrastructure that provides assistance and advice to travelers abroad with medical needs. Their services include:

- Worldwide medical referrals and advice

- Connectivity with doctors who can assess and direct you to medical providers
- Evacuation and repatriation coverage
- Dispatch of medication and medical supplies for emergencies
- Assess to ISOS clinics
- Medical monitoring
- Medical alerts
- Emergency translations and interpreter services

Pregnancy and Childbirth

If you're pregnant or planning to have a child in China, you will have some decisions to make. Some expats choose to travel back to their home country to give birth. The reasons range from ensuring birthright citizenship to increased comfort with medical practices in a home country. I also know a few Western women who chose to give birth in Shanghai's modern hospitals, and they were more than happy with the outcome. If you do become pregnant in China, you'll have to learn to deal with Chinese superstitions surrounding pregnancy and some interesting fads. The latter include avoiding exercise during pregnancy (I cannot recall EVER seeing a woman in late pregnancy walking around the city), avoiding funerals and spending a whole month in pajamas post-delivery.

DETERMINING YOUR BABY'S GENDER

China's one-child policy resulted in a years-long preference for boys, and now China finds itself with a hefty gender imbalance. As a result, it is against Chinese law for any member of the medical staff to inform would-be parents of a baby's gender. If you want to know your baby's gender, consider getting a sonogram outside of China, or, as one friend did, wear down the medical staff with begging.

Face Masks/Air Filters

To wear one, or not to wear one, that is the question. Air quality is still one of China's most pressing issues. Images of China's frequent air apocalypses have been broadcast across the world. There is good news on this front. Under pressure from the citizenry, China has done much to improve its air quality. Shanghai is no longer ranked in the top 20 most polluted cities in Asia, or in the world. Thanks to its location next to the sea, Shanghai's air quality is usually far healthier than Beijing's, which is encircled by mountains that trap pollutants. The bad news is that air quality is still an issue of significant concern. The air quality has improved by leaps and bounds over the past five years, and China's environmental goals ensure that this trend should continue.

After a water cooler, your second purchase should be an indoor air filter. There are a number of good brands and many places to buy them. Lightly used indoor air filtration systems from outgoing expats are abundant on many of Shanghai's "used" exchanges. The Chinese have turned facemasks into an example of haute couture. Wearing a standard white or blue surgical mask is fine when you are walking or exercising outdoors, but you won't be making any fashion statements. Patterned cloth masks are available everywhere, but Chinese residents are more likely to wear facemasks than expats. The reason may be due to studies showing cloth masks really aren't very effective in combating PM 2.5.

MONEY MATTERS

Moving to China requires serious forethought about money matters. Issues that will need to be considered such as how to communicate to home country financial institutions from abroad, how to apply for foreign bank accounts, or how to deal with the complexities of maintaining accounts in multiple countries, all need to be ironed out before you arrive in Shanghai.

Renminbi, yuan, or kuai

Distinguishing between the many words for Chinese currency can be confusing for new arrivals to Shanghai. The official name for Chinese currency, established by the People's Republic of China in 1949, is the *renminbi* (RMB) which quite literally means "the people's money." However, the formal abbreviation used at currency exchanges and banks *within China* is CNY, which refers to *Chinese renminbi yuan*. Technically speaking, *yuan* is merely a unit designation of *renminbi*—you might pay five *yuan* for a sweet potato from a street vendor, for example. However, *yuan* has taken on a life of its own in China and it is now commonly used to refer to Chinese currency generally. To further complicate matters, China divides its currency into offshore currency CNH (money that is allowed to be traded internationally outside the mainland) and onshore currency, which retains the CNY designation. Just when you think you've gotten hold of it all, you'll hear the word *kuai*, a common colloquial term for *yuan* and a word that is even more commonly used in Shanghai when referring to Chinese currency.

Banking

If you plan to live in Shanghai for any reasonable length of time, opening a bank account is a necessity. As with nearly everything, the language barrier will be your biggest hurdle. Many employers help new hires complete the paperwork necessary for these transactions, but if yours does not, find a translator you can trust. The cost to open a basic bank account is as little as ¥200 (US$29). You will need your passport, residence permit, and possibly your police registration for proof of address in China. ATMs are generally located in shopping malls and bank branches, but it's easiest to choose a bank that has ATMs accessible to both your home and place of work.

Historically speaking, China bypassed the plastic credit card system to which the rest of the world remains tethered. Getting a credit card is nearly unheard of in China. If you'd like to rely on credit, it's best to maintain an account in your home country. American Express cards are nearly impossible to use in China, but UnionPay, VISA, and Mastercard are still accepted in places that deal with tourists. Beware of incurring painful currency exchange fees.

China Merchant Bank (CMB), the Bank of China, and ICBC (Industrial and Commercial Bank of China) are the three largest banks that cater to expats. A number of Western international banks have locations in Shanghai and can be your best method of accessing foreign funds outside the country, though they can charge inordinately high fees. China frequently changes its rules about how much money can be removed from the country, and it sets limits (currently the equivalent of US$50,000) that apply to foreigners as well as locals. If your employer pays in RMB, these rules will dictate how much money you can transfer to accounts outside the country. Many expats tend to keep their Chinese bank balances on the low side. If in doubt, ask your employer.

WeChat Pay and Alipay
Most new arrivals in Shanghai are astonished by the streamlining of China's mobile payment platforms. In a relatively brief time span, the convenience and cutting-edge

nature of Chinese technology has dramatically changed the lives of ordinary citizens. Within a three-year span of our arrival in Shanghai, the city transformed from a place where "cash was king" to one in which it became increasingly difficult to find vendors who would accept a ¥100 note. Most shoppers in Shanghai need to carry nothing more with them than a cellphone.

Historically speaking, when consumers in China turned to plastic payments, they used debit cards, which are themselves quickly disappearing in favor of mobile payments. Unlike mobile payment systems in most Western countries which require users to download any number of individual apps, China's mobile payment industry is dominated by just

A local street food vendor offers mobile payment QR codes to customers.

two companies: WeChat and Alipay. Downloading both apps is nothing short of imperative for expats who plan to stay in Shanghai for any length of time. By 2018, the Chinese mobile payment industry was already fifty times larger than its U.S. counterpart and growing rapidly. Virtually everyone in Shanghai uses these two apps to pay for everything from medical expenses to restaurant bills. Even wet market vendors and local street vendors accept third party mobile payments from WeChat for as little as 5 *kuai*.

To link the downloaded WeChat and Alipay apps to a funded bank account, expats will need their Chinese cell phone number, their passport number, and their debit card number. Users must enter their names *exactly* as they appear on their bank account—entries are case sensitive. Once mobile payment accounts are funded, money can easily be transferred between the apps and bank accounts as needed.

QR code scanning technology (see Chapter 4) makes payments as simple and automatic as adding contacts. Renting bikes through Shanghai's ubiquitous bike share

ALIPAY

Alipay first exploded on the scene when Alibaba replicated PayPal's mobile payment design and transformed Alipay into one of the world's most comprehensive mobile payment apps. Shortly afterward, Tencent Holdings Ltd. developed WeChat Pay, a widely used mobile payment system run from its social media platform. WeChat's Wallet function is slightly better than Alipay's, and WeChat is the more comprehensive of the two systems thanks to its social media dominance. On the other hand, Alipay was the first third-party payment system linked to the Shanghai metro system, and it is the only way to make purchases on Taobao, China's largest online marketplace also run by Alibaba. Both WeChat and Alipay allow for the seamless transfer of money between their platforms and bank accounts, and they enable easy person-to-person cash transfers as well. Both also stash user's funds in interest bearing mutual funds—just another way that payment platforms in China are encroaching on the banking system.

program or paying a restaurant bill is simply a matter of scanning the QR codes of businesses or users. It's also simple to transfer money between friends or pay an *ayi* or a driver. Hospitals regularly accept Alipay for payment of medical bills and local businesses and restaurants text coupons and run membership programs via the WeChat app. Beginning in 2018, the Shanghai Metro System began installing Alipay scanning functionality on its turnstiles, with plans to accept WeChat Pay in the future.

Money kept in both Alipay and WeChat Pay accounts will earn interest just like a traditional bank account since the funds are held in two of the world's largest money market mutual funds. Both companies are branching out to offer additional financial and banking services as well. Security features for the apps are strong, but a general rule is to keep fairly low balances in case cell phones or payment accounts are hacked. An increasing number of businesses are refusing to accept debit card payments in Shanghai, and there are rumors of foreign tourists arriving in some regions of China with cash, only to find that no one will accept that, either. Of the two platforms, WeChat dominates mobile payment life. With each passing day an increasing number of handwritten notes appear on shop doors explaining that WeChat is the only form of accepted payment. Its convenience isn't just versatile, it's addictive.

Accessing Financial Accounts at Home

Getting access to your home-country financial accounts from inside China can prove challenging. Many Western financial institutions have multi-step online security systems that track VPN (Virtual Private Network) use and ISP (Internet Service Provider) locations. Using an ISP address in China raises alarm bells in many countries. The resulting identification checks—texts to an overseas phone number, multiple verification passcodes, phone calls, and emails—can prove maddening given China's own restrictions on Internet technology. Even if you've informed your bank that you are living in China, some financial institutions may still mistake you for a Chinese hacker.

The best strategy for ensuring access to financial accounts is to maintain a cell phone account in your home country as well as a home SIM card. It's wise to use your home country SIM card when trying to access bank accounts or when making phone calls to financial institutions. There are other benefits of using two cell phone numbers and two SIM cards as well. Moving between countries is challenging, and a yearly account can pay for itself just by helping you avoid roaming charges.

MAIL SERVICE

Receiving mail in China is unpredictable at best, and your privacy is never guaranteed. The few times foreign mail actually arrived at our Chinese residence, it clearly had been opened and read. There are a healthy supply of postal offices in Shanghai if you should have to mail something back to your home country, but you'll need basic language skills or a good cell phone translation app. Packages in and out of the country will have to clear customs and may take up to a month to arrive. Express mail services are the most reliable way to receive mail from your home country, and many expats who need to receive or send mail do it through their employer, which can prove a more reliable strategy.

In the age of technology, most expats don't bother risking the vagaries of Chinese mail, opting instead to receive mail

THE TAXMAN COMETH (FOR AMERICANS ONLY)

The U.S. is one of the only countries in the world (along with Eritrea and Hungary) that taxes the income of expatriate, non-resident citizens. The Foreign Account Tax Compliance Act (FATCA), passed in 2010, compels foreign banks to report overseas accounts held by American citizens. The law has raised hackles in many countries, including China, for increasing paperwork and decreasing foreign banking privacy. This can make it difficult for Americans to open bank accounts overseas. American citizens with foreign bank accounts that exceed $10,000 USD are required to file an FBAR (Foreign Bank Account Report) with your U.S. tax return. Some U.S. states will still consider you a state resident if you have not given up your local accounts, and they may require you to pay state income taxes, especially if you retain property or a driver's license. It's wise to retain the advice of a financial advisor specializing in expat services before moving overseas.

AMERICANS AND INVESTMENTS

Further complicating overseas banking for Americans is the fact that many U.S. investment firms will no longer want your business. Increased regulation by the U.S. government on overseas investments has made the U.S. financial industry wary of foreign rules governing potential overseas customers. Most U.S investment firms will not sell mutual funds or open new accounts for Americans living overseas. Informing your current investment company of your plans to move to China may endanger your accounts. Stories abound of U.S. expats being forced to liquidate retirement and other personal investment accounts after moving overseas. A financial advisor can help you navigate the complications of a stint living overseas.

in their home country either by eliciting the help of family members or by setting up an electronic mail forwarding account. There is a dizzying number of virtual mail companies for expats to choose from. Most companies will allow you to handle mail in virtual reality. These companies provide a range of services including scanning and emailing digital copies of mail, shredding nonessentials, forwarding, and even paying bills—all for a fee, of course. Since mail forwarding services handle personal or financial information for you, it's good to do your research and use a reputable company. Different countries have differing laws about virtual mail services, so do some research in your home country ahead of time. As of this writing, U.S. citizens are able to file their tax returns using a U.S. virtual mailbox.

INTERNET

Setting up Internet service in Shanghai is relatively straightforward. Your service provider will likely be one of China's three telecom giants: China Unicom, China Telecom or China Mobile. Most large apartment buildings and compounds catering to expats will automatically provide an Internet connection along with a modem. If you're technologically sophisticated, it's possible to bring a digital VPN modem with you from your home country, but you risk having it confiscated when passing through customs. Most international employers, (businesses and schools), have better Internet access than the average Shanghainese, and many expats get used to using the Internet services at work to accomplish personal tasks.

Internet usage can be one of the most frustrating aspects of life in China. While it might seem improbable to expats living in Shanghai, the city's Internet is considered excellent by the standards of the rest of the country. Unfortunately, China's Internet speeds are some of the slowest in the world thanks to the work of censors and China's Great Firewall. It can take an impossibly long time to upload any file larger than an email. And, of course, anything you send or receive can be monitored.

The Great Firewall

Chinese citizens are among the least "free" people in the world when it comes to their online behavior and access to information. Examples of international election interference have further emboldened the Chinese government, giving it a compelling argument in favor of censorship for the sake of stability. There is no other irritant as often denounced by expat residents and business professionals as the constant impediments to their Internet access on the mainland.

Many foreigners wonder how Chinese citizens feel about these blocked sites. The position of the government regarding search engines and social media is that China already provides its own Chinese versions of everything. Indeed, China has its own version of Google called Baidu. Chinese websites and search engines are monitored and heavily censored by the government, but their popularity is soaring among Chinese citizens. Baidu is the primary search engine used by the Chinese, and it has introduced an English search function as well. Many expats find it easier to use Baidu for local Internet searches than trying to circumvent the restrictions on Google and other Western search engines.

The list of foreign websites and news sources that China blocks with its Golden Shield Project—the official designation for the Great Firewall— is unbearably long. It includes the vast array of Western social networking sites along with streaming sites like Netflix, as well as many European, Japanese, and American news outlets from Bloomberg to Le Monde to The New York Times. For those who think information about Western financial markets will be easy to access, think again. That said, China is also far more politically concerned with censoring internal news and keeping tabs on disruptive Chinese citizens than it is with foreigners and their opinions. Blogs and Internet postings by Westerners living inside China are usually ignored.

The technology of the Great Firewall relies on a series of tactics to censure users on the mainland, all of which will make Internet access somewhat laborious. The Firewall isn't just one unified strategy, instead it relies on a number of techniques: slowing downloading time, censoring texts and online comments, filtering methods that weed through search terminology and URLs, and rerouting of inappropriate searches. As a result, China's Internet isn't just slow, it is unpredictable—exactly how unpredictable varies. China's broadband connectivity generally ranks between 91st and 134th in the world. Many foreigners who live in Shanghai, regardless of statistics, come to feel that it has the slowest Internet speeds in the world.

While it is possible to use virtual private networks (VPNs) to bypass the Great Firewall in a megacity like Shanghai, don't expect them to be one hundred percent effective, especially when traveling in China's more rural areas. Despite China's plans to improve high speed broadband access in rural China, firewall workarounds are often much less effective there. In some sections of the country, especially in contentious areas such as Xinjiang, there are no extant VPNs available to the population. The Chinese government takes a slightly lax approach to things in the rebel city of Shanghai thanks to the requirements of international businesses. Internet connectivity can be an especially big source of irritation for many of Shanghai's Asian foreigners, since the fastest Internet speeds in the world are generally located in neighboring countries such as Korea, Japan, and Singapore.

(VPNs) Virtual Private Networks (VPNs) and TOR

Virtual Private Networks are fee services that provide downloadable software to help circumvent China's Great

Firewall. They work by hiding IP (Internet Provider) addresses and making it seem as if an Internet connection is actually outside of mainland China. Data is encrypted and rerouted through the VPN servers, cloaking your location. Most VPN's will offer a choice of which country outside of China you want to route the connection through.

When we first arrived in Shanghai, my daughters loved staying in fancy Chinese hotels like the Hyatt because they catered to foreigners by providing free VPN service with their hotel rooms. Those were the good old days when everyone had a working VPN and accessing Western information was easy. In recent years, China has taken a more aggressive approach to censorship, and expats can no longer count on gaining access to VPNs through a 5-star hotel, since, they too, have been forced to comply with China's restrictive Internet laws. I was shocked to see a notice in 2017, in a 5-star hotel, informing me that I would not be able to access a long list of American news organizations. Of course, with two personal VPNs, it wasn't an issue, but it was a reminder that after a period of openness, China is currently in retreat again.

Expats have to buy and install their VPNs on personal phones and computers before arriving in China. It can be difficult to update these apps (as well as many other Western apps) without travelling outside the country. For those planning to stay in Shanghai for a considerable length of time, subscribing to more than one VPN is best. Every year, the list of "best VPNs for China" seems to change. The Chinese government occasionally cracks down on specific, widely used VPN services, which is why having a second one in place is handy. There are free VPN services available online, but you get what you pay for. Research the VPNs that work best in China before you leave, and don't balk at the cost. Better yet, ask a friend or your employer which VPNs are working best.

Keep in mind that VPNs are illegal in China. The government recognizes an underlying benefit, primarily that (slow) international access to English-speaking sites is necessary for an elite slice of society, and it generally turns a blind eye to their use. The most widely available VPN services to which companies and international schools subscribe, are often "registered" with the government. This means that access is granted to institution-wide VPN services on the school campus or in the office. (Yes, your child will have good Internet access on his or her school campus). Expats who move to China as high-level employees can obtain a "registered" VPN router for their homes or apartments. But be aware that if a VPN is "registered," activity that crosses it is likely monitored.

Some technologically sophisticated expats in China have tried using TOR, a type of worldwide anonymity network, hosted by volunteer servers. TOR provides free downloadable software to help users connect via their network and to protect against Internet surveillance. The free software encrypts communications, which is then relayed (bounced, really) around the world to a network of host sites, which makes tracking activity difficult. While TOR gives its users privacy, it does not protect anyone from seeing that you are using TOR, a fact that has made it easier to block inside China. In the continual game of cat and mouse that occurs between the Chinese government and those who want to get around the Great Firewall, China has been winning the battle against TOR users.

Jaywalking: Big Screens and CCTV

Facial recognition technology is widely used throughout China to surveille the population. Increasingly, it is being used to shame, ticket, or fine jaywalkers—proof that there really isn't that much crime in Shanghai. The city has a few intersections where faces of jaywalkers can be projected on a large public screen, and people in Shanghai do get ticketed by the police for ignoring traffic lights at intersections or crossing in the middle of the road. For some unknown reason, scooters appear largely immune to consequences.

Your chances of getting a ticket are pretty minimal, but if you are stopped by a local traffic cop, he will ask for your ID or passport number, and fine you on the spot if you don't know it. Jaywalking remains endemic in Shanghai, and the fines are paltry. Many view jaywalking as part of the chaotic charm of the city. In the older sections of the city, where the streets are twisting and narrow, people jaywalk with impunity.

CABLE AND SATELLITE TV

Cable and satellite television services that offer access to Western or English-speaking broadcasting networks are widely available in Shanghai. These provide access to sports and even news channels such as the BBC and CNN. Television is blocked occasionally by Chinese censors, especially when worldwide conflict, protests, or demonstrations are reported, and most definitely when Western media reports on Chinese politics. There are televisions available for purchase in some shops in Shanghai, usually in expat-dominated areas, that carry built-in VPNs to assist with access to Western media.

According to Netflix, there are only four countries in the world without *any* access to its services: Syria, North Korea,

Crimea, and China. When we first moved to China in 2014, streaming services could be easily accessed using our personal VPNs. That's not always the case currently. Some streaming services grew wise to the use of VPNs, which allowed access to programming outside of subscription service areas, and in 2016, many began using software to identify customers who log in using a VPN. There are still VPN locations that will allow you to access your streaming networks, but it's another game of cat and mouse. Expats need to contact their VPN service providers and ask tech support to provide the geographical locations that will make their particular streaming service accessible from within China.

CELL PHONES

Life in Shanghai without a cell phone would be virtually impossible. Although it is easy to buy a cell phone in China, the brands common in Western countries are significantly more expensive in Shanghai. The best option is to purchase an *unlocked* cell phone in your home country and then purchase a Chinese SIM card along with a long-term mobile phone plan when you arrive. If possible, keep cell service activated in your home country and switch SIM cards as you travel back and forth.

As with Chinese Internet providers, your cellular phone service will likely be with one of China's three telecom giants: China Unicom, China Telecom or China Mobile. The two largest companies, Unicom and Telecom divide up their services geographically, while China Mobile is primarily an option for residents in larger, modern cities. China Mobile has offices everywhere in Shanghai, including a large one downtown with English speaking customer service representatives, which makes it one of the most popular among expats.

That said, in 2018, the American Chamber of Commerce issued a warning from the National Telecommunications and Information Administration that recommended blocking China Mobile from providing telecommunication services in the U.S. for reasons of national security. This shouldn't affect your service in China, but it's another reason to maintain a mobile plan and SIM card in your home country. If you're determined to use one of Shanghai's smaller, lesser-known service providers, you'll require a Mandarin speaker to accompany you when you set up a plan.

Data plans vary, and both monthly and yearly prepaid plans are available. For monthly plans, unless you can read Mandarin, you'll likely receive a bill in the mail that will require a trip to a brick and mortar office to pay. For that reason, most people prefer an annual plan. Another option is to buy a prepaid plan, where a certain amount of money and data are set. Self-service machines are available in stores to reload plans when the data runs out. Foreigners will need a passport and residency papers to set up a plan since foreign cell phone accounts are linked to passport numbers.

FOREIGN AND INTERNATIONAL SCHOOLS

Moving children to Shanghai can be challenging. Not only will they experience a new city, a new language, and a very different lifestyle, they will have to adjust to a new school culture. Finding the right fit for children is important. The number of international schools in Shanghai is a bit staggering, and the choices are really varied. It's likely you'll find what you're looking for, but the process will require some research and some sorting. The majority of Shanghai's large international schools are well-known and reputable, and the quality of international education in Shanghai is among the highest in the world.

Like all things in China, the list of international schools gets exponentially bigger each year. There are a growing number of fly-by-night (often for-profit) schools popping up that should be avoided. Some of them cater to local Chinese students who want English language schooling and a leg up in international college admissions. The number of high-quality, reputable international schools is long, so it's best to focus your energy there.

When choosing a school, you'll have to decide whether you're trying to reproduce a home country experience (American, British, French, German international schools) or expose your children to a more Chinese educational experience. Chinese law forbids Chinese nationals from attending international schools, but Shanghai has a high number of repatriated expat Chinese families whose children hold foreign passports, so even if you choose a Western-style international school, your student may still study alongside many Chinese students. There are positives and negatives to having children immersed in a mostly Chinese educational system: Avoiding the prospect of having children educated in an expat bubble is wonderful for many families, but on the flip side, many Western students do not blossom in the academic pressure cookers that some predominantly Chinese schools have become.

If you're set on living in a particular area of the city, location will narrow the school choices. If the reverse, find the school, and then decide on the housing—the choice most expats with families make. Ask your employer for recommendations.

Most international schools advertise copiously and allow prospective families to visit. Acceptance rates and academic reputations vary. Some international schools have wait lists, so it's best to contact schools as early in the transition process as possible. In the Resource Guide in Chapter 10, I have listed the most well-known and well-established international schools. It's not an exhaustive list but will offer a place to begin the research process.

CHAPTER 6

FOOD CULTURE

> ❝When the noble man eats,
> he should not stuff himself.❞

— *The Analects of Confucius*

EAST VS WEST

The first time I sat down to a family-style Chinese meal with a large group, I wondered how we would possibly finish the enormous array of hot and cold dishes on our table. Ordering continued throughout the afternoon (it was lunchtime). Item after item arrived despite the many unfinished plates of food still sitting on the table's lazy Susan. I found it hard to reconcile the restraint shown in other areas of Chinese culture, which emphasizes humility and moderation per *The Analects of Confucius*, with the plethora of food sitting in front of me.

I soon learned that mistaking an overabundance of food as an enticement to gluttony was wrongheaded. Leaving

The traditional Chinese table includes a huge variety of foods.

some food untouched is exactly the point, and it is often viewed in China as an example of luck and hospitality. The entire enterprise of eating is a great Shanghainese pastime. A large family-style meal offers the real substance of life in China. Important events, holidays, celebrations, and business meetings almost always involve food. A Chinese host never wants guests to leave the table hungry. In Shanghai, people are eating everywhere: at street corner tables, in cafes, in wet markets, while walking to work. The very act of enjoying food is woven into daily life, on and off the streets.

Chinese Food: Healthy or Not?

China's cuisine has long been characterized as one of the healthiest in the world, thanks to its emphasis on vegetables. Generally speaking, the Chinese still eat far more green vegetables and less sugar than a typical Westerner, and Chinese sweets are not very sweet. But the amount of meat consumed in China is mind boggling.

SUKHBIR

The international media have thoroughly documented the obesity epidemic in the West, a result of its penchant for an unhealthy excess of salt, fat, meat, and sugar. Yet, fatty meats and oily stir fries play a central role in Chinese cuisine as well. While traditional rural diets are still predominantly vegetable-based (meat is expensive), a triumvirate of new social circumstances is changing the face of Chinese eating. Growing wealth, widespread popularity of fried foods and dough, and an imported taste for sweets, are bringing the diabetes epidemic to China's front door.

When it comes to food, fat, sugar, and salt are the building blocks of flavor, and authentic Chinese cuisine is rich in all of these. In fact, the diversity of the country's cuisine, a direct result of diversity inside the country, deserves far more acclaim than it receives—Chinese food can hardly be viewed as a monolith. Likewise, Shanghai's local food scene is more hybrid than holistic. The city's history as a magnet for migrants from across China have created a foodscape that offers broad entry into Chinese cuisine in addition to local preferences. Expats who enjoy food will find Shanghai to be something of a food nirvana—eating in Shanghai quickly becomes a favorite pastime for foreigners.

You can (and should) experiment with an array of Chinese cuisines. Cantonese food is widely available, along with choices from the predominantly Muslim northwestern provinces of Xinjiang and Shaanxi, where lamb is a central ingredient. Sichuan and Hunan restaurants serving food laden with a slew of *tien tsin* (red peppers) and numbing peppercorns, are abundant. And there is ample opportunity to experiment with the vegetable-heavy Dian cuisine of Yunnan, or the less oily offerings of Hainan cuisine. When it comes to food, everything is at your fingertips in Shanghai.

Table Etiquette

Eating in Shanghai revolves more around customs and practicalities than around social etiquette. When at a loss in any situation involving a meal, just do what everyone else does. Generally speaking, Chinese food etiquette is common sense. During family-style meals, take small portions so that everyone can sample the plate, (unless you are dining at an upscale restaurant, most Chinese restaurants will serve family-style meals). When dining with a group, meals are likely served at round tables. At the center of the table, a wide lazy Susan ensures that everyone can snap up a share of the endless stream of hot and cold dishes.

A typical serving of authentic Chinese meat dishes may be full of bones requiring a "hands on" approach. It is not uncommon for diners to stack cleaned bones or shrimp shells directly on the table when no discard plate is provided. In small, street-side food establishments, bones are sometimes dropped directly on the floor (or sidewalk). More upscale restaurants typically offer sets of serving chopsticks and spoons so that individuals do not have to use their eating chopsticks to serve themselves. That said, it's common practice in many situations for diners to use their own chopsticks to move food from serving dishes to their plates.

There seems to be universal agreement that resting a pair of chopsticks standing up in a bowl of rice is bad luck, but this admonition seems more like folklore than an actual rule of etiquette. At some point, the words "table etiquette" may strike many foreign expats as humorous given how boisterous meals in China can become. Behaviors such as belching are not necessarily considered rude. But Shanghai is a wealthy city with many Chinese who have traveled abroad, and Westernized cultural practices, especially at high-end restaurants, generally prevail.

The elderly and senior members of a family always deserve a place of honor at a Chinese table. Similarly, a guest of honor, should always be served first at a meal.

The elderly and senior members of a family always deserve a place of honor at a Chinese table. Similarly, a guest of honor, should always be served first at a meal.

THE FOOD CULTURE

Shanghai is the foodie capital of China. Not to disparage Chinese food in Western countries—authenticity can be found in many places—but many Western Chinese restaurants have inevitably adapted their dishes to the non-Chinese palate. The difference between Chinese food in China and Chinese food in the West is so vast that many experts consider them wholly separate cuisines. Don't go to Shanghai looking for General Tso's chicken. And if you *do* find it, don't eat it.

Regardless of their views on meat, most expats (vegetarian or not) will quickly come to terms with the wide array of meat presentation in Shanghai, including whole dead animals and a host of animal parts. The Chinese are not as squeamish as many Westerners when it comes to handling animals for food, largely because food production has not yet been industrialized on the same scale. Even big-box grocery stores in Shanghai sell live eels, turtles, and frogs for consumers. Likewise, when shopping locally, many expats will have to adjust to different standards for food handling. The Shanghai Food Bureau has increased its health inspections of food stalls and street food stands, but fly-by-night street food vendors are still quite common. By way of example, my

Live frogs are sold in the cooler sections of standard supermarkets.

favorite local chicken purveyor once smoked his cigarette down to the nub before picking up my chicken, placing it on a wooden chopping block, and prepping it for me without washing his hands. As I stood on the sidewalk, he sliced and gutted the bird, stuffed its feet into the cavity, dropped the chicken into a plastic grocery bag, and handed the bag to me with his blood and gut-stained hands.

Even if you choose not to buy your chicken from a local shop or wet market, your *ayi* is likely to shop locally unless you provide specific instructions otherwise. If you prefer that your *ayi* shop in Western stores, you may have to provide a means of transportation as most *ayis* will only have electric scooters.

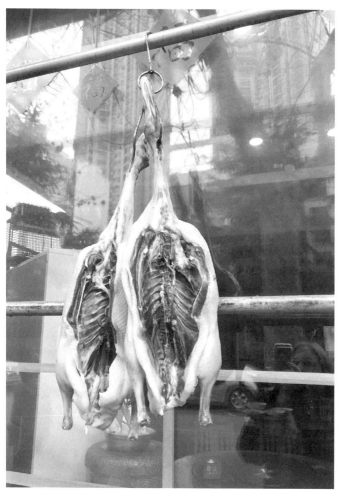

Smoked whole goose is a popular winter time food in Shanghai.

There is no compartmentalizing about food in China. An average dinner at a local restaurant may contain the head, feet, and other unmentionable parts of whatever creature is on the menu. Neat geometric cubes of meat are rarely in sight. Menus in Shanghai often include dishes such as stewed sea cucumber, braised donkey meat, stewed pork intestines, carp tail, and pig's knuckles. In China, the reality of death stares you, quite literally, in the eye—from the sidewalk, at street food stalls, in supermarkets, wet markets, and sometimes with every bite you take.

In her memoir, *The Woman Warrior*, Chinese-American writer Maxine Hong Kingston, writes about growing up with Chinese parents and hearing tales about "big eaters" in Chinese folklore. As Kingston explains it, in China, capable eaters defeat ghosts. Kingston's mother told stories of emperors who ate duck tongues and monkey lips. Wei Pang, a historical figure from the Tang dynasty, whom Kingston calls "the most fantastic eater," consumed birds, rabbits, scorpions, snakes, cockroaches, worms, slugs, beetles, and crickets.

Kingston's portrayal of her family epitomizes the clash of food and animal culture that typifies Western and Chinese worldviews. In Chinese folklore, Kingston says, "big eaters win." Growing up, she viewed her world with the sensibilities of an American child. She describes hiding under the bed with her fingers plugging her ears "to shut out the bird screams and the thud, thud, of the turtles swimming in the boiling water, their shells hitting the sides of the pot." She describes her mother dismembering skunks on the kitchen chopping block and cooking animals like raccoons, hawks, and snakes. "I would live on plastic," she concludes.

FOOD SAFETY

Food scandals in China typically create a stir in the international community, and stories about food danger can seem quite terrifying to the uninitiated. A man who did business in China told me a harrowing story about the inexpensive strawberries his American company procured for export from China to the U.S. When company officials became suspicious of the prices, they dispatched an employee to inspect the Chinese processing facility. Conveniently, the strawberry fields adjoined the processing plant, but they were also growing adjacent to a large sewer waste-processing facility. That was the end of cheap strawberry imports to the U.S. This story is not meant to scare you away from eating strawberries in China as much as to illustrate an important point: no matter where we live, the food we eat can always be suspect.

There are no guarantees in life. One of the most frequent questions I'm asked is whether or not we eat the local food. The answer is, "yes, of course." One of the greatest pleasures of life in Shanghai is the array of delicious and exotic foods. Buying produce in wet markets was one of my favorite shopping experiences in China.

There are two Chinese products that most foreigners typically choose not to take a gamble on: milk and baby formula. Ample supplies of imported milk and formula (usually from Europe and Australia) are available in Shanghai. However, if you're going to live in China, don't cut yourself off from the authentic human experience of eating and sharing the local food. It never hurts to play it safe, but your motto should be: Enjoy!

Drinking Water

China has made tremendous progress toward modernizing its infrastructure, but those improvements still do not extend to Shanghai's drinking water. The Ministry of Environment remains under pressure to improve China's access to clean water. Many areas, including Shanghai, rarely meet international or environmental clean-water standards. Shanghai's lakes, rivers, and other water sources have suffered from years of heavy pollution.

While most locals drink the tap water in Shanghai, foreigners and expats should not. Will something immediate and catastrophic happen if you drink the tap water in

Shanghai? Probably not. Many guidebooks suggest boiling tap water to 100 degrees centigrade, but this is far from foolproof. Boiling will kill bacteria, parasites, and other germs, but no amount of boiling will clear the water of industrial contaminants or heavy metals, which are the source of much of Shanghai's drinking water contamination. After a few months of feeling miserable, one expat friend of mine who regularly drank his tap water was diagnosed with arsenic poisoning.

Many travel resources advise using bottled water for brushing teeth as well as drinking, but most expats take their chances with brushing. Others install built-in water filters for both bathroom and kitchen faucets. One of your first purchases in China should be a large, refillable water cooler that dispenses cold and hot water. Your *ayi* can handle ordering the replacements. Remember that when children are drinking bottled water in Shanghai, their exposure to fluoridation is non-existent, thus a visit to the dentist for fluoride treatments is advisable.

WATER SAFETY TIPS

- Some *ayis* wash fruits and vegetables in a mixture of white vinegar and water to help kill bacteria. You may want to ask your *ayi* to wash your produce this way. Large bottles of white vinegar can be purchased from most Western-style stores and stashed under the kitchen sink for convenience.

- Drinking a large glass of ice water is inconceivable to the average Chinese. The ancient medicinal concepts of balance often mean that extremes are frowned upon. According to the Chinese, the most advantageous temperature for drinking water is lukewarm (precisely at body temperature) so as not to disrupt the body's internal systems. Many Chinese drink plain hot water, since ice water is believed to slow the blood and disrupt its flow. Remember: yin = cooling effect on the body; yang = warming effect.

SHANGHAI'S REGIONAL CUISINE

Shanghai cuisine, also referred to as *benbang* (local) or *ben bang cai*, is young by Chinese standards, and much of what is considered native to the city's foodscape is more broadly a product of the entire southeastern coastal region. Like the cuisine of nearby Hangzhou, local Shanghainese dishes are often sweeter than food from other areas of China. Rarely is a Shanghainese dish naturally spicy. Most local meat and seafood dishes have sticky sweet-and-sour combinations with wine or soy sauce. The addition of sugar syrups and Shaoxing wine (a rice cooking wine) contributes to the sweet taste, as does the tendency to brush meat with glazes.

Shanghai has a wide variety of specialty dishes that use seafood and sea plants found along the city's coastline and in nearby rivers and lakes. Chicken dishes are popular, too, but aquatic offerings are ubiquitous. Carp, yellow croaker,

Noodles hung on a rack to dry.

hairy crabs, eels, turtles and frogs—all local favorites—are readily available for purchase in wet markets and grocery stores and frequently show up on local menus throughout the city. While Shanghai cuisine is known as focusing on steaming, stewing, and braising dishes, in reality there is an abundance of deep-fried and stir-fried dishes rounding out the local repertoire as well.

If frequently eating at street-food stalls, noodle stands, and wet markets isn't your style, there are plenty of high-end restaurants with international flavor in Shanghai to whet your appetite. A slew of well-known international chefs has found tremendous success in Shanghai by appealing to the tastes of the new, wealthy classes. On the other hand, when Michelin-star restaurants are budget busters, a large selection of affordable, internationally-oriented restaurants and bars await. The many historic buildings along the Bund play host to rooftop bars and restaurants that are popular among expats and Chinese alike. Sunday brunch in Shanghai is a popular weekend tradition, and Shanghai's numerous hotels offer brunch selections at all price ranges. Dining out while enjoying a stunning view of the Huangpu River and the Pearl Tower is not an unusual experience in Shanghai, and it can be accomplished on even a teacher's income.

FINE DINING

Shanghai boasts a surprising number of restaurants at the top of International "Best Restaurants" lists. In 2016, Michelin, the famous red guide to restaurants around the world, created a dedicated guide just for Shanghai—the only one in mainland China. As of 2019, there are 34 Michelin-star restaurants in the city, although only one, Paul Pairet's Ultraviolet (a multi-sensory food experience), has been awarded the coveted 3 Michelin stars. An evening of nibbling your way through 20 courses at Utlraviolet will set you back about ¥6,000–7,000 (US$872–1017) per person.

FOOD BASICS

Much of Shanghai's regional food mirrors the diet staples of China's larger food culture. The basic building blocks of the Chinese diet—tea, rice and soy—are important parts of Shanghai's local cuisine as well.

Tea

The history of tea in China is long and complex enough to be the subject of doctoral dissertations. One of the many commodities that made its way from East to West along the Silk Road, tea has been a central part of Chinese culture for thousands of years. Suffice it to say, tea is still one of China's most valuable commodities. While Chinese teas are often categorized into three main types—white, red, and green—there are actually hundreds of types of Chinese teas. What separates one particular type of tea from another can come down to simply using different processing methods. In

Tea brewing and serving are a ritual in China.

fact, many different types of Chinese teas actually originate from the same plant, yet are dried, roasted, or fermented in unique ways accounting for their different colors and flavors.

While all Chinese tea drinkers will have individual preferences, two of the most popular types of tea in Shanghai are Oolong and Longjing tea (also known as Dragon Well tea). Oolong tea occupies a special space somewhere in between green and black teas. Made from the same leaves as these other types of tea, Oolong has a darker color than green tea (from partial oxidation) but retains some differences from traditional black teas which are fully oxidized. Longjing is one of China's most popular green teas. Grown in neighboring Hangzhou, it is a favorite of the local Shanghainese for its medicinal properties and elevated taste. Many Shanghainese *ayis*, drivers and laborers can be seen drinking clear containers filled with the steeping leaves of Longjing tea all day long.

Bags of tea leaves are sealed and ready for delivery.

All tea in China is consumed as loose leaves steeped (floating) in hot water. When pouring or drinking tea in China, it's necessary to wait until the leaves settle to the bottom of the cup or teapot. Tea shops selling specialty brands of tea, along with all manner of tea paraphernalia, from clear glass tea pots to small candle burners, can be found throughout the city, but some of the best are found in Xuhui area. High-end tea shops will often carry tea bricks, large (usually round) blocks of compressed tea wrapped in elegantly and artistically decorated paper.

British colonialism has made a mild reappearance in Shanghai in recent years, as traditional British afternoon tea has become a popular afternoon activity among Shanghai's wealthier Chinese families. A surprising number of exclusive hotels in Shanghai, including the Fairmont Peace Hotel and the Four Seasons Pudong, offer formal high tea with fancy biscuits (usually requiring reservations). Less formal afternoon teas are served in many establishments around the Bund.

Rice

It should come as no surprise that China is both the world's leading producer of milled rice as well as the world's largest importer of rice. As in much of Asia, rice is the base grain of the Chinese diet. The low wetland regions around Shanghai, along the Yangtze River Delta, provide fertile ground for China's rice production, although the grain is harvested in different seasons throughout the country. Archeologists have determined that inhabitants of the areas immediately surrounding Shanghai, in neighboring Zhejiang province, began growing rice as far back as 3,000 to 4,000 years ago.

Stir-fried rice is an important component of Shanghainese cuisine, and dishes such as *cai fan*, stir-fried rice with salt pork and bok choy, or stir-fried rice with green onions and bean sprouts, are classic examples of the centrality of rice in the Shanghainese diet. In addition to being used as an accompaniment to meat and seafood dishes, rice is the base grain for Chinese alcohols, noodles, and glutinous deserts.

Soy

Along with mung beans, soybeans form another staple of the Shanghainese diet. With 1.4 billion people to feed, it's hardly surprising to learn that, along with rice, China is also the world's largest importer of soybean products; the country simply cannot produce enough soybeans to meet the demands of Chinese consumers. In Shanghainese cuisine, soybeans are primarily eaten as tofu in soups, stews, and stir fries and it is often braised, fried or fermented.

Tofu is also a frequent accompaniment to fish dishes in Shanghai, where it is sometimes glazed with the signature sweet Shanghai sauces. *Douchi*, fermented black soybeans, are a popular accompaniment to meat and seafood dishes, and are used as a base for a variety of sauces. Fermented soy can be quite salty (although unsalted versions exist), so if you are experimenting, a little goes a long way. Packaged, fermented, soybeans and tofu are sold in just about every Chinese grocery in Shanghai.

Alcohol

The Greeks have *uzo*, the Japanese have *sake*, and the Chinese have *baijiu*, a clear grain alcohol distilled from fermented rice or sorghum. If not for China's tea industry, *baijiu* ("*jiu*" means alcohol) might be considered the national drink of China. The alcoholic content of *baijiu* can be very high, topping 50 per cent—a fact more than one expat has learned the hard way.

A popular drink for celebrations, *baijiu*, like water, is served at room temperature with a meal. Distributed in small glasses, the drink is swallowed in one gulp, like a shot. Drinking in China, like eating, can be a loud and protracted affair, and if you are hitting your limits, you will have to be discreet and pace yourself. Refusing to take a shot of *baijiu* with a group can be considered rude, and the Chinese can be quite convincing, often times holding small cups of *baijiu* directly up to your mouth.

The Chinese are also beer drinkers, attested to by the fact that China has the world's largest beer market. *Pijiu*, Chinese beer, is popular among local and expat diners in Shanghai, and can be found in most restaurants. Shanghai's most popular beer, according to *The Drink Magazine*, is the brand Tsingtao, an internationally known beer whose brewery, China's second largest, was founded by Germans. Across China as a whole, the brand Snow beer enjoys the greatest popularity, but accounts for less than a quarter of beer sales in Shanghai.

Fermented and Pickled Foods

In Chinese cuisine, pickling and fermenting foods is a popular way to enhance flavor and increase shelf life. Large, cloudy vats of pickled vegetables (or eggs) adorn the counters in many street food stalls and food stands. The Chinese use a variety of spices and flavors, including hot chilies, in their pickling liquids, with garlic, ginger, soy sauce, and vinegar making up the basic four pickling ingredients. Occasionally, vegetables and fruits are fermented with spices, wine, and salt.

Meats (think pig's feet) are often pickled in China, as well as fruits and vegetables, such as white cabbage, radishes, turnips, carrots, long beans, and cucumbers. Pickled cabbages are frequently found in stews or as an accompaniment for a plate of meat. But by far, the most popular fermented food in Chinese cuisine is the humble soybean.

Gelatinous and Glutinous Foods

The Chinese have a special affinity for gelatinous and glutinous foods. The texture of these sticky, viscous, and wobbly edibles is a food hurdle for many foreigners. If blood tofu, jellyfish salads, and mung bean jellies sound less than delectable, a path forward can be found. Chinese sweets, which are seldom very sweet, are commonly made from glutinous rice—grown throughout Asia—and filled with sweet bean paste. When glutinous rice (which contains no actual gluten) is cooked, the high starch content breaks down into a glue-like texture that can be pounded, stretched, shaped, then filled with sweets. *Qingtuan*, a bright green glutinous rice ball, is popular during the April Qingming Festival (Tomb-Sweeping Day) and is a treat that appeals to many foreign palates. Social media and e-commerce have brought *qingtuan* to the attention of young people in China, which has significantly increased the snack's popularity in recent years.

DID YOU KNOW?

The preparation of traditional *qingtuan* begins with adding juice from wormwood grass, which only grows in the month of April. *Qingtuan* is a popular savory and sweet treat throughout the Yangtze River Delta region in southern China.

SHANGHAINESE DISHES

Shanghai's regional cuisine has been heavily influenced by its border provinces and often makes use of vinegar and wine combinations that form sticky sauces. Glazed meat dishes are popular and account for the city's reputation for enjoying "sweet" tastes over spicy. Seafood dishes are popular fare, as are meat dishes with chicken, goose, and pork.

Xiaolongxia (crawfish)

Xiaolongxia is to Shanghai what crawfish is to New Orleans. This seasonal food is available during the hot, humid summer months, and is typically popular in many of the cities along the Yangtze River Delta. Many menus will list crawfish as lobster, so make sure you know what you're ordering. *Xiaolongxia* are steamed whole in the shell. Peeling crawfish is the same as peeling shrimp, but make sure the tail of your *xiaolongxia* is curled under. A straight or mushy tail could indicate the crawfish was not alive when cooked. In Shanghai, crawfish and peeled shrimp are dipped in black vinegar sauces.

Stir-fried shrimp / Yellow croaker

Shrimp and yellow croaker fish are abundant along Shanghai's alluvial plains. Plates of oily, spiced and stir-fried peel-and-eat shrimp are popular lunch and dinner options. Yellow croaker fish shows up in both noodle and stir-fry dishes in Shanghai.

Mao xie (hairy crab)

Seasonal hairy crabs are a local specialty best plucked from nearby lakes, although demand is now so great the crabs are widely farmed and imported. The crabs, also known as "mitten" crabs, need both fresh and saltwater for successful breeding. Hairy crabs are abundant in Shanghai during the autumn months, when temporary street-side storefronts pop up and are suddenly full of water tanks filled with live crabs. Hairy crabs are served steamed and whole with a sweet dipping sauce of dark rice wine vinegar and ginger. Other types of crabs (*xie rou*) are sold throughout Shanghai as well, so make sure you are purchasing the correct variety.

During autumn, empty storefronts are filled with tanks of hairy crabs.

Shansi leng mian (cold eel noodles)

Eel is extremely popular in Shanghai. Live eels are such an essential part of the local cuisine that you can purchase them in big-box Western-style grocery stores like Metro, as well as in local wet markets. A variety of eel dishes will top the menus in many local restaurants. The most popular is eel with noodles, although eel is also braised and stir-fried in both sweet and savory sauces.

Cold eel noodle dishes are an important part of Shanghai cuisine.

Zui ji (drunken chicken)

Drunken chicken is a popular cold chicken dish that originated in neighboring Zhejiang province. The chicken is first steamed or boiled with ginger and spring onion (leaving the skin pale and pliable) and soaked in Shaoxing wine, a sweet rice wine popular throughout this part of China. Drunken chicken is typically served sliced cold with rice or added to a bowl of clear broth for easy access with chopsticks.

Shizi tou (lion's head meatballs)

Lion's head meatballs are exactly what you'd expect: jumbo meatballs. Stewed for as long as three or four hours, the meatball is large enough to eat as a single serving. The unique, soft consistency of the meat is achieved by chopping the fatty pork into a paste, which tenderizes the meat by breaking down the fiber. Tofu is added for moisture, and water chestnuts for crunch. The meatballs are first blanched in water and then braised in a rich broth of soy sauce, Nappa cabbage, and Shaoxing wine, and served in the broth with chopped bok choy. A different version of the dish features a lighter broth and the addition of vermicelli noodles.

Braised tofu dishes

Soft, braised tofu dishes are popular in Shanghai, and a number of varieties exist in which soft tofu is served in a warm clear broth. A variation on these tofu dishes is a Sichuan- influenced dish with stir-fried eggplant, soft tofu, and ground pork with chili oil. One version or another can be found on local menus and in the recipe repertoires of many Shanghai *ayis*. Foreigners are sometimes surprised to see the amount of oil in authentic Chinese stir-fry, and this dish is no exception.

Dumplings

Dumplings occupy an enormous category of food types in Shanghai and have become something of a high art form. By far the city's most popular and well-known cuisine, they are truly in a category of their own. As with so much of Shanghai's cuisine, many of the most popular dumplings have actually been imported from other regions, and the food stalls of Shanghai have tried their own turn, selling dumpling varieties from around the country, including Cantonese (dim sum) and the humble wonton, which originated in northern and central China. The varieties are too numerous to catalogue here, but I've tried to choose the best and most common, those typically found at Shanghai's street vendors, restaurants, and local dumpling shops.

Most types of dumplings in Shanghai are generally known as *baozi* or simply *bao*, which refers to a yeasty steamed bread with filling inside that are Shanghai specialties. Prices can vary according to the number of tourists nearby, but a good plate of four to five dumplings shouldn't cost more than about 10 yuan (US$1.45). Seafood dumplings are popular in China, and inexpensive if the seafood is mixed with pork (about 30 yuan / US$4.36 per order). Crab dumplings are also quite popular in Shanghai and a single order can be costly, setting you back as much as 100 yuan (US$14.50) for a plate of five or six in some areas. The out-of-the way streets hidden behind the Park Hotel at People's Square are a prime location to find local dumpling shops in Puxi that sell all varieties.

Xiaolongbao (pork soup dumplings)

The pork soup dumpling, *xiaolongbao* is legendary in Shanghai. No other dumpling in the city has achieved equal renown or been the subject of so much debate. The dumpling's popularity comes from the surprising burst of pork filling with delicious hot broth inside. But it is the thickness of the *bao* wrapper that makes these bite-sized steamed dumplings the subject of many heated discussions. An excellent *xiaolongbao* must combine delicious pork, a significant amount of hot broth with an extremely thin wrapper sealed with as many top-pinched pleats as possible.

The perfect plaits of Din Tai Fung's *xiaolongbao* are hard to match.

In order to get the broth inside *xiaolongbao*, the chopped pork filling is mixed with solidified, cooled pork gelatin that melts into a delicious soup when the dumpling is steamed. Everyone has a favorite approach to eating soup-filled dumplings. Some people like to poke a hole in the dumpling and carefully suck out the broth. The preferred method seems to be to hold the dumpling over a wide Chinese soup spoon and poke a hole in the dough, allowing the broth to spill into the spoon. Since *xiaolongbao* must be eaten hot, both methods protect diners from burning their tongues. Others prefer to wait until the soup cools barely enough to pop the entire thing into the mouth all at once. An accompanying dipping sauce of vinegar and soy sauce completes the meal.

The popularity of *xiaolongbao* has given rise to a well-regarded, if humorous, local publication called *A Guide to Soup Dumplings in Shanghai*, by Christopher Cavish, a long-time Shanghai expat. Cavish calls his book, which is available in boutique shops in the French Concession, a "pseudo-scientific guide" to choosing the best *xiaolongbao* in the city. Cavish's Soup Dumpling Index, a self-described scientific formula for rating soup dumplings, considers *xiaolongbao* "an engineering challenge."

Cavish rates dumplings based on the thinness of the wrappers, the weight of the filling, and the percentage of soup inside, all balanced against freshness (dumplings can't have been sitting around). He visited and ranked the *xiaolongbao* at fifty-two dumpling establishments in Shanghai and fleshed out (literally) the best eighteen. Just for good measure, he is also bold enough to warn readers away from a couple of the more terrifying dumpling restaurants. His book is worth a read if you're a dumpling fanatic.

Sheng jian bao (pan-fried dumplings)

Sheng jian bao is a rather generic word for dumplings that doubles as a colloquial name for Shanghai's popular round, pan-fried dumplings. Also referred to as *sheng jian mantou* or simply *sheng jian*, these dumplings are a bready, yeasty version of *xiaolongbao* that are often sprinkled with white or black sesame seeds. *Sheng jian* are ubiquitous in street food stalls and local dumpling joints throughout the city. The fillings of *sheng jian* are typically some combination of pork and vegetables with *broth*. As with all pan-fried dumplings, *sheng jian bao* aren't really fried, but instead browned on one side in a hot, oiled skillet. *Sheng jian bao* vie with *cong you bing* and *jian bing* as some of Shanghai's most popular breakfast treats.

DUMPLINGS IN SHANGHAI

Din Tai Fung's *xiaolongbao* are rated one of the best in Shanghai. It is a chain restaurant with multiple locations and by far the easiest place, especially if you're new to the city, to sample a variety of dumplings. Another good option is Jia Jia Tang Bao, located at 90 Huanghe Lu.

For some of the best *sheng jian bao* in the city, try these two places: Yangs, a Shanghai institution located at Nos. 54 and 60 Wujiang Lu (behind the Park Hotel, People's Square); and Gaochi, located at K11 Art Mall, 300 Huaihai Zhong Lu.

Baozi (pork buns)

Popular for breakfast or on-the-go lunches, traditional Shanghai *baozi* (literally, "bun") are made with a yeasted dough setting them apart from traditional dumplings. *Baozi* are cooked everywhere along sidewalks or in small food stands and are best eaten hot straight out of a stacked bamboo steamer. What you'll experience is a puffy, cloud-like parcel containing every manner of sweet or savory filling— from barbeque pork, shrimp, crabmeat, and veggies, to

Bamboo steamers full of *baozi* are a common sight during the breakfast hours.

sweet bean paste and custards. Despite their reputation as humble street food, *baozi*, along with other local street foods, have become popular haute cuisine abroad at upscale Asian restaurants. In Shanghai, the best *baozi* won't set you back much more than a few *kuai*.

Jaozi / Jian jaozi

Jaozi refers to a broad class of crescent-shaped steamed dumplings that Westerners often confuse with pot stickers (see *guo tie* below). *Jaozi* are everywhere in Shanghai—in street food stalls and restaurants, and all home cooks or *ayis* worth their salt can make excellent ones. The fillings vary widely, depending on the whim of the cook, but typically include pork, shrimp, cabbage, greens, herbs, scallions, and garlic.

A popular sibling to *jaozi* is the *jian jaozi*, or pan-fried version of *jaozi*. Like most pan-fried dumplings, *jian jaozi* are first steamed, then browned in an oiled pan to add color and crunch on the bottom. An authentic Shanghainese *jaozi* will include a local herb known commonly as shepherd's purse (capsella bursa-pastoris). Considered a weed in Europe and North America, shepherd's purse adds the unique peppery flavor also found in Shanghainese wontons and soup broths. Reliably good *jaozi* can be found almost anywhere between Wuyuan Lu and Fuxing Lu.

Guo tie (pot sticker)

Marry the crescent shape of a *jaozi* (although the shape can vary) with the pan-fried style of a *sheng jian bao* and the result is a typical *guo tie*. These are the pork and cabbage stuffed pot stickers most Westerners are familiar with. Most dumpling joints in Shanghai usually serve a variety of types. If you find good *xiaolongbao*, you'll likely find a delicious *jaozi* and *guo tie* as well.

Among the many types of *bao* in Shanghai, *sheng jian bao* and *jian jaozi* are some the most popular breakfast dumplings.

Hun tun (wontons)

Regional versions of the humble *hun tun* are found throughout China. A true Shanghai wonton, like a *jaozi*, will have a pork or shrimp filling and a generous amount of shepherd's purse. Wontons are not always eaten in soups in Shanghai, and the

MRS CHUNG'S DUMPLINGS

Our *ayi* for our first two years in Shanghai was an extraordinary cook. A native Shanghainese, her jaozi recipe (culled and cajoled with the use of a translation app), yields the best homemade dumplings in the world. Like all authentic recipes, the measurements aren't exact, but rather, to taste.

1. Filling (mixed in stages):
1 lb. ground pork mixed with ½ cup oil
1 tsp dark soy sauce
1 tbsp light soy sauce
1½ piece ginger, grated then chopped finely
1 large bunch green onions chopped

2. Add and mix well:
1 tsp black pepper
1 cup (plus a little more) finely chopped oyster mushrooms (squeeze out juice)
3 handfuls of grated and chopped carrot
A huge amount of finely chopped shepherd's purse, an herb in the mustard family. As with the mushrooms, squeeze out the juice. Substitute a mix of watercress and *bok choy* for shepherd's purse if you must.

3. Fill dumpling wrappers:
Peel off individual dumpling rounds, which are easily available packaged. Spread water around the edge, add 1 tsp or so of filling, flatten, then fold in half and seal top middle. Starting from one edge, make small pleats all round to seal.

4. Cook:
Place about 1 tsp butter or oil in non-stick frying pan. Cover bottom of the pan with dumplings, let fry a few seconds (until very lightly browned on bottom), then add water to cover the bottom of the pan. Cover with a lid and cook (steam) ten minutes. Continue with next batch.

NOTE: Shepherd's purse can be hard to find in the West since it's considered little more than a common weed. Many Asian markets that import from China will carry it in the summer months.

bite-sized versions are popular breakfast snacks. Wontons are served in a chicken broth two different ways. Small wontons often show up in a broth flecked with shepherd's purse, while a single large wonton in broth, sometimes in a spicy red broth, makes a common lunch entrée.

The Internet is brimming with suggestions about where to find the best dumplings or the best street food, but local businesses in Shanghai come and go with alarming speed. You're just as likely to find amazing dumplings at a no-name street stand you chance across on a daily walk. Some of the best *guo tie* I've had have been made by small sidewalk vendors with no name to advertise.

STREET FOOD

Street food, or *xiaochi* (literally, small snacks) is China's answer to Spanish tapas. Think of it as Cantonese *dim sum* on the fly. *Xiaochi* plays an important role in the food culture of Shanghai. While city life may have transformed in other ways to a high-end shopping mecca brimming with exclusive designer labels, it is the *xiaochi* that keeps the city's denizens grounded.

In the past few years, Shanghai has gained a reputation as one of the world's best street food cities. With 25 million hungry inhabitants

The underground tunnels of Shanghai's metro lines are a good place to sample a variety of Chinese snacks and many types of street food.

squeezed into an area one-third the size of Beijing, street food stalls are far and away the best place to pick up a quick, inexpensive meal. The fact that Shanghai is also a city of migrants means that a wide variety of street food is available, much of it original to other areas of China.

Most of the popular water towns (ancient towns that run on the water, like Venice) near Shanghai have an abundance of street food possibilities, though maybe not always the best quality. Chenghuangmiao Old Street, near the Yu Garden Bazaar and City God Temple (along with the surrounding commercial district) is one of the most popular street food destinations in Shanghai. The street food stalls in this area are extremely popular among Chinese tourists and locals who work nearby. The huge variety of street food in Chenghuangmiao is unmatched by any other location in Shanghai, but the crowds can make it feel like a less authentic experience. Try to explore side streets in Jing'an and the Former French Concession to find street food stalls that residents visit daily.

Wujiang Lu (in Jing'an) is not much more than a narrow line of kitschy shops, but it is conveniently located near the Starbucks Roastery (the world's first and largest, of course). For the most authentic street food (and to eat the way the locals do) explore the underground world of food stalls inside the metro tunnels, including the People's Square underground market. To pick up quick street side snacks for breakfast or dinner, stroll the back roads around Jing'an commercial areas as well Qibao old street near Fuxing Rd, Wulumuqi Middle Rd and Huai Hai Rd in Xuhui.

Below, I've tried to choose the most common and widely available street fare around town.

Liangpi (cold noodle dishes)

Liangpi, cold dishes of rice noodles covered in peanut sauce, are popular throughout the summertime in street side noodle shops. Some noodle dishes are served with cold vegetables such as bamboo shoots, scallions and meat such as cold chicken and eel.

Bing (round cake)

Bing in Mandarin is one of those words that endlessly confuse non-Mandarin speakers. Depending on the tone, accent, context, and Chinese character, the word itself can have as many as twenty different meanings, which is only made more confusing by the Romanized pinyin. In reference to street food, *bing* has one clear meaning: a flat, disk-shaped pastry or cake. However, even in this context, the type of pastry or cake can

Bing dough before being fried in oil.

be wide-ranging: *Bing* can refer to a sweet cookie, a pancake, a crepe, a bread pastry, a mooncake, or something like a small pizza. Shanghai street vendors offer up an amazing variety of *bing*, ranging from *naan*-like flatbreads to donut-like fried breads for dipping. Chinese *bing* can be fried, grilled, steamed, or baked. While I've tried to highlight some of the most common *bings* found on Shanghai streets, my list is by no means comprehensive.

A local street food seller shapes his *bing*.

Jianbing (fried pancake)

Jianbing, a popular pan-fried, stuffed and rolled crepe, is the king of street food *bing*. Although it originated in northern China, it is ubiquitous in Shanghai's street food stalls. The name translates literally to "fried pancake." True *jianbing* closely resembles a French crepe, which probably accounts for its skyrocketing international appeal—a situation that has prompted a local trade commission in Tianjin, a city outside Beijing, to release a series of "rules" outlining the proper size and fillings for an authentic version of this common street food.

Watching a street vendor make *jianbing* is almost as fun as eating it. A wide ladle of mung bean batter is skillfully poured onto a round, oiled griddle—some griddles are spinning like a potter's wheel, and the best *jianbing* cooks are truly food artists. As the dough firms up, a beaten egg is brushed across the crepe with a wooden spreader. Sometimes the *jianbing* is flipped, sometimes not, before receiving a topping of meat, seafood, scallions, vegetables, and Chinese sauces. A crispy piece of fried wonton is often placed in the center before the *jianbing* is rolled and folded like a burrito for easy on-the-go eating.

Cong you bing (scallion pancake)

Cong you bing is the once-removed cousin of *jianbing*. This, rather than *jianbing*, is the true "scallion pancake" of Shanghai (*cong you* literally means "scallion"), although the Internet is rife with videos confusing the two snacks. More pancake than crepe, *cong you bing* is made with dough, not a batter, which produces a smaller, thicker and oilier fried cake. Bits of meat, typically pork, and an array of sauces are added. A thin *cong you bing* is often folded into a half-moon shape, while the thicker, puffier version is eaten whole.

Shou zhua bing

The pan-fried dough of *shou zhua bing* has a consistency more like a cross between *naan* and croissant. These puffed up pancakes are the slightly crazier siblings of *cong you bing*, stuffed with sandwich-style foods including ham, fried eggs, bacon, ground pork and chili sauces.

You dunzi (shredded radish cake)

Another fried-dough favorite in Shanghai is *you dunzi*, the closest thing Shanghai has to a savory funnel cake. To make *you dunzi*, a dollop of doughy batter is unceremoniously dropped into a round mold, covered with a mixture of shredded *bailuobo* (white radish), scallions, and seasoning, then topped with another layer of dough and fried until it forms a puffy, greasy doughnut. After the dough is removed from the oil, additional fillings or sauces are added to a hole poked in the center.

Youtiao (Chinese churro)

The elongated churro-like shape of *youtiao* is primarily what distinguishes it from the disc-shaped *bing*. To make *youtiao*, a yeasted dough is rolled flat and segmented into long strips. Although the final shape can vary, the most artistic *youtiao* should have four puffed ridges, a shape easily accomplished by laying one strip of dough on top of another and pressing them together in the center with the long side of a knife or a metal pin. When the dough is fried, the edges puff out, creating the ridges.

Unlike a churro, *youtiao* is not covered with sugar, but instead used as a dipping bread (more like a biscotti), in congee (rice porridge) or *douhua* (tofu pudding).

A wide selection of meat, seafood and vegetables are sold as nighttime snacks.

Shaokao (BBQ meat skewers)

Unlike dumplings and cake-like street foods, which are often eaten for breakfast, *shaokao* are essentially Chinese kebabs—smoky spiced skewers of BBQ meats, popular for afternoon and evening snacks. While pork and chicken are popular, in Shanghai the sea is king. Skewers of shrimp, sea plants (like lotus) and flatfish are common. Another popular skewered treat is kebabs of small quails, skewered whole (including the heads) and glazed with a sticky sweet sauce of soy and Shaoxing wine. Skewered quail are often found in food shops along Huai Hai Road and near Yu Yuan Garden Bazaar. Vegetable skewers are also popular and usually include tofu, cauliflower, mushrooms and beans.

Kao di gua (roasted sweet potato)

Roasted sweet potatoes are a popular snack during the winter months. As soon as the cold air sets in, sweet potato vendors pop up all over the city, with their portable barrel stoves, sometimes balanced on the back of bicycles or pulled on two-wheeled carts. Sweet potato vendors are often migrants, frequently Uyghers from the Xinjiang region. A large, smoky, roasted sweet potato typically costs between 4-5 *kuai*.

Sweet potatoes roasting on a street vendor's cart.

Dou hua (soft tofu pudding)

Dou hua is a soft bean-curd pudding popular for breakfast and early afternoon snacks. Sweet versions of *dou hua*, made with sugar syrup, have a silky texture and flavor similar to a Spanish flan. Both savory and sweet versions can be found in Shanghai, with savory versions sporting the ever-present topping of scallions. Although the best dou hua is available in restaurants and market stalls, it's also commonly purchased pre-packaged (like chicken feet) from super markets and take-out food shops.

Zongzi (bamboo leaf-wrapped sticky rice)

Zongzi is a Chinese version of sticky rice dumplings found throughout Asia. While these are sometimes eaten as seasonal treats during the June dragon boat festival, they are widely available in street-food stands throughout the winter and spring. To make *zongzi*, sticky rice pouches, filled with pork or salted duck eggs, are steamed or boiled inside triangular pouches of bamboo leaves, and tied with string.

Chicken feet are often fried and glazed with a sticky sweet sauce.

Fengzhao (chicken feet)

Chicken feet are widely available in Shanghai's wet markets, hot food stalls, and street-food stalls, as well as in supermarkets and restaurants. They are one of the most sought-after food snacks in China. The most popular version of chicken feet in Shanghai is, of course, deep-fried and coated with a sweet glaze. But chicken feet can also be found boiled, spiced, and mixed into stews and stir-fry dishes. Chicken feet have been at the center of a long trade dispute between China and the U.S, but the tensions seem not to have diminished China's appetite for these gelatinous goodies. Some locals even eat the bones instead of spitting

Sidewalk fruit shops offer a wide variety of regional fruits such as leechee and nashi pears.

them out. When buying chicken feet be sure to avoid using literal translations on translation apps which often use the word *ji zhua*, referring to actual chicken feet. When chicken feet are no longer part of a living chicken, but instead have become a food item, the translation is *fengzhao*.

Fruit stands

Local fruit stands carry a wide variety of Chinese seasonal fruit worth sampling, including nashi pears, juju dates, and lychees. Wet markets also sell seasonal fruits, including spring strawberries, mangos, bananas and other familiar fare. Becoming a regular customer at a particular market stall usually means shop owners eventually stuff your bag with extras and freebies to keep you happy.

Many fruit vendors in Shanghai sell their fare from mobile pull carts.

EVERYTHING MADE OR DELIVERED

The service economy in China, as in much of Asia, often feels paradoxical to Westerners. Certain aspects of service that many Westerners are accustomed to—an attentive restaurant wait staff, for example, or a friendly smile from the grocery checker, are often in short supply in Shanghai (excluding high-end restaurants or hotels, of course). Don't be surprised to find yourself sitting alone ready to order while the wait staff seem oblivious to your presence.

On the other hand, almost anything that can be built, bought or brewed can easily be delivered to your front door quickly and efficiently. This is one of the best parts of life in Shanghai. Most restaurants deliver food. The creation of the English version of the food delivery app Sherpas makes ordering takeout food a breeze. With a touch of your finger, any type of food within range can be delivered to your home.

CHAPTER 7

ENJOYING
SHANGHAI

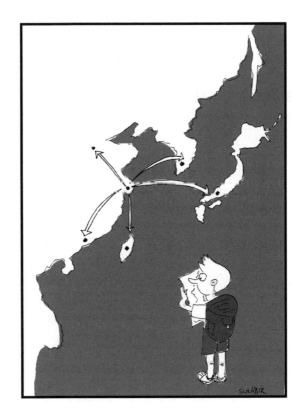

❝Who can go out except through the door?❞

— *The Analects of Confucius*

GETTING IN AND OUT OF SHANGHAI

Shanghai's coastal location makes it the perfect jumping off point for travel throughout Asia. To the east, Japan and Korea are a hop, skip, and jump away. To the west, lies the vast expanse of China's diverse provinces and autonomous regions. The Philippines, Taiwan, and Hong Kong are easily accessible for weekend travel, and Southeast Asian countries like Thailand and Vietnam are popular vacation spots for expats during holidays. Regional travel is affordable and comfortable on China's state-of-the-art bullet-train system, which now connects more than five hundred cities within China.

Airports

Any city that is home to the headquarters of more than 550 multinational corporations can rest on its laurels. Yet, Shanghai persists. Not one, but two international airports flank the city's eastern and western edges. Shanghai Pudong International Airport, the primary entry point for overseas passengers, is a sprawling complex located on the eastern edge of Shanghai, along the East China Sea. With a stunning seventy-four million passengers moving through its facility, Pudong Airport is the ninth busiest airport in the world and second busiest in China, after Beijing.

Transportation from Pudong airport to the city center is streamlined and efficient. The Maglev, the world's fastest train, offers a short ride from the airport to Longyang Road metro station where visitors can pick up Lines 2, 7, 16 (and the future Line 18) of the Shanghai Metro System. From there, nearly all the city is accessible. If a ride on the Maglev isn't your cup of tea, direct access to metro Line 2 is also available at the airport. Buses and airport shuttles are conveniently located in the lobbies once you've cleared customs.

Exiting the baggage area at Pudong requires walking through a gauntlet of hired drivers feverishly waving signs and shouting names as they look for passengers. The crush of people gathered along the walkway can seem overwhelming for first timers. In addition to hotel drivers, random taxi drivers are lined up shouting and looking for customers. In general, these drivers are legitimate, but it's best to make sure your taxi is cleaner and newer (Volkswagen is an official taxi brand) and working for one of Shanghai's official companies. Nearly all hotels offer transport service from the airport.

Most domestic travelers, as well as those moving between a handful of other Asian countries, will depart from the Hongqiao International Airport, located just west of downtown. Although Hongqiao has been in operation since the 1960s, the newest terminal was constructed during a multi-billion *yuan* expansion in 2010, making it a bit more architecturally interesting than Pudong, which opened in the late 1990s. Traveling from Hongqiao Airport is the epitome of convenience, with Terminal 2 offering a direct connection to the Hongqiao Railway Station, the largest railway transit hub in Asia. Walking between the airport and the railway is the easiest and most efficient method of traversing the two facilities.

THE SHANGHAI RAILWAYS

Shanghai has four large, modern railway stations that run both traditional and high-speed train service to every

Chinese province. High-speed trains alone (known as bullet trains), offer service between Shanghai and most major cities, including Beijing, Hong Kong, Guangzhou, Hangzhou, Chengdu, and Xian. Shanghai's train stations look remarkably similar to its airports, chock-full of shopping outlets, restaurants, and snack shacks.

Train tickets can be purchased in locations throughout the city as well as in each of the stations. TravelChinaGuide is a website that offers the best online ticket-booking services for English speakers; it includes train schedules, ticket purchases, and ticket delivery directly to a location in Shanghai. Look them up on WeChat or visit their web page.

China now has some of the fastest trains in the world.

Hongqiao Railway Station

Hongqiao Railway Station is one part of the undisputed king of Asian transit centers, the Hongqiao Transportation Hub (HTH). Connected by a series of passenger tunnels and walkways directly to Hongqiao Airport, as well as to Lines 2, 10 and 17, of the Shanghai Metro System, this station is a hive of activity that offers visitors real insight into how prodigious Chinese crowds can be. During holidays, especially, the throng can feel impenetrable.

As the newest, largest and most popular station in Shanghai, Hongqiao Railway provides extensive bullet-train service from Shanghai to the greatest number of Chinese cities. In addition to its role as a major artery for planes, trains and buses, the HTH has the capacity to house a Maglev train. Signs and routes are clearly marked in pinyin and English, and navigating between stations and airport provides an example of the best of Chinese efficiency.

Shanghai Railway Station

Shanghai's second largest, the Shanghai Railway Station (referred to by locals as the "new station") replaced the old Shanghai North Station back in the late 1980s. This station offers a healthy bullet-train service and provides traditional train service to areas north and south of Shanghai. Shanghai Railway is most convenient for travel to nearby locations such as Suzhou and Hangzhou as well as major cities in China, including Beijing, Xian, and Chengdu. The Railway is more commonly used by travelers as a connecting station on longer routes between cities, like Hong Kong, and Beijing. Shanghai Railway Station has fewer high-speed train routes than Hongqiao, which means a greater number of more affordable train tickets. The station is accessible from metro Lines 1, 3 and 4.

Shanghai South Railway

Accessible via metro Lines 1 and 3, the Shanghai South station is identifiable by its unique round architecture. The station provides traditional train service to many of China's smaller southern cities and river delta stops. The station and its metro tunnels are host to the typical underground fare of snack shacks and small shops peddling fake goods.

Shanghai West

Shanghai West is the smallest and least used (and therefore, least crowded) of Shanghai's four stations. Only a handful of bullet trains run between Shanghai West and regional destinations such as Nanjing and Wuxi. The station is accessible by metro Line 11.

CHINESE HOLIDAYS AND TRAVEL

Navigating Shanghai's airports, train stations, highways, and metro stations during Chinese national holidays is something that requires serious planning. Nearly all business comes to a halt during both Chinese New Year and the Mid-Autumn Festival, and many of the city's main roads are closed, making travel by driver and car challenging. Regular delivery of household essentials is nearly impossible, so it's important to stock up on supplies like water ahead of time. Many expats choose to leave the country during the longest holidays; even so, nearby Asian destinations can feel overrun with the crowds of Chinese tourists who also travel during the holidays.

Shanghai is also a chief destination for many families from elsewhere in China, especially since children are out of school. During a few holidays, there have been dangerous stampeding incidents involving large crowds on the Bund. As a result, expect to see a healthy presence of military and police forces around the city during these times.

DAY TRIPS FROM SHANGHAI

Short adventures can bolster the spirits of even the most homesick expat. Getting out of Shanghai for the day or overnight can reignite your sense of appreciation for Chinese culture and provide opportunities to see how people outside the big city spend their time. While the following suggestions are by no means comprehensive, I have tried to focus on favorite activities and accessible locations that have broad appeal to expats of all stripes.

Water Towns and Ancient Villages

A large network of ancient villages and water towns surround the suburban perimeter of Shanghai. Visiting these towns offers great insight into hundreds, or sometimes thousands, of years of village life along the waterways, canals, and wetlands that make up the entirety of the Yangtze River Delta. In many of the villages, ancient Chinese architecture (mostly restored) dates back nearly two thousand years.

From Shanghai, the closest and most accessible water towns, Zhijiajiao, Zhouzhuang, and Qi Bao Old Town, have become quite popular among visitors, and can become overcrowded and touristy. Commercial construction around

Boats offer rides in the scenic canals of Zhijiajiao water town.

the perimeter of these towns is encroaching on the ancient village centers, and abundant tourists during spring and fall make visits uncomfortably close. Even with the crowds, these towns are well worth a visit. The narrow lanes and ancient bridges, as well as local residential areas, provide a stark contrast to most of suburban Shanghai. Boating vendors and restaurants now line the canals and walkways of Zhijiajiao, while the alleys are jammed with street-food vendors and trinket merchants. Local Chinese citizens no longer live inside the most touristy water towns, but a short stroll beyond the central area can yield pictures of local life worth experiencing. Many residents of the area wash dishes and utensils in the canals, which are quite polluted, so consider carefully where you eat.

Both Tongli and Luzhi water towns are extremely picturesque, sporting beautiful architecture, Chinese covered bridges, ivy covered walls, and spectacular gardens. Although slightly further from Shanghai (about an hour and a half by

Residents of Yangtze Delta water towns live alongside an expansive canal system.

(This and facing page): The scenic water town of Longmen village is a three-hour drive from Shanghai.

car), they are worthwhile one-day trips. While Tongli can feel extremely touristy, it is located just outside the beautiful city of Suzhou, a trip in its own right. Luzhi feels a bit more local.

If you absolutely must get away from people, Longmen ancient village, a lesser-known water town a few hours outside Shanghai, offers views of quiet mountain life. Longmen is an actively occupied village, still inhabited by local residents who are usually playing cards, sweeping sidewalks, or stringing badminton racquets, the manufacture of which provides a livelihood for many. The biggest attraction of Longmen village is its ancient (and restored) architecture, many of which are old family compounds dating back thousands of years to the Ming and Qing Dynasties

Taxis to Tongli, Luzhi, and Qi Bao can cost as much as ¥800 (US$116) round trip. Public buses have routes to all the villages but can be somewhat challenging to navigate. Tongli is accessible by bullet train to Suzhou. Zhijiajiao is

accessible via Line 17 of the Shanghai metro, but still requires a fair amount of walking to get from the metro to the village. Although local tourist guides regularly run trips to most water towns via expat societies, many Westerners find hiring a private driver, who will wait during the visit, is the easiest and most convenient way to make the trip. Taxis tend to drop off tourists at main gates, which charge fees to enter (at Zhijiajiao, in particular), but paid entry to most towns is not compulsory, and there are a multitude of entrances via bridges and sidewalks that connect the water towns to the surrounding villages.

Suzhou

Just as Shanghai has been historically compared to Paris, Suzhou is frequently referred to as the "Venice of China." With nearly twenty-five hundred years of history to claim, Old Town Suzhou is essentially a scenic water town

Tourists take a ride on the beautiful canals of Suzhou.

surrounded by a city of ten million people. Known especially for its classical Oriental gardens, picturesque bridges, and gondola rides through the canals, Suzhou has become the weekend destination of choice for Shanghai urban dwellers looking for relaxation. Travel to Suzhou is especially popular in the spring when the city's many flowering plum trees are in bloom. Getting to Suzhou from Shanghai, a mere thirty minutes by bullet train, is easiest via Hongqiao Railway Station. If a weekend getaway is in your future, the city boasts a number of five-star hotels, spas, and resorts that cater to every size pocketbook.

Houtouwan

For the adventurous at heart, a trip to Houtouwan Village (known locally as Green Heaven) makes a nice weekend outing. The abandoned fishing village, which has become rather scenically overrun with vines and other vegetation, offers an escape from the typical crowds and hawkers that populate the water towns. The village itself is a favorite of expat photography buffs. Located on Shengshan Island, one of the four hundred Shengshi Islands that dot the eastern coastline, the trip requires a rather long ferry ride. It's possible to see Houtouwan in one day (with most of your day involving travel back and forth), but an overnight stay on one of the nearby islands makes the trip more relaxing.

Ferry tickets can be purchased online or at bus stations in Shanghai. Houtouwan village can be viewed from a raised platform on an adjoining hillside, but if you've come this far, you'll want to amble over the walkways and see the eerily quiet houses up close. Boats from the central village on Shengshan Island take visitors to the island for a hefty fee (¥100 / US$14.5).

Chongming Dongtan Nature Reserve

Even long-time residents of Shanghai are frequently unaware that the estuaries along the Yangtze River form important stopovers for millions of migratory birds each year, including the spectacular hooded crane. The Dongtan Nature Reserve on nearby Chongming Island—China's third largest island— was established to protect the habitat of these birds, twenty percent of which are listed among the world's endangered species. Hooded cranes can sometimes be spotted in Dongtan during February, which is the time visitors are least likely to venture out to the park.

Like many things in China, Dongtan is more like a mishmash of culturally Western concepts adapted to fit into

A boardwalk at the Dongtan Nature Reserve.

Chinese framework. Part nature reserve, part amusement park, part conservancy, the park is exactly what you'd expect from a bird sanctuary in China: bikes for rent, boat rides, tram rides, a petting zoo, and, of course, an alligator park. Avoid holidays as it can feel more like Disneyland than a nature reserve. There are also many lovely kilometers of natural beauty to be found in the park's wetlands. The reserve is huge, and lazy bike rides offer the quietest and most relaxing way to explore the park. In nice weather, it's not uncommon to see children flying kites, or find that Chinese families have set up tents and hammocks and other camping equipment for impromptu "campouts" in the grassy areas.

Getting to Dongtan is quickest by car and driver, although a metro line to Chongming island from Pudong is slated for future construction. Driving offers the added benefit of crossing one of Shanghai's more impressive engineering ventures, the Yangtze River Tunnel and Bridge, a combined tunnel and bridge complex that connects Pudong to Chongming Island via Changxing Island. Check Dongtan's website for seasonal hours of operation.

People set up tents for "camping out" at the Dongtan Nature Reserve.

Nanjing Memorial Hall

There are many good reasons to make the short one-hour train ride from Shanghai to Nanjing, but none is as sobering as a visit to the Memorial Hall of the Victims of the Nanjing Massacre by Japanese Invaders. This important monument pays tribute to the more than 300,000 Chinese people who were tortured and killed in Nanjing by the Japanese Imperial Army during the Second Sino-Japanese War in 1937.

The memorial is subdivided into parts, consisting of both indoor and outdoor sections. Outside, a sculpture park depicts floating scenes of children and families fleeing from the massacre, while the large indoor facility is built directly over the Jiangdongmen burial site. Be advised that the Jiangdongmen portion of the memorial preserves exposed skeletons and bones of victims that were discovered in mass graves. Young children especially may find the memorial frightening. Hours and directions to the memorial from the Nanjing train station are widely available online.

WEEKEND EXCURSIONS FROM SHANGHAI

Hangzhou, a city of beautiful gardens and parks, is in Zhejiang Province. It is the corporate headquarters of Alibaba, and the location of the beautiful West Lake, a UNESCO Heritage site. Visit a tea farm and participate in a formal tea ceremony. The Leifeng Pagoda on the southern end of West Lake offers a stunning view of the city and the mountains surrounding it. Other special sights include Lingyin Temple and the Feilai Feng grottoes, a stone peak with 450 Buddhist carvings made between the 10th and 14th centuries.

Nature lovers should take the train to Moganshan and hike in its famed bamboo forests.

Scenic West Lake in Hangzhou.

Located at the entrance to Lingyin Temple in Hangzhou, the Feilai Feng Grottoes include more than 400 rock buddha reliefs in stone.

Plan a visit to Lake Tai just north of Suzhou. Lake Tai is easily accessible if you are staying in Suzhou for the weekend. The best views of Lake Tai can be had at the Dragon Light Pagoda in Xihui Park in Wuxi. Lake Tai is one of the largest freshwater lakes in China. The area is home to resorts, the golden grand Buddha, and a number of ancient water towns.

Although Ningbo has a reputation an industrial city, it is a popular shopping destination for expats who want to buy Chinese style furniture, some of which is manufactured there. Ningbo also has a large number of old Buddhist temples.

Anji County is a mountainous region located in northwestern Zhejiang Province. Hike up to the Hidden Dragon Waterfall and explore the mountains and bamboo forests that contain the widest variety of bamboos found in China. The mountains around the Tianhuangping Scenic Area are home to the

The mountains of Anji county in neighboring Zhejiang Province contain the widest variety of bamboo in China.

Huadong Power Station, the largest power station in Asia and the second largest in the world. Mountain views from the Power Station are stunning.

TEMPLES

Much of Shanghai's Buddhist history has been destroyed through thousands of years of war. While there are a host of small "village temples" in residential areas that may entice those seeking lesser-known sites, the three most important temples in Shanghai offer the last real look at different strands of Buddhist life in the city.

Jing'an Temple

Fully renovated in the early 1980s after being used as a factory during the Cultural Revolution, the Jing'an Temple offers visitors an exercise in perspective. The temple's curved lines and imperial architecture create a vista in stark contrast to the shimmering glass of surrounding high-rise buildings. Located at the juncture of metro Lines 2 and 7, and adjacent to Jing'an Park, the temple is open to visitors most days of the week. The temple is located in one of the busiest sections of Jing'an. Admission gates are across the street from Jing'an Park. A mishmash of art and Buddhist artifacts from different eras, including China's largest jade Buddha, are on display in the temple's many halls.

New skycrapers rise above the Qing Dynasty era Jing'An Temple.

The reclining Jade Buddha was brought to Shanghai from Myanmar.

Jade Buddha Temple

Originally built in the late 1800s to house a collection of jade Buddhas from Myanmar, the Jade Buddha Temple is still an active home for monks. The temple's location away from other tourist points of interest makes it one of the more pleasant temples to visit. Aside from its central attractions—a large white, reclining jade Buddha, and a smaller reclining jade Buddha—the temple has a number of huge gold-plated Buddhas as well. The temple also has a large hall dedicated to The Four Heavenly Kings. Be sure to bring cash—as of 2019, the temple still does not accept mobile payment.

Longhua Temple and Pagoda

Although the full history of Longhua Temple stretches back nearly two thousand years, the temple complex has been destroyed, rebuilt, and restored numerous times. Most buildings inside the temple complex were rebuilt in the mid 1800s, with a modern restoration completed in the 1950s. Unlike Shanghai's other temples, Longhua is a sprawling complex of gardens and buildings with many halls, Buddhas, a drum tower, and the Longhua Pagoda. As the oldest and most spectacular temple in Shanghai, Longhua's history is inextricably intertwined with Shanghai. During the Chinese civil war, the Kuomintang executed suspected communists on the grounds and ten years later, the Japanese used the complex during the Second Sino-Japanese war. The Longhua metro station is on Lines 11 and 12. Walking tours of the temple grounds are available during the week.

Wenmiao Confucian Temple

Shanghai proper has only one Confucian temple, the Wenmiao Temple, located in the old city, which is a worthwhile trip. The temple was badly damaged during the Cultural Revolution but renovated by the government in the mid-1990s. The area surrounding the temple is the site of one of the biggest used Chinese book markets in Shanghai, and the best time to visit the temple is on Sunday mornings when the market is full of activity. Rumors of the book market closing constantly circulate in Shanghai, so check local resources before making a trip especially for that.

If Confucian temples are a special interest, Chongming Island has a lovely Confucian temple, and it is one of the area's oldest surviving temples. Originally constructed in the thirteenth century, the temple was reconstructed during the late Ming Dynasty. It's easy to combine a visit to the temple with a visit to the Dongtang Nature Reserve.

City of God Temple

The City of God Temple (also officially called the City Temple of Shanghai) is probably the most visited temple in the city. Although now maintained as a Taoist Temple, it is actually an example of a Chinese folk temple. Visiting this temple offers insight into how Chinese religious history is connected to folk belief and local customs. The temple houses Shanghai's three city gods, all of whom were historical figures who eventually became folk heroes: Huo Guang, Qin Yubo, and Chen Huacheng. Located in the midst of the Chenghuangmia commercial district (connected to the Yu Garden Bazaar area), expect the streets around the temple to be crowded with shops and street food shacks.

PLAYING THE ROLE OF TOURIST

Shanghai has a healthy round of must-see attractions. Many visitors will enjoy spending a day touring Shanghai's Old City, a collection of winding streets, small buildings with tile roofs, and local wet markets. Although the old city abuts some of Shanghai's busiest tourist attractions, life here remains distinctly Chinese, and very local. The area was once surrounded by a large defensive wall that in later years separated the Chinese residential area from the colonial concessions. Although the walls were removed during the early twentieth century, a small remnant is still viewable.

Adjacent to the Old City, the surrounding Yu Bazaar tourist area is a series of reconstructed Chinese-style buildings making up a confusing labyrinth of stores and restaurants. The classical Ming Dynasty Yu Yuan Garden (often shortened to Yu Garden) stands in the middle of the tourist bazaar and charges an entry fee. It's best to avoid this area during Chinese holidays and weekends, as the

The Ming Dynasty Yu Yuan Garden is a beautiful example of ancient Chinese architecture and garden design.

narrow alleyways become so congested, pedestrian traffic comes to a virtual halt.

Tours of Pudong's famous triumvirate of skyscrapers—The Jin Mao Tower, The Shanghai Financial Center (the "bottle opener"), and The Shanghai Tower, never fail to impress visitors. Skyward views of the three buildings are spectacular from the Lujiazui Pedestrian Bridge in Pudong. All three buildings allow visitors to ascend to observation towers or decks. The glass floor of the Financial Center observation deck gives visitors a queasy look at the city below. The Shanghai Tower has the world's highest observation deck, and the world's fastest elevators, two high-water marks that make the trip especially impressive. A number of architectural tours are available in Shanghai, which explore the construction of the city's towering skyscrapers on its soft alluvial soilscape.

If you prefer an escape from the famous skyline—and the crowds that come with it—Shanghai's parks offer a bit of respite. The Jing'an Sculpture Park, with its myriad animal and human sculptures constructed from a variety of materials, is a favorite for young children. Not to be confused with the sculpture park, Jing'an Park is located across the street from the Jing'an Temple, and is regularly filled with groups of elderly Chinese drum groups, *tai chi* practitioners, ballroom dancers, and a host of street performers, along with cafes and an impressive collection of stray cats that soak up attention (and food) from park visitors. In Pudong, Century Park is modeled after New York's Central Park. Its cultivated gardens and meandering walking paths along a lake make this park an excellent exercise place for children. The park also has on display a wide variety of horticultural sculptures.

The People's Park is located adjacent to People's Square. Initially constructed by the British as a horse racing track, the park is now a green space at the cultural and political heart of Puxi—Shanghai's municipal government buildings are located at the park's southern end and the park is surrounded by museums, a theater, hotels, and a new expo center. The landscaped park is also the much-discussed location of the weekend Shanghai Marriage Market (see below).

Tianzifang and Xintiandi, are two sections of the city with wide appeal to foreigners. The trendy cafes and boutiques of Xintiandi, located in the heart of the Former

The narrow alleys of Tianzifang are a good place to shop and experience the old shikumen style buildings.

French Concession, feel more Western than Chinese. The primary tourist attraction in this area is the collection of *shikumen* buildings that make up the Site of the First National Congress of the Chinese Communist Party. Similar to Xintiandi, Tianzifang is also home to a large number of cafes and boutiques, surrounding a renovated *shikumen* village tucked away between the main city roads. Entrances to the Tianzifang alleys are squeezed between buildings along the main sidewalks. Most shops and restaurants in the area are quite touristy, but the neighborhood that skirts the borders of the *shikumen* has a large, modern, wet market worth visiting.

Last, but certainly not least, families may want to make a trek out to the ultimate Shanghai tourist destination: The Disney Resort and Theme Park in Pudong. A joint venture between Disney and a Chinese investment firm, the park was opened to great fanfare in 2016. The resort contains all of the traditional accouterments of other Disney theme parks (the food has a slightly more Chinese bent to it), and the park sees about 10 million visitors per year. Like everything else in mainland China, the Disney Shanghai is extremely crowded during holidays and weekends.

THE ZOTTER CHOCOLATE THEATER

Located on the Pudong side of the river, The Zotter Chocolate Theater is as close as you will get to experiencing Willy Wonka's chocolate factory in real life. Zotter is an Austrian chocolatier with an international reputation. The Shanghai facility, the site of chocolate production for Zotter's Asian market, doubles as an offbeat chocolate "theater" that is part entertainment and part marketing. Zotter runs both English and Chinese tours of the factory, which include a short film, walks through "air locked" rooms, and many, many opportunities for tasting—from bite-sized truffles to melted chocolate drinks. Zotter is known for its unusual combinations of flavors (chocolate and blue cheese, for example), as well as its colorful and creative decor. Moderate your chocolate consumption early on or you will be under-the-weather by the tour's end. Visit www.zotter.cn.

MUSEUMS

A surprising number of contemporary museums, dedicated to everything from glass and automobiles to film and contemporary art, have exploded onto the scene in Shanghai since the city hosted the 2010 World Expo. Although many of Shanghai's museums are privately operated, a spate of impressive new state-backed museums is cropping up along Pudong's newly developed East Bund area. At least three new museums anticipate opening for visitors in 2020, including the 105,000-sqm Shanghai Museum East, which will display a notable collection of Chinese antiquities. For Chinese art lovers who survived the Cultural Revolution, the trend of promoting art and culture has cemented Shanghai's reputation as the country's most progressive city. For expats, Shanghai's museum scene offers a window into Chinese history, art, and culture. This list represents only a handful of the most popular museums (new and old), chosen for ease of access and topics of interest.

Contemporary Art

A collaboration between The West Bund Group and the French Centre Pompidou to build a new branch of the iconic Pompidou museum in Shanghai feels like a natural extension of the historical East/West comparisons between the two cities. Located in a wing of the brand new West Bund Art Museum, Le Centre Pompidou Shanghai opened in 2019. As an homage to authentic cultural exchange, the Shanghai branch showcases collections from Paris, while the Paris branch displays works by contemporary Chinese artists.

Three other contemporary art museums opened in 2018, adding to the long list of places for China's growing number of artists to showcase cutting-edge conceptual pieces. The

Silo of 80,000 Tons is an industrial-style exhibition complex in Pudong constructed from the largest silo facility in Asia. The architecture of the museum itself is as exciting to see as the galleries. Additional new contemporary art museums appearing on the scene in 2018 include the HOW Museum and the LONG Museum (www.thelongmuseum.org).

The Power Station of Art (powerstationofart.com), and the art deco Rockbund Art Museum (www.rockbundartmuseum.org) are established museums that promote Chinese contemporary and conceptual artists. The China Art Museum located in Pudong, constructed for the World Expo in 2010, is dedicated to displaying works by modern and contemporary Chinese artists. Last but certainly not least, the Museum of Contemporary Art Shanghai (MoCA) (www.mocashanghai.org) was founded as the first independent, non-profit museum in the city. Located in the center of People's Square, MoCA exhibitions regularly showcase the work of international artists.

Science, History and Culture

A mainstay of the People's Square complex, The Shanghai Museum (www.shanghaimuseum.net) is home to the city's largest collection of Chinese antiquities, some of which are estimated to be five to ten thousand years old. Although the museum itself predates the Cultural Revolution, the current building was constructed in the 1990s, after a massive fundraising drive by the Chinese archeologist and former museum director Ma Chenguan. The building's unique rounded architecture was conceived as an homage to the museum's treasured masterpiece, the *Da Ke Ding*, a bronze cooking vessel on a tripod, dating back to 1046 BCE. The extensive collection of ancient calligraphy, oracle bones,

Neolithic pottery, hand-painted scrolls, jade, ceramic pottery, furniture, and bronze figurines is so large it will soon be shared with the newly constructed Shanghai Museum East in Pudong.

Family favorites spanning both sides of the Huangpu River, The Shanghai Natural History Museum (www.snhm.org.cn) and the Science and Technology Museum (en.sstm.org.cn), are great day-outings with children. Both museums offer enough interest and entertainment to keep children engaged and busy for hours. As a bonus, the Natural History Museum, situated adjacent to the Jing'an Sculpture Park, is an adventure of Alice-in-Wonderland-like sculptures that captivate the imagination of its visitors. The Science and Technology museum serves as an anchor complex on the edge of Pudong's enormous Century Park. The museum is home to no less than four IMAX theaters and contains a wide range of interactive exhibits that celebrate state-of-the-art advancements in technology.

History and political buffs can spend a worthwhile afternoon hunting down the inconspicuous Shanghai Propaganda Poster Art Center (www.shanghaipropagandaart.com), a small, privately run museum hidden in the basement of a vanilla apartment complex in the Former French Concession. The museum is popular with the expat community since it offers great insight into the historical depictions and attitudes toward Westerners from posters that were created during the Mao years. Before the government offered official sanctioning of the collection, the owner displayed it secretly, which explains its unusual location. Many of the posters, valuable as much for their artistic form as for their politics, display anti-Western, racist, and xenophobic Communist mottos that characterized the years of the Cultural Revolution.

Americans, for example, are often portrayed as Jews with caricature-style features and stereotypic depictions as money lenders. Other images promote the technological superiority of China. The Center also runs a small museum shop next to the exhibition where reproductions of Chinese propaganda posters (and some originals), are available to purchase, along with postcards, and a large collection of Mao memorabilia. The museum is not well marked but is locatable on map apps. Stop at the gate when entering the apartment complex and the guard will hand you a small paper directing you to the correct building.

SHOPPING

As contrary as it may seem to the Communist Party position, conspicuous consumption is alive and well in Shanghai. In the past decade, Shanghai has transformed into a shopping mecca for thousands of Chinese tourists from other provinces who flock to the city's high-end shopping districts during national holidays. Shopping in the city can feel like a cultural experience of its own. Certainly, the scores of designer brands and cheap knock offs are part of the attraction, but the city is also teeming with specialty markets, local tea shops, and underground shopping malls where tourists can buy almost anything from faux designer prescription glasses to tailored suits.

Brand Name Shopping

Upscale shopping districts in Shanghai are typically clustered around hotels and tourist destinations. The famed Nanjing Road, which bisects the city into northern and southern halves, stretches from the Bund to well past Jing'an Temple and offers some of the best brand name and designer shopping in the city. East Nanjing Road (Nanjing Dong Lu), has been blocked off to traffic—except for a continual stream of tourist trams—and reconfigured into a pedestrian boulevard. Although generally viewed by expats as a congested tourist trap, it's a great place to witness Shanghai's version of capitalism at work. Western stores along East Nanjing are often interspersed with small Chinese curio markets on side streets and at the metro entrances. Prepare to be accosted on a regular basis by people hawking fake watches and handbags. For a more interesting experience, try exploring the backroads in this area and sample the Chinese street food.

Shanghai's equivalent of New York's 5th Avenue is West Nanjing Road (Nanjing Xi Lu) which begins near People's Park and runs past the Ritz Carlton and Shanghai Exhibition

Starbucks chose Shanghai to launch its first Roastery, the largest Starbucks in the world.

Center. The area is dotted with shopping malls and iconic fashion labels like Gucci, Prada, and Burberry. You'll also find the world's largest Starbucks along this stretch. Additional high-end shopping malls can be found along Huai Hai Lu in Xuhui and bordering Pudong's Lujiazui Pedestrian Bridge. For some reason, many Chinese shopping malls are constructed with circular architecture, which can turn them into a confusing labyrinth of escalators and elevators. The high-end Super Brand Mall in Pudong, is a good example.

The Fake Markets

Living in China means learning to accept an uneasy relationship with piracy. Fakes are so embedded in life, and so integral to the Chinese market economy, that "fake" is not even a pejorative term for the Chinese. In his book, *China in Ten Words*, the Chinese writer Yu Huan chooses the word "bamboozle" to discuss the Chinese fondness for fakes. By some estimates, nearly sixty percent of the world's counterfeits originate in China. In Shanghai, tour guides advertise special trips to the best fake markets. Shopping in fake markets in Shanghai may make you uneasy, but it is part of the culture. Just remember what you are buying.

Vendors who sell counterfeit goods are commonly referred to in China as *shanzhai,* which translates literally to "mountain fortress." The best fake markets are located in the labyrinthine underground tunnels of the metro system. Metro stations at both People's Square in Puxi, as well as the Science and Technology Museum in Pudong, are good entry points for those wanting to shop for designer fakes or just pick up a pair of knock-off sunglasses. The AP Plaza under the Science and Technology Museum is full of notoriously aggressive vendors, so be prepared for an onslaught of hawkers shouting and following you. When bargaining in this market, walk away if you cannot get the price down significantly. The commercial district areas around Yu Bazaar are also loaded with fake stalls and storefronts selling Chinese "antiques."

Good deals on freshwater pearls can be found at the Hongqiao Pearl Marekt if you are willing to bargain.

The Hongqiao Pearl Market is a perennial favorite for buying leather goods, scarves, and of course, freshwater pearls (which are actually authentic). Haggling over price is expected. Don't buy pearls without bringing the price down to at least half the opening quote. A common practice is to start as low as 25 percent of the asking price and walk away if you don't get the price you have in mind. There are plenty of other pearl stalls with the very same items. Tailors, who will copy practically any article of clothing you have in mind, can be found on the top floors of the Hongqiao Pearl Market and are quite affordable.

Pirated DVDs are sold with impunity out of storefronts that look exactly like legitimate businesses. What strikes expats as odd is that most of the Western movies and films sold in DVD shops are banned in China, but the government turns a blind eye to these local operations. If you plan to watch movies on DVD in China, there is little point bringing legal ones from home because most Chinese DVD players are configured to work only with the pirated DVDs purchased in China. Western books are also widely pirated and sold over WeChat in downloadable formats. For those who don't want to fight the Shanghai crowds, Taobao, China's largest online shopping vendor (and the world's largest purveyor of fake goods), has set up an English language website. Nearly everyone in China has a Taobao account, and it has become one of the best go-to places for shopping and front door delivery.

Specialty Markets

Shanghai has a variety other specialty markets that make fun outings for tourists and residents alike. Many markets in China are nothing more than a series of stalls selling one particular item, usually located inside shopping malls and old commercial buildings. It's not uncommon for the smaller specialty markets to disappear and reappear in new locations, or even be razed entirely without warning (such was the fate of the Shanghai "antique" market).

Painter's Street, which used to be located in a rambling series of alleyways, has been relocated to an adjacent building. At this popular market, local painters have created

It's possible to leave the glasses market with a few new pairs of prescription eyeglasses in 20 minutes.

An indoor wet market where local residents and ayis buy produce.

a type of collective where they sell their (mostly) copied paintings, along with some original work. While Painter's Street is still a great place to pick up an odd piece of artwork, the new location lacks some of the charm of the former street market. Similarly, the Confucius Temple Book Market has a tendency to come and go. A favorite Sunday hangout for intellectuals, this is one of Shanghai's largest used book markets. Unless you can read Mandarin, purchasing books here is mostly an artistic endeavor.

The Shanghai Glasses Market, located in an old mall next to the Shanghai Railway Station, consists of four or five floors of eyeglass stalls. Eye exams typically are included in the price of prescription glasses and lenses. In a 20-minute visit, most vendors will give an eye exam, develop a prescription, and hand you multiple pairs of made-to-order glasses with "designer" lenses. The average price for a pair of prescription glasses is between ¥200-350 (US$29–51). More eyeglass stalls are located in the People's Square metro station tunnels, but these are slightly pricier than the larger market.

Local produce markets, known as wet markets, are one of the best places for foreigners to catch a glimpse of daily life in Shanghai. These go-to markets are often hidden down alleys and between storefronts downtown. Chinese families and *ayis*, as well as many expats, buy their produce, eggs, tea, fish, fruit, and spices from these local vendors. Some wet markets also sell live animals, such as chickens, turtles, eels, and frogs. It's not uncommon to find an impromptu wet market set up on blankets along the sidewalk, where local farmers sell produce like cabbages, strawberries, and bok choy. Every neighborhood in Shanghai has at least two or three local wet markets that are worth exploring.

One of many roadside wet markets that pop up on Shanghai sidewalks.

Live markets are a fact of life throughout Asia, and Shanghai is no different. Some foreigners find these markets difficult to visit, since the standards for animal treatment can be different in China than in the West. The Pet Market targets residents looking to buy a pet in Shanghai, and many families bring children here expecting something akin to a petting zoo. In reality, it is a claustrophobic maze of caged puppies, kittens, and birds with questionable provenance. While some expats do purchase pets from this market, the health of animals is dodgy at best.

The Bird and Flower Market, one of Shanghai's most popular live markets, offers a better, more uplifting experience for most expats. Flowers, ceramics, and bird cages are the go-to ticket items at this market. The Cricket Market is a fascinating journey into the Chinese world of buying and selling crickets, which are used for betting games and "cricket fights." Crickets have long played an important role in Chinese culture and literature. Valued for their musical abilities, crickets, like birds, have been kept as pets in China for nearly 2,000 years. The market is located on the edges of a residential neighborhood and can be quite crowded on weekends. Many locals will not appreciate foreigners taking photos at this market.

Cricket cages at the Shanghai Cricket market.

For anyone looking for a tailored suit, a fitted winter coat, or new drapery, the South Bund Fabric Market is an unrivaled outlet for buying fabric and ordering just about anything custom made. The choices are overwhelming as are the number of tailors vying for your business. Ask long-time Shanghai residents to recommend a tailor.

ART AND CULTURE

In the past two decades, Shanghai has set its sights on playing an international role in the arts. Whether it's a performance of *Swan Lake* or traditional Chinese opera (*Yueju*), you'll likely find the performing arts scene in Shanghai more than satisfactory. Aside from a number of theaters and concert halls that host performing arts, the Shanghai Symphony Orchestra has its own twelve hundred-seat concert hall. The state-of-the-art Shanghai Grand Theater, located in People's Square, includes three separate theaters with more than 2,700 seats between them. The Grand is the performance home of the Shanghai Opera House (a Western-style opera company) and also hosts visiting performances from around the world, including Broadway shows. In addition to traditional performance, a large array of Western pop entertainers perform annually at the Mercedes-Benz Arena in Pudong. The city also has a vibrant (and more intimate) live music scene.

In addition to its focus on performing arts, Shanghai has also made a name for itself in the visual arts. The annual Shanghai International Film Festival has grown over the past fifteen years into one of the largest and best film festivals in Asia. The Shanghai Arts Festival and the ever-growing Shanghai Literary Festival, both continue to expand their international bona fides by hosting writers, thinkers, journalists, and filmmakers from China and overseas.

NIGHT LIFE

Since its heyday in the 19th century, Shanghai has maintained its reputation as China's party town. That said, nightlife in Shanghai still operates under the watchful eyes of the government. While the club and bar scene are really not comparable to cities like Bangkok or New York, there is no lack of places to eat, drink, and be merry in "The Hai." Clubbing in Shanghai offers the whole range of dance and live music: Western jazz, blues, rock and pop. Some bars cater to younger crowds, with high-rise pool parties and pole dancers, while classic venues, like The Long Bar at the Waldorf Astoria, are mainstays for older residents who prefer a classic jazz scene.

Clubs in Shanghai can be exclusive, partly to limit the clientele, but more likely to avoid the radar of Chinese authorities. A common practice is for clubs to require an RSVP (or private invitation) to access the party. This is especially true for gay clubs and venues. Some "clubs" in Shanghai completely lack brick and mortar. Organizers create a mailing list, and change venues regularly—often renting the city's best hotels and party facilities—and then "invite" guests to the venue. After a night of partying, Sunday brunch at any of the city's four- or five-star hotels is the premier way for Shanghai expats to shake off the excesses of Saturday night.

A Word about Drugs in Shanghai

Although cannabis has some historical roots in traditional Chinese medicine, recreational use of pot is illegal in China. This may seem ironic given that nearly fifty percent of the world's cannabis is grown in China. The legalization of cannabis in many Western countries has increasingly led to some sticky situations for companies and schools that hire foreigners. Don't be surprised if a future employer makes an inquiry about recreational use of cannabis in your home country. Remember that new expat residents in Shanghai undergo a medical exam, which requires both urine and blood samples. Marijuana and other drugs are definitely present in Shanghai, especially in the bar and club scenes. Many Western consulates now warn their citizens about raids at local Chinese bars, which started to become more common beginning in 2015 and occasionally target primarily foreigners.

STREET LIFE

One of the most enjoyable aspects of living in Shanghai comes from just experiencing the daily life unfolding around you. On warm spring and autumn evenings, the parks and city squares are filled with the sound of Chinese music and with the swish of dancers "exercising." During humid days, drivers often line up along quiet lanes, smoking or napping in their vehicles. Many Chinese take naps on the back of bicycle loads, in doorways, sitting on park benches, or even on their parked scooters. There is no defined way to nap in China, but when the mid-afternoon slump hits, the Chinese close their eyes.

Streets like Wulumuqi Lu are bustling with activity throughout the day. Chicken vendors sell whole birds to *ayis* in the mornings and close their shops by noon.

A man takes a nap on his cart.

THE SHANGHAI AVOCADO LADY

The Avocado Lady runs a celebrated storefront grocery on Wulumuqi Lu in the Former French Concession. She received her nickname years ago for selling avocados when they were nearly impossible to find elsewhere in Shanghai. While avocados are now widely available in the city, she is still well-known for selling imported items that expats cannot find elsewhere. Indian spices, curries, grains, specialty cheeses, meats, yogurts, breads, as well as jarred and canned goods from overseas that are nearly impossible to find in the rest of Shanghai are usually available in her shop. If she doesn't have it, ask and she will get it. The shop is small and always busy.

Knife sharpening vendors ply their trade surprisingly close to pedestrian traffic, and hairy crab venders set up temporary markets during the autumn season. Street food is as abundant as fancy local shops on Wulumuqi. On warm spring evenings it's not uncommon to hear the sound of bamboo flutes. The roads are jangling with traffic, and scooters zip across the sidewalks. Enjoying Shanghai is easy if you bring the right attitude and an open mind.

Fresh chickens are sold in an open air street stall.

Shanghai's Favorite Party Drink

The well-known Yunnan cuisine restaurant Lost Heaven on the Bund is a favorite dinner locale for expats and locals. Aside from the spectacular food and the exotic décor, Lost Heaven is the home of the Thai Zeed—a sweet-salty-sour drink made with spicy vodka, lime, and coconut, that has become a well-established trademark drink with a "secret recipe". After many meals at Lost Heaven and a few experiments, I concocted a recipe that, if not exact, is close enough to satisfy our Thai Zeed cravings without having to leave the apartment. As with any drink imitation, proportions are estimates, and you should make the drink to taste (we like ours limey). Lost Heaven garnishes its drinks with a Thai chili and both lemon and lime slices.

A man offers knife sharpening services on the sidewalk.

MAKE YOUR OWN THAI ZEED

Ingredients
Thai chili infused vodka
Coconut rum
Fresh lime juice
Sugar syrup
Splash of water
Salt for the rim

Directions
To make Thai chili infused vodka: Add
5-6 sliced red Thai chilies to a half bottle
of vodka for a few hours. For two drinks:
Salt the rims of two glasses

Fill a shaker with ice and add:
¼ cup chili infused vodka (chilled in the freezer)
¼ cup coconut rum (chilled)
¼ cup (and a splash more) of freshly squeezed lime juice
1/8 cup sugar syrup (equal parts dissolved water/sugar)
Splash of water (this can help control for spiciness too)

Adjust ingredients to taste. Shake it well so it gets foamy. Garnish with cut
lemons or limes and a sliced red Thai chili on the rim.

CHAPTER 8

THE LANGUAGE

> ❝If a man wishes to move a mountain,
> he must begin by moving small stones.❞
>
> — *The Analects of Confucius*

OVERVIEW

Trying to define the language known as "Chinese" (especially for a non-linguist), quickly leads down an *Alice in Wonderland*-like rabbit hole of forked passages, each with doors opening onto new and divergent pathways, some with dead ends, and others that loop back in circles. In other words, getting lost is easy. Even native speakers of Chinese struggle to explain the linguistic branches that compose the Sino language groups.

The long and short of it is this: almost 92 per cent of China's population is Han. As a result, the dominant spoken and written Chinese language has long been Hanyu or the Han language. Hanyu is further classified into seven distinct language groups, although some linguists argue there are actually between ten and fourteen different classifications of *mutually incomprehensible* language groups within it. Each of these distinct groups is further divided into a dizzying array of sub-dialects. Adding to the confusion is the fact that hundreds of different regional languages exist, spoken by non-Han people living in mainland China.

When most English speakers hear the word *dialect*, they imagine something like a Cockney dialect in England that competes with the standard "Queen's English." In other words, dialects typically refer to mutually understandable versions of the same language. However, dialect speakers of Hanyu generally do not understand one another, as any Mandarin speaker will tell you when s/he lands in Hong Kong and cannot understand the Cantonese spoken there. This has led to some controversy over the use of the word *dialect* at all when referring to categories of Hanyu or Chinese languages more generally. In response, sinologist Victor Mair, in 1991, coined the word "topolects" to identify the linguistic and regional characteristics of Chinese language groups that differ broadly, and whose speakers cannot understand one another.

The seven traditional topolects of Hanyu are: Guan, Wu, Yue, Min, Hakka, Xiang and Gan language groups.

Standard Mandarin Chinese, the official language of mainland China, is a Guan topolect of the Hanyu language family. Its roots are firmly established in northern China and Beijing. In Chinese, the word for Standard Mandarin is *putonghua*, or "the common language," and historically speaking, this name was assigned to avoid any sense of unfairness among speakers of other regional topolects, dialects and languages.

Chinese is a logographic language with no alphabet and over 50,000 known characters. Memorizing Chinese characters is an essential part of literacy. The fact that written Chinese is symbolic, not phonetic, creates a fascinating situation in China. Speakers of many different topolects, who cannot understand one another when speaking, are able to communicate in writing. As a result, the government's push for literacy in Standard Chinese Mandarin has been forceful. Although statistics vary, China reports as much as 90 per cent of its population is literate at least in basic reading and writing.

The Beijing dialect of Mandarin Chinese first assumed a prominent national role in mainland China in 1911, when Dr. Sun Yat-Sen overthrew the Qing Dynasty and founded the Republic of China. The seat of power resided in Beijing, so the Mandarin topolect of northern China was adopted as a standardized national language. In 1949, with the formation of The People's Republic of China, literacy rates in China hovered around 20 per cent, and Mandarin was again officially designated as the country's standard language. In a national push to improve literacy, the Communist government directed schools to stop teaching local dialects in favor of standard Mandarin.

Currently, more than 70 per cent of mainland China's population *speak* Mandarin Chinese. It is the official language of Taiwan, and one of four official languages in Singapore. Mandarin Chinese is now spoken by nearly one in six people on the planet, making it the most commonly spoken language in the world. Despite that staggering number, upwards of 400 million people in mainland China still do not speak the country's national language.

OLD CHINESE

Old Chinese, a precursor of modern Chinese Sino-Tibetan languages, dates back to 1250 BCE, and is considered the 4th oldest language in world, predating both Latin and Sanskrit. Oracle bones, ancient tools for divination, contain the earliest examples of Old Chinese symbols.

LEARNING CHINESE

Spending any length of time in China without speaking Mandarin will certainly present some daily challenges. That said, Shanghai is by far the easiest mainland city to navigate in English. Carrying some basic spoken Chinese phrases in your back pocket will go a long way toward endearing yourself to Chinese locals, who are more than happy to engage. There is a deep sense of appreciation and respect for expatriates who make the attempt, even if the effort results in blank stares and confusing conversations.

Chinese has a reputation for being one of the most difficult languages to learn, and this certainly is true if you are learning to read and write. A second language learner can take up to eight years to memorize the three thousand characters needed for general literacy. An educated native of China typically knows as many as eight to ten thousand characters, each of which can represent things as various as syllables, entire words, or even phrases.

The interpretative aspect of Chinese characters can present major comprehension hurdles for learners when they try to make *literal translations* of characters. For example, the Chinese character for *electric* may be used in combination with other characters to describe items such as telephones, trains, or computers. The Chinese character for computer literally translates to "electric brain," a somewhat confusing image for English speakers.

Fortunately, learning to *speak* Chinese doesn't require the same commitment as learning to read and write. Depending on the length of your stay, many expatriates with a good ear have learned to speak Chinese through daily "immersion." Taking a few classes before and after your arrival goes a long way toward arming you with some basic survival vocabulary, and once you move to China, phrases will come quickly by listening and engaging with street sellers, drivers, *ayis*, friends, and shop owners.

My daughters, both of whom took Chinese language in secondary school, like to joke that Chinese has "no grammar." While their assertion isn't exactly true, Chinese grammar rules sometimes seem happily minimal compared to English, which is one reason why learning to speak can be easier than expected. Verb forms in Chinese are fixed. There are no verb conjugations to indicate number and tense (past, present, future), among other things. For example, the verb to walk is the same regardless of whether walking is happening in the past, present, or future.

Chinese speakers indicate verb tenses in other ways, by using context clues and time clues (yesterday, today, tomorrow), as well as by attaching specific suffixes and prefixes to sentences that may only need to be stated once in order to establish a time frame. After a time has been established (I am speaking about something that happened yesterday), there is no longer a need for the speakers to continue to use the suffixes or context clues until the time frame switches again. Grammatically speaking, this makes Chinese vastly different from Romance languages, since Chinese language learners have fewer grammatical rules to remember. By contrast, put yourself in the shoes of a native Chinese speaker, and imagine the frustration that comes from having to constantly conjugate verbs when learning English.

SIMPLIFIED VS TRADITIONAL CHARACTERS

Whether or not you choose to study Chinese, you will find yourself needing at least one translation app on your cell phone. The first baffling decision you'll face, after typing in words from your home language, is whether to translate your words into traditional or simplified Chinese characters. On mainland China, you should always choose simplified characters. In Taiwan, traditional characters are still in use.

As the names suggest, the primary difference between simplified and traditional Chinese characters is their level of visual complexity. Traditional characters have been used for centuries, and over time these characters evolved to form an increasingly complicated series of strokes as people tried to refine meanings. Some traditional characters have so many strokes it can be difficult to distinguish minor differences among characters.

In the 1950s and 1960s, when improving literacy across the country became a paramount goal of the newly established People's Republic of China, the government took on the enormous and fascinating task of simplifying traditional characters using methods such as reducing strokes, eliminating variants of a character, simplifying shapes, and replacing characters entirely. What emerged is known as the Table of General Standard Chinese Characters, which now includes more than 8,000 simplified characters. The new system enables students of Chinese to memorize strokes and characters more fluently.

TONES

Chinese is a tonal language, which means that tone or pitch (the high or low quality of a sound) contributes to the actual meaning of words. Tonal languages tend to have a musical quality to their speech. While less challenging than memorizing Chinese characters, the nuances of learning tones for different syllables can present its own frustrations to Western speakers, at least in theory. Individuals with musical training often start with a leg up, since they are used to listening for subtle changes in voice pitch.

In practice, the five tones of the Chinese language help distinguish meanings among the language's many homonyms.

Reverse the situation for a moment and imagine the difficulty Chinese speakers face when learning English. They face learning hundreds of homonyms (words like "grave" or "duck") that are spelled the same but have entirely different meanings, only to learn there are no vocal markers like a rising or falling tone to help distinguish shades of meaning. English homonyms and homophones sound exactly the same in every context! Although words in Chinese may have the same sound, *how* the words are spoken changes their meaning. The oft-cited example of this is the syllable "ma", which can mean "hemp," "horse," or "mother," depending on the tone used. Even more confusing, "ma" can indicate a question such as when your neighbor asks, "Ni hao ma?" (How are you?). Likewise, "ji" can refer to a chicken, a small table, quantity, or jealousy, depending on the context and the tone.

Mispronunciation of tones has led many new expats into conversations resulting in, if not shock and awe, at least complete bafflement on the part of their Chinese counterparts. One friend of mine likes to tell the story about explaining to her taxi driver that she saw a ghost, when in fact, she was trying to relay some directions. Nearly everyone learning Chinese will find themselves in a beginning class learning the five tones. The tones are numbered for instruction, and each tone is represented in pinyin (see below) with a specific visual mark, always over a vowel, sometimes called a tone mark. On close inspection, the tone marks themselves are symbolic representations of the direction of each tone.

Chinese linguists have developed a system for visualizing Chinese tones (flat, up, down) in a graph. The fifth neutral tone is short and lightly spoken at the end of a sentence to make the sentence into a question, as in this example of

Tone one is a flat, high level tone represented by flat line over a vowel.
Tone two is a rising tone represented by a rising mark over a vowel.
Tone three is a falling-rising tone represented by a falling-rising mark over a vowel.
Tone four is a falling tone represented by a falling mark over a vowel.
The fifth tone is merely a neutral tone and carries no written symbol.

the word "ma." "Ni hao" means "hello" (literally, "you good").
"Ni hao ma?" means "how are you?" (literally, "you good?").

Tone Chart				
#1	#2	#3	#4	#5
mā (mother)	má (numb)	mǎ (horse)	mà (scold)	ma (question particle)
high	rising	falling-rising	falling	neutral

PINYIN

Pinyin is a Romanized system of pronunciation based on the Latin alphabet. It is also the saving grace of visitors to China from just about everywhere. Hanyu Pinyin, as the system is formally known, uses an alphabet roughly corresponding to English, to translate the phonetic *sounds* (not the characters) of spoken Chinese into comprehensible words. If you're an English speaker, this means you will be able to pronounce (mostly) the names of metro stops and roads in order to communicate.

Pinyin is not the only Romanized system for speaking Chinese but is the most widely used system in mainland

China and throughout the West today. Since Russian linguists developed pinyin, some of the vowel and consonant sounds may still feel foreign to native English speakers. But in general, learning pinyin and recognizing the tonal marks in written pinyin will help you communicate during your time in China. The following is a rough pronunciation guide to get you started.

Consonants

Pinyin has 23 consonants (b, d, g, p, t, m, f, n, l, h, c, s, z, ch, sh, zh, r, j, q, x, w, y), most of which are similar in pronunciation to their Standard American English (SAE) equivalents. The table below contains pronunciations for the consonants whose sounds vary the most from SAE.

Consonant	Pronunciation
c	ts in fits (tongue forward; aspirated)
s	s in supper (tongue back; sharper)
z	dz as in tsunami (unaspirated)
ch	ch(r) (chop, with tongue curled)
sh	shrug (tongue and mouth position of sh in shrug is more forward vs. sh in harsh)
zh	dj (j with tongue curled back)
j	cheap (tongue forward)
q	change (tongue back)
r	r in red
x	harsh

Vowels

Vowels are a complicated matter in pinyin, and I'll only touch on them here. Mandarin has six basic vowels (a, o, e, i, u, ü), but those vowels combine with each other, and with a few different consonants (c, n, ng, r), to produce a *myriad* of vowel combinations that range from two to four letters long. In pinyin, vowels are written differently depending on whether they follow a consonant, as in "di" and "bi", or stand alone, in which case the vowel "i" becomes "yi". The same rule applies to compound vowels, such as: "-ia" to "ya," or "-ing" to "ying."

The chart below contains examples of SAE approximations of Chinese vowel and vowel combination sounds. Your best bet, rather than relying on reading about sound-alike words, is to listen to the audio of pronunciations, which are available on several websites. I've provided a short list of sites at the end of this chapter. One of the best is the Yabla website (https://chinese.yabla.com/chinese-pinyin-chart.php), where you can click on a vowel or vowel combination, all of which are marked for tone, allowing you to hear the pronunciation *and* read the marked vowel at the same time. Notice how the pronunciation can differ depending on tone, varying, for example, from "you" to "yo" in the pronunciation of "iu".

Vowel	Pronunciation	Example
a	ah	father
o	aw	law
e	er	per/her
i	ee	feet
u	oo	mood
ü	shape lips like when whistling, then say "ee"	the "u" sound in French

A Sampling of Vowel Combinations

ai	long i	aisle
ao	ow	cloud
ei	ay	bake
er*	er, ar	earth, car
ia	ya	yard
iao	yeow	meow
ie	yeh	sierra
io	ee-yo	your
iu	eew	yo-yo
ou	oh	blow
ua	wah	wand
uai	why	why
ue	yoo-air	share
ui	way	weigh
uo	waw	water

* Whether er is pronounced like ear in earth, or like ar in car differs by region in China.

NAVIGATING STREET SIGNS

All metro stops and signs in Shanghai are written in pinyin, and it's best to learn the pinyin directional words before trying to navigate your way around the city. Chinese street signs have five directional words (north, south, east, west, and middle) that separate the actual name of the street from the word "lu" (which means "street"). The street sign for East Nanjing Road will say Nanjing Dong Lu, literally translating as Nanjing East Road.

Directional words on road signs designate the *actual section* of a particular road. A sign that says Maoming Bei Lu means the northern part of Maoming Road. Local address or block numbers usually follow the street names. Chinese street signs also use a fifth directional marker—"zhong," which means middle and refers to the center section of a road. A street running north/south through Shanghai will typically have three location markers in the street name: north, middle, and south. On Wulumuqi Zhong Lu, one is standing on the middle part of the north/south running Wulumuqi Lu.

DIRECTIONAL WORDS ON STREET SIGNS

"bei" means north
"dong" means east
"nan" means south
"xi" means west
"zhong" means middle

SHANGHAINESE

Shanghainese is part of the Wu topolect of Hanyu, meaning it's in a different language category than Mandarin (Guan topolect). Shanghainese is native to the city, and is actually related more to Tibetan language families than to Mandarin. As a consequence, Mandarin speakers are unable to understand Shanghainese. The topolect itself has many versions, or dialects, from traditional to modern, can have two, three or five tones (unlike Mandarin's four) depending on the region, and is the largest subgroup of Wu Chinese languages spoken along the entire Yangtze River Delta. Other dialects similar to Shanghainese are spoken in neighboring cities like Hangzhou, Suzhou, and Ningbo and nearby provinces, but Shanghainese is considered the primary connecter language between provinces in this area.

Interactions with local government officials will benefit a lot from having a Shanghainese speaker on the team.

While many young people no longer speak Shanghainese, attempts have been made by the local government of Shanghai to create programs to retain the language and keep it from dying out. With the tremendous influx of migrants to Shanghai, and the increasing foreign influence, Shanghainese is beginning to wane. From the early 1990s, schools began discouraging the use of Shanghainese, and only English and Mandarin Chinese are taught in schools. Many children born and raised in the region at that time did not learn the local dialect. Even today, many young children are only exposed to Shanghainese through older family members. As with many dialects in China, Chinese characters can be used to write in Shanghainese, which allows people who are unable to communicate orally, to communicate in written form. Below is a chart with common Shanghainese words and phrases.

CHINGLISH

Outside mainland China, Chinglish is a term that bilingual speakers of Chinese and English sometimes employ to describe switching back and forth between Chinese and English in conversation. Many bilingual speakers and first-generation English speakers enjoy the word play of combining words from pinyin and English to form new Chinglish spoken words.

Many Westerners enjoy seeing "Chinglish" translations on public signs.

SHANGHAINESE (Wu topolect)

Common Words

Nóng hō	Hello
Nóng hō va?	How are you?
Zōlǎng hō	Good morning
Wö ä	Good night
Zä wēi	Goodbye
Zǐ e	Yes
Fé zǐ e	No
Jǒu kū nēng	Maybe
Yá yà	Thank you
Fé yōng kē qì	You're welcome
Dēi fé qì	I'm sorry, Excuse me
Hō e	Okay
Nóng gāng...?	Do you speak...?
Yīng vēn	English
Fā vēn	French
Wú jiō...	My name is...
Yē dēi	Some
Dahsoeke lalaq rahlitaq?	Where is the bathroom?
Ngu eh nóng	I love you
Qiuming a!	Help!
Chin la ke xin ye	Bon appétit
Ngú ba shede	I don't know.
Ngú ban dong	I don't understand.
Qǐng nóng zóng fō yē tān	Please repeat that.

Numbers

0: líng, 1: yē, 2: liáng, 3: sä, 4: sī, 5: n, 6: ló, 7: qīe, 8: be, 9: ǐu,
10: zé, 11: zé yē, 12: zé ní, 20: nä, 21: nä yē, 30: sä se, 40: ì se,
50: n se, 60: ò se, 70: qīe se, 80: be se, 90: jīu se, 100: yē be, 1,000:
yē qī

However, inside mainland China, Chinglish refers to the somewhat unfortunate, and always hilarious, non-grammatical translations of Chinese into English, which routinely appear on signs throughout the country. The ubiquity of Chinglish has become so well known that publications as staid as *The New York Times* and *The Guardian* (both inaccessible in China), have published photos capturing some of the funniest Chinglish translations.

While Chinglish provides foreigners, especially English speakers, with boundless laughter, Chinese speakers may, and do, sometimes take offense. The humor of Chinglish is seen as pejorative inside China since it makes fun of ungrammatical translations, points out malaprops, and highlights errors in syntax that result in nonsense phrases. Most expats who find themselves giggling over Chinglish signs see the phenomenon as part of China's charm. However, you may want to temper your responses around Chinese acquaintances who may not appreciate humor at the expense of their countrymen. The Chinese are sensitive about their international image, and it's appropriate defer to their worldview when living as a guest in the country. Native Chinese see hypocrisy in English speakers who struggle with the complexity of Mandarin yet laugh at poor English translations.

In the end, it may not matter. Chinglish is rapidly disappearing in China, and cities like Shanghai have far fewer examples now than in the past. Eliminating Chinglish in public signs in hospitals and transportation hubs ranks very high on the to-do list of the People's Republic. As far back as 2009, the government made a priority of eradicating Chinglish signs throughout the country. A renewed effort began in 2017 that aimed to create a standardized list of acceptable English translations and grammar. For a brief period in 2016, Shanghai was awash in rumors that city officials were considering removing pinyin signs and all signs containing English in the city, making it virtually impossible for those not literate in Chinese characters to navigate. In the end, the pinyin and English remained.

CHAPTER 9

WORKING IN SHANGHAI

❝The most important thing for you to do in the next three years isn't about money. It's about reputation.❞

— Josh Gardner, CEO and cofounder of Kung Fu Data and E-commerce Group

THE FOREIGN EMPLOYMENT SECTORS

Many guidebooks about foreign employment in China approach working overseas as exclusively the purview of business and industry. There's good reason for this. As China opened up to the world and instituted market reforms in the early 1980s under the leadership of Deng Xiaoping, foreign trade and business investment were priorities. Flash forward to 2016. Shanghai's Commission of Commerce reported that more than five hundred and fifty foreign-owned multinational corporations had regional headquarters in the city, making Shanghai a truly international hub when it comes to business.

Shanghai's foreign employment opportunities have expanded in the past ten years.

In fact, it's far more common for foreigners in Shanghai to work for multinational corporations than for local, Chinese-owned businesses.

As with most of China, the economic composition of Shanghai's workforce continues to undergo seismic changes. Although the city is still home to some large manufacturers of steel, automobiles, plastics, and technology, recent market analysis suggests the tide of manufacturing is moving away from Shanghai—and away from China more broadly—in search of lower costs in countries like Vietnam and India. At the same time, cities like Shanghai now have a larger

High end retail stores are abundant in Shanghai and account for growing service sector employment.

local population with discretionary income. A new service economy is growing up from the fertile ground of increased Chinese wealth.

As a result, twenty-first century Shanghai is attracting a far wider range of foreign workers than merely those in the world of business. The city's employment sectors are expanding well beyond manufacturing and business, similar to those of Western economies, with overseas employment being increasingly driven, not only by the financial and service industries, but also the education and healthcare industries. Indeed, Shanghai has a large and well-established healthcare network, with numerous international hospitals and smaller medical facilities that employ ever-larger numbers of foreign medical staff.

Perhaps no other employment sector in Shanghai has seen its growth skyrocket in the past ten years as quickly as the education industry. The Chinese Ministry of Education reported in 2017 that 489,000 foreign students studied in China. According to the Shanghai Education Commission (SEC) more than 56,000 of those international students (from 187 countries) were studying in Shanghai alone. University students now account for nearly one-quarter of Shanghai's foreign resident population. At least 70 per cent of these students will study for more than six months. And the numbers are only expected to grow.

The obvious attraction for students and teachers moving to Shanghai is the city's huge number of educational institutions. More than 35 institutions of higher learning, including two top-ranked universities, are located in Shanghai. Fudan University and Jiao Tong University are both members of China's C9 League (the Chinese ivy league) and are recognized as two of the world's most distinguished institutions of higher education. Other well-respected Chinese universities in the city include Tongji University, and East China Normal University. Additionally, esteemed American schools such as Duke University, New York University, Rutgers, and UC Berkeley have all opened satellite campuses in Shanghai and are attracting students and faculty from abroad. Universities in Shanghai now regularly offer courses in both English and Chinese and host visiting scholars and professors from around the world.

The traditional split between the worlds of business and higher education is quickly closing in Shanghai. Much of China's push in the education sector has occurred in response to the tremendous brain drain China suffered in the years between the Cultural Revolution and the early manufacturing boom three decades ago. Many of the country's most talented citizens emigrated abroad in search of educational and employment opportunities. China is now working diligently to reverse this trend, encouraging expat Chinese citizens to return and enticing foreign talent, including students, to stay.

In addition to offering generous scholarships to some foreign students, China has tried to keep the best foreign students in the country by creating better access to internships and part-time employment at Chinese institutions. China continues to adapt and ease its residency requirements for certain populations (while simultaneously making policies more stringent for others). In general, the higher your level of education, the more urgent your field of study (tech innovation is paramount), and the more talent you bring to the table, the easier it will be to find employment in Shanghai. Residence permits for foreign workers are typically based on income gradations—higher earners receive longer residency permits—but other permits are geared to enticing bright foreign students to enter the workforce. In 2016, the Shanghai Education Commission estimated that more than 1,500 foreign students in Shanghai were employed as interns at various institutions.

BUSINESS AND EDUCATION FACTS*

- Shanghai is home to nearly 15 per cent of China's total foreign investment opportunities.
- Nearly 70 per cent of Shanghai's GDP can be attributed to service industry sectors.
- Shanghai is home to 242 foreign-invested financial institutions.
- Nearly 9 million overseas tourists visit Shanghai each year.
- Shanghai is mainland China's largest consumer market (among cities).
- In 2017, 489, 200 international students studied in China. 50 per cent of those students were degree seeking. The top five countries sending students to China are: South Korea, the U.S., Thailand, France and Germany.
- The number of graduate students in China increased 18.2 per cent between 2016 and 2017.

For information on studying in China, see: www.campuschina.org

*Sources:
2016 Stats from Hong Kong TDC Research Group:
http://china-trade-research.hktdc.com/business-news/article/Facts-and-Figures/Shanghai-Market-Profile/ff/en/1/1X000000/1X06BVOR.htm

Ministry of Education of the People's Republic of China:
http://en.moe.gov.cn/News/Top_News/201804/t20180403_332258.html

---

Beyond the extensive university system, Shanghai boasts more than 30 international schools—including Chinese schools with international divisions—that educate elementary through secondary students. Most of these schools employ both foreign and Chinese nationals. Indeed, my own family arrived in Shanghai to work in and attend just such a school. With such a rich educational environment, one can safely assume that "working" in China now encompasses a wide range of employment circumstances.

Despite the wealth of opportunity, working in China is not always a bed of roses. Lower wage foreign workers (including teachers) are finding it increasingly difficult to stay in Shanghai, not only because it is a very expensive city, but also because China is focused on retaining high-earning talent. Foreign employers learn quickly that the worker is king in China, and companies or international schools that payroll PRC staff can find that Chinese worker protection laws leave them little wiggle room to replace ineffective employees. Transferring Chinese employees in and out of positions can be a very expensive proposition. Investing in employee training and review before hiring Chinese staff is essential.

Even more challenging is the fact that foreigners will have to deal with constantly changing Chinese regulations related to their employment, from Visa requirements, to work permits, to mandatory retirement ages. Currently, foreign workers are legally mandated to retire at specific times, typically age 60. Chinese workers face forced retirement as early as age 55. Of course, exceptions are made for high-earning (Class A) foreigners and workers with special skills, but in general, arriving in China as a middle aged-employee can be daunting. One reason there are so many elderly people dancing in Shanghai's parks is that they were mandated to leave the workforce. Many foreign teachers have been shocked to learn that they must leave the country (and their jobs) when they turn 60.

Perhaps the most formidable challenge about working in Shanghai is dealing with the Chinese government. All foreigners in executive or human resources positions must be ready to view the government as an ongoing partner in

Forced retirement in China leaves time for many people in their early 60s to enjoy park dancing.

work—it is the government in Shanghai that can stall or stop a project at any time. If you're working in Shanghai, you must build relationships and never burn any bridges with city officials.

FRIENDS IN HIGH PLACES

The city of Shanghai operates outside China's wider system of provinces. Shanghai's local government functions as essentially its own province—it is one of four municipalities that report directly to the central government in Beijing. But Beijing does not control everything in Shanghai: The city has its own series of administrative bureaus and ministries that dictate how local rules are enforced. Unless you have a high-level position in a foreign company, you aren't likely to interact with the municipal government very often.

Nevertheless, you will feel the results of government

decision-making at all levels of employment—from securing your employment paperwork to filing your housing locations with the local police department to verifying your educational or marital credentials. The involvement of the local government in so many aspects of business life means that bureaucracy and inefficiency sometimes rule the day.

SHANGHAI GOVERNMENT WEBSITE

The Shanghai government has its own English language website that provides a host of useful information
www.shanghai.gov.cn/shanghai/node27118/node27386/node27400/index.html

Since foreign business and school leaders must regularly deal with municipal officials, navigating the bureaucracy that is the Shanghai city government—a government that is often entrenched and inflexible—requires making use of all the *guanxi* you can muster. For this reason, many businesses and schools hire Chinese speaking government liaisons to help smooth the communication process between foreign companies and Chinese government officials. Likewise hiring and using translators to navigate communications between Chinese officials and local businesses is almost always required. Many multinational companies and international schools prefer to use their own translators to ensure accurate communications, since the cultural practices around hierarchy (fear of offending superiors) can sometimes crimp the reliability of Chinese translators.

WORKPLACE ATTITUDES

Workplace attitudes in China are dictated by the same cultural frameworks that govern other aspects of daily life. The concepts of *mianzi* (face) and *guanxi* (social currency), as discussed in earlier chapters, are vital for understanding workplace interactions. Viewing these concepts in isolation would be a mistake, as they are the very bonds that link the Chinese people's employment lives (and opportunities) directly to their social and family lives.

Saving or giving face, and developing *guanxi*, play out daily in the workplace. If an unexpected problem occurs, these will be the two most essential cultural practices to navigate through. Culturally speaking, the Chinese value careful planning and long-term thinking, and they rarely appreciate surprises. When conflicts arise, figuring out a solution that allows each party to save face is paramount for moving things forward. A spectacular example of this occurred after an incident in which my husband's institution was blindsided by an unexpected media crisis. Local government officials immediately called an emergency meeting. The official in charge of the meeting had been chastened by his Beijing superiors for not providing adequate oversight, and now the very same official needed to save face in the eyes of his superiors and his employees. Both sides arrived at the meeting with an entourage of interpreters and cultural liaisons.

During the tense discussion that followed, the government official never explicitly blamed my husband for the crisis. Such an overt criticism would be viewed as a personal insult and would fail to acknowledge the respect his position demanded. Yet, the official needed to save face in the eyes of his own superiors. His strategy was to lecture the group (sternly) about official protocols. In this way, he took a stab at the institution (not an individual), and publicly saved face. Clearly, he did not want my husband, who had built significant *guanxi* by that point during his tenure, to lose face. This meant each leader had a role to play in the "theater of face," and my husband's group needed to determine how best to respond. Instead of showing frustration or arguing, his team thanked the official,

and made clear how valuable this new information was to them. The official saved face—he got to demonstrate that he was doing his job—and my husband's team set themselves up for positive treatment in the future.

Broadly speaking, the rules of doing business in Shanghai, and China more generally, are the opposite of typical Western rules, although that is changing in more international contexts. Making deals with directness and efficiency is not the Chinese way. Since the long game is important to the Chinese, this can result in a noncommittal attitude during business negotiations. If wrapping up a deal or achieving a definitive reply from business associates (or government officials) is your goal, facing a tangled and meandering bureaucracy can seem like an exasperating task. Best to remember the importance of chain of command. Many smaller players may be involved in the process before a final decision is reached.

That said, the Chinese can be very keen on people who are innovators, since so much of China revolves around systems. Western creativity and willingness to think outside the box is one of the things the Chinese like most about the West. This perspective is especially prevalent among Chinese who have studied or lived in the West.

Typical Western communication styles of direct confrontation and speedy decision making are not the correct avenues to take in China, where a more considered approach is common. Western directness can feel offensive to some Chinese, and if you find yourself about to be critical of a Chinese employee or colleague, do not do so in public (because of face), but rather in a private conversation. This doesn't mean you won't be privy to Chinese anger and direct confrontation. The Chinese are quite practiced at confrontation in the right context. Situational awareness matters. When interacting with those whom the Chinese do not know well, formality is the rule. Once you become part of the system, the formal rules of business etiquette may very well fly out the window.

Finally, you'll do well to remember that Communist party membership is required of all government workers and of some business people as well, especially if they aspire to any sort of career advancement. The Chinese take pride in their country, and in the great advances China has made on the world stage. Never make negative comments about the Communist party to your Chinese coworkers and try to appreciate the fine balancing act required of many Chinese citizens. In her book, *Little Soldiers*, Lenora Chu, a long-time Shanghai expat, suggests that China has created a duality in its citizens. While many Chinese pledge their loyalty to the Party outwardly, internally they cultivate "alternative thoughts." As a foreigner, you are unlikely to be privy to such private thinking, so be respectful of Chinese pride in their country.

Yin Yang: Tipping the Balance Sheet

Business is a formal affair in China, and traditional Chinese values play important roles in the workplace. These values are typically Confucian in origin, emphasizing order, harmony, and hierarchy. Senior members of any Chinese company, business, school, or team will be ceded a place of authority and importance in any discussions or deal making. Junior members of the staff are expected to fall in line. Submission to authority, and the primacy of the interdependent group over the individual, all dictate how the Chinese view their responsibilities and their roles in an employment environment. As in other areas of Chinese life, reverence for experience, age, and social position are also important factors to consider when trying to get things done in the world of business.

Exactly how seniority functions in a given employment situation can be determined by a number of factors. Time spent in a position or at a company is highly valued, but age, educational background, and experience play roles as well. Each situation will be evaluated independently. An oft-cited frustration about working in China for many Westerners is the sense that building relationships can seem so transactional. In Western cultures, transactional exchanges often are viewed as paving the road to corruption, and corruption in the form of bribes and favors no doubt plays a peripheral role in the Chinese workplace. However, a system of reciprocity and balance exists—a kind of yin yang of checks and balances, which mitigates corrupt influences by supporting the Chinese preference for harmony. Accepting the existence of a transactional culture right from the start will make your work life easier in the long run. One executive we know likes to describe the employment culture as "tipping the balance sheet" in someone's favor, preferably his own.

The image of a financial balance sheet is a useful metaphor when approaching the workplace in Shanghai. Your imaginary balance sheet will accrue tallies of indebtedness and opportunity. Understanding this means understanding that a Chinese executive or government official might feel "indebted" to you for decisions that, in Western culture, typically carry no strings. Conversely, government officials and business clientele may expect you to be indebted to them for decisions in your favor. For leaders who frequently deal with government offices, understanding the concept of indebtedness can mean the difference between quick approval of a project— bypassing bureaucratic red tape, for example, versus a project that gets "lost" in the system. If you breach the rules of etiquette, or cause an important person to lose face, you may face a new kind of "great wall."

As a school head, my husband often faced a problem wherein admitting a child to the school resulted in a family feeling a sense of personal indebtedness to him, despite the fact that he had absolutely nothing to do with the process. When the Chinese feel indebted, they expect to realign the imbalance by paying back the debt, or by creating some new circumstance that favors their own position. As the head of a culturally Western institution, the proffering of favors posed a tricky position for him. Furthermore, some gestures, voiced as appreciation or expressions of gratitude, come with their own strings attached—strings having to do with something entirely outside the local interaction. Always be attuned to the deficits and surfeits on your balance sheet. In China, everything is connected.

The Indispensable Business Card

The exchange of personal business cards has become a high art form in Shanghai. It is not uncommon to see professionals with elaborately decorated card cases, or to find all manner of decorated card holders front and center on desks. As a professional working in the city, you should never be without your business cards.

The standard practice for printing business cards in Shanghai is to use both sides of a card, with your title and contact information in Mandarin on one side, and in English on the other. Business cards are the de facto way to exchange contact information, even in a non-business setting.

Gift Giving and Graft

The Chinese love to give gifts for all sorts of personal and professional occasions. Gift giving is an important part of Chinese culture, and you should expect to both give and receive many gifts if you are employed in Shanghai or living there for any length of time. But deciding *when* and *what type* of gift constitutes an appropriate gesture can be more difficult to discern. The boundaries between business etiquette, gratitude, and bribery aren't always clear. As in the West, bringing gifts to hosts is expected. Offering gifts of gratitude is more nuanced.

The Chinese-American author Lenora Chu writes about the bribery that often occurred via luxury gifting at her young son's Shanghai elementary school. Although none of the Chinese parents in Chu's world seemed offended (or surprised) about teachers receiving gifts like expensive designer handbags, such exchanges would elicit rebuke among international school employees and most businesses. Graft at the higher levels of the Chinese and international business world is still somewhat common, although in recent years, Xi Jinping has made rooting out corruption a central theme of his government. While some international corporations undoubtedly "get things done" in unethical ways, the practice is becoming less acceptable.

The best approach is to avoid the appearance of bribery by offering smaller gifts, such as Chinese sweets, tea, or other edible treats. Food makes a safe and popular choice for holidays and thank yous. Other modest gifts, like business card holders are always popular choices since they are usable and contextual. Since Chinese holidays are typically linked with certain types of foods (mooncakes during Mid-Autumn Festival, or glutinous rice balls during

Lantern Festival), these also make good gift choices. Proper Chinese gift shops do an excellent job of packaging and wrapping gifts, and these items are unlikely to be construed as graft.

For business leaders and executives, offering home-country gifts upon arrival for special meetings is common practice. A good general rule to follow for gift giving in the workplace is to consider whether your gift creates an imbalance in the professional relationship. You can think of this as the yin yang of social currency. Equality and inequality of status matters a lot when it comes to the unwritten rules of gift giving.

One of my biggest gift-giving faux pas occurred with our driver. Since I frequently traveled back and forth between Shanghai and my home country, I made a habit of returning to China with sports memorabilia for my driver and his young son, both of whom were avid soccer fans. To me, this was simply a way of bringing a bit of my culture back, as well as a way to show my appreciation for his long hours. One day, my husband pointed out that I was creating a "gift" imbalance. Since our driver could not repay this imbalance, he thought my gifts may be making our driver uncomfortable. Unfettered generosity is often not well received in China, nor in other Asian cultures where high value is placed on interdependence and reciprocity.

If you happen to find yourself on the receiving end of a gift that exceeds the bounds of propriety, creative solutions can be always be found. While playing dinner host to a Chinese family whose children attended the school, my husband once received a very good bottle of wine as a gift. What seemed like a natural fit for the occasion turned into a problem when he discovered much later that it was, indeed, a *very* good bottle of wine: The vintage commanded upwards of US$1,800. Unable to return or refuse the wine by that time, he decided to publicly share the bottle with his staff over a working dinner.

Drinking and Dinner

In Western countries, invitations to the home are not uncommon, but in China, this practice is seldom encouraged. Dinners and lunch meetings (both business and personal) nearly always take place in public restaurants, and they make up some of the highest-value work interactions between foreigners and Chinese. Luckily, Shanghai has no dearth of excellent restaurants for working meetings. Shanghai is bursting at the seams with Western restaurants, and your working dinners may seem no different from those in your home country.

Business dinners or lunches at Chinese restaurants generally follow the food etiquette rules laid out in Chapter 6. Chinese meals are served family style and shared among guests with serving chopsticks used. Drinking can be serious business in China in both personal and professional meals (and celebrations).

For many foreigners, drinking games can take on an urgent feeling as there is a clear expectation that all members participate. When *bajiu* makes an appearance, the party is underway, Chinese etiquette usually stipulates that everyone at the table partakes. My husband tells a funny story about secretly dumping out his *bajiu* under the table when it became clear he needed to moderate his consumption. If you can no longer indulge, a self-deprecating comment about your weakness usually provides an acceptable way out of the situation.

Make Use of Shanghai Business and Trade Organizations

Similar to the foreign network of overseas consulates and embassies, nonprofit Chambers of Commerce have been established by a large number of Western countries to assist businesses and others who live and work overseas. Shanghai is currently home to more than fifteen, including one of the earliest American Chambers of Commerce, all of them linked primarily to Western countries.

Whether you're an educator or business professional, your home country Chamber of Commerce will offer invaluable resources to assist you in navigating the world of business, Chinese government regulation, Chinese culture, and upcoming legal changes by the Shanghai municipal authorities. The "chams" also offer convenient expat services such as tax filing (for U.S. citizens), professional development, networking opportunities, speakers, medical and insurance programs, and Visa assistance. Chinese regulations regarding expat employment and residence credentials are in constant flux and Chambers of Commerce make it their job to keep their members duly informed. Some of the most active of these are listed in the Resource Guide (Chapter 10).

Working in Shanghai can be a thoroughly rewarding experience. Chinese business etiquette is not complicated and learning just a handful of rules about Chinese culture and expectations will go a long way toward smoothing a path for success. Above all, build relationships, overproduce, and enjoy the experience.

CHAPTER 10

FAST FACTS

Official Name
People's Republic of China

Capital
Beijing

Flag
The Chinese flag was designed in 1949 during a competition
held by the Communist Party. It features a large yellow star
in the top left-hand corner with four smaller stars adjacent
in a semi-circle. The five yellow stars stand out against a red
field which is symbolic of blood spilt during the revolution.
The large golden colored star symbolizes the leader of the
Communist Party while the four smaller stars represent the
Confucian vision of the four classes of people in China—*shi*,
nong, *gong*, and *shang*: the working class, the peasants,
urban petite bourgeoisie and national bourgeoisie.

National Anthem
The national anthem of the People's Republic of China is
known as the "March of the Volunteers" and was composed
in 1934 by the poet Tian Han. The following year the
composer Nie Er set it to music. The anthem, which honors
the soldiers who fought against the Japanese during the
1930s, was not made the official song until 1949.

Time Zone

Although China is a very large country, it uses a single standard time and does not observe daylight saving time. The official standard time is known as "Beijing Time," which is eight hours ahead of the Universal Time Coordinated (UTC).

Telephone Country Code

+86

Currency

Yuan renminbi (RMB), also called just *yuan* and *kuai*. On stock exchanges China's currency is abbreviated CNY for China Yuan.

Land Area of Shanghai

6,340.5 square kilometers, (not counting urban sprawl)

Population of Shanghai

24.15 million (2016)

Military

China has the world's largest military, numbering over two million members

Employment Sectors in Shanghai

Shanghai's primary employment sectors are business, manufacturing, healthcare, education, finance, and the service sector.

Manufacturing

Shanghai is a top manufacturer of automobiles, chemicals, petroleum and steel.

Business

The strongest business employment sectors in Shanghai are in communications, information technology, biomedical engineering, finance, insurance, real estate, and tourism.

Education

Shanghai has more than 30 international schools and the highest primary and secondary test scores in the world (PISA).

Local Government Structure

As a direct municipality in China, Shanghai has a dual-party governing structure. The city's mayor is the senior ranking executive of the local Shanghai government bureaucracy. The Communist Party Committee Secretary of Shanghai (Party Chief) outranks the mayor as a member of the national government.

Number Of Billionaires from Shanghai (2019)

17

Ethnic Groups

40 per cent of Shanghai's population are migrants from other regions of China.

Electricity

220v, 60hz

Famous People Born in Shanghai

- **Victor Chang**, who helped to pioneer the field of heart transplantation, was born in Shanghai in November of 1936.

- The Chinese American actress and screenwriter **Joan Chen** was born in Shanghai in 1961.
- **J. G. Ballard** wrote about his childhood in Shanghai during the Japanese occupation of the city in his novel **Empire of the Sun**. He was born in the International Settlement in 1930.
- Chinese NBA All-Star basketball player **Yao Ming** was born in Shanghai in 1980.
- Contemporary model and actress **Angela Yeung (Angelababy)** was born in Shanghai in 1989 to a Shanghainese mother.

Major Celebrations
- The actual observance dates for most Chinese holidays vary since they change according to the lunar calendar.
- January 1: New Year's Day
- Chinese New Year (Spring Festival): Begins on the 12th lunar month of the Chinese calendar, usually falls in early February or late January. Sometimes referred to as New Year Golden Week.
- Late February or early March: Lantern Festival
- Early April: Tomb Sweeping Day (Qing Ming Festival or Ancestor Day). Connected to the spring equinox
- May 1: Labor Day
- May 28: Dragon boat festival
- October 1: National Day. Begins the Golden Week holiday or the Mid-Autumn Festival (typically one to two week observance)

Interesting Facts
- The Yulan Magnolia (White magnolia) is the official city flower of Shanghai. A native of the Yangtze River

Delta, Yulan Magnolia is an ornamental tree with spring flowers resembling the lotus. Yulan magnolia blooms in Shanghai just prior to tomb-sweeping day, and its petals, extending outward, are said to symbolize the vigor of the city.

- White Magnolia Plaza, located on the Puxi side of the Huangpu river, is a skyscraper complex completed in 2017 that bears the name of the city flower.
- The Long Bar at the Shanghai Club, located inside the Waldorf Astoria Shanghai, is far from the longest bar in the world today, but in 1910, this mahogany beauty held the world record.
- The Shanghai Stock Exchange (SSE) is one of the two independently operating stock exchanges in mainland China. By market capitalization, it is the world's fourth largest stock market.
- In 1910, a "rubber bubble" economic crisis known as the Shanghai Rubber Stock Market Crisis shut down nearly 50 per cent of Shanghai's local banks. The crisis was the result of an over inflation of rubber stocks.
- The Shanghai Tower is the second tallest building in the world. As of this writing, it has the highest observation deck in the world along with the world's fastest elevators.
- Shanghai has its own professional baseball team called The Shanghai Golden Eagles.
- The English author J.G. Ballard, who wrote *Empire of the Sun*, was born in Shanghai.
- The *Protection Plan for the Old City Historical Cultural Scenery Area* was enacted in Shanghai in 2006. Designed to preserve the Old City's roads and remaining ancient walls, the area is now a designated scenic location.

- In 2018, the Global Financial Centers Index ranked Shanghai as the third most competitive financial center in Asia after Singapore and Hong Kong.
- According the *China Daily*, Shanghai is the most expensive residential city in Mainland China.
- In 2018, Mercer's 24th Annual Cost of Living Survey ranked Shanghai as the seventh most expensive city in the world for expats.
- Both the Longhua and Jing'an Temples were founded during the Three Kingdoms Period.
- Shanghai, the world's most densely populated city, grew from 16.7 million in the year 2000, to over 24.2 million in 2018. In 2016, Shanghai's population surpassed that of nearby Taiwan. The population has been capped by the government at 25 million.
- As of 2013, China's Education Ministry reported that nearly 400 million residents of the country could not speak Mandarin.
- According to *China Daily*, Shanghai has the world's highest life expectancies (age 83).
- Shanghai's high school students posted the top math, reading, and science scores in the world on the 2013 Program for International Student Assessment. The newest results of this test will be released in December 2019.
- Shanghai has the world's fastest train, the Maglev, which runs from the Pudong Airport.

CULTURE QUIZ

SITUATION 1

You set up a meeting in Shanghai with local government officials involving both foreigners and Chinese nationals at your company. It has been months of waiting for the local government to allow your company to press forward with a new initiative that requires its approval, yet the official in charge has largely ignored your requests. When you finally get everyone in the room to discuss the initiative, the official keeps telling you that your project is still under consideration. Your options are:

Ⓐ Find someone who the official is indebted to, and have them set up another meeting

Ⓑ Aggressively press the official for a yes or no answer in the meeting

Ⓒ Get angry and yell at the official

Ⓓ Thank the official for his time and end the meeting

Comments

This is an unfortunate situation. Becoming angry or aggressive will break every single Chinese rule of etiquette and risks alienating your long-term relationship with the local government. Not only will an angry response be highly ineffective, but it will also sabotage your future and make it virtually impossible for you to build guanxi. The most likely answer is D, which involves finding a different path for your project. If you have built strong relationships and can manage to find someone who has guanxi that the official respects, (answer A), then you are far more likely find success. Saying no outright to things is not the Chinese way. A bold "no" would cause you to lose face. Instead, it's more common for Chinese officials to put off dealing with requests or pass them down the line, all the time hoping the request will go away, which is what this official may be doing.

SITUATION 2

You are living in Shanghai but travel frequently to other countries. You have been raised to show your appreciation for those who work for you by giving them small gifts at different times of the year. When you return to Shanghai, you return with a generous gift for the daughter of your *ayi* as a way of showing appreciation for the hard work she does. Even though it is not a Chinese holiday, you offer the gift to your *ayi*. However, you are confused when she seems ungrateful for the gift and even appears uncomfortable with it. Why?

Ⓐ She would rather have a raise than this gift

Ⓑ Her idea of polite behavior is different from yours

Ⓒ She doesn't like the gift

Ⓓ She feels she cannot reciprocate the gift

Comments

While it may be true that your *ayi* would enjoy a raise, the correct answer is actually that she may feel she cannot reciprocate (answer D). Confucian philosophies of balance and harmony mean that many Chinese prefer to keep their relationships in balance and do not like to experience indebtedness. Since your *ayi* cannot likely repay the gift or give you a similar gift, her sense of indebtedness may make her uncomfortable. Of course, every situation is different, and this is not *always* the case, but overdoing gift giving can make things uncomfortable for some Chinese.

SITUATION 3

You are a manager who oversees five Chinese employees who are considered your subordinates. One of your employees has made a serious mistake in accounting, and the financial error has been noticed on a spreadsheet during a meeting. You cannot immediately figure out who made the error, and when you ask the entire group about it during the meeting, no one takes responsibility. Later, you find out who is most likely responsible for the mistake. You should proceed by doing which of the following:

Ⓐ Talking directly to the person in private
Ⓑ Pointing out the error to the person during the next meeting
Ⓒ Asking another subordinate of yours to handle the situation
Ⓓ Ignoring the situation altogether

Comments

The correct answer is a little more nuanced in this case and can be either answer A or answer C. Because saving face is so important in public situations in China, it's not uncommon for groups of Chinese to avoid admitting to a mistake, especially in public. Asking an intermediary to handle the situation is a fairly common Chinese practice, and it will help save face for the employee if the "big boss" is not calling attention to it. As an alternative, a private conversation is another good choice, and this makes the mistake known to the least number of people. A personal conversation can also help avoid future misunderstandings. The employee will appreciate not having his/her mistake made public.

SITUATION 4

The Chinese New Year holiday is just a day or two away and you are about to leave the country for a vacation. You know that your *ayi* and driver are expecting their "13 month pay." You have taken out a large number of ¥100 bills to pay out your *hongbao*, and as you are ready to stuff the envelopes, you remember there is a rule about giving *hongbao* that has to do with good or bad luck. The rule is . . .

Ⓐ Never give *hongbao* in person
Ⓑ Never leave an even number of bills
Ⓒ Never leave an odd number of bills
Ⓓ Never give the *hongbao* on a Tuesday

Comments

The Chinese have so many superstitions related to good and bad luck that it can be difficult to remember them all. When giving *hongbao* for the Chinese New Year holiday, putting an odd number of bills in the red envelope is considered bad luck (answer C). An easy trick to remember this is that "balance" is an important Confucian principle in China. Even-numbered things are always balanced.

SITUATION 5

You are out to dinner with a large group of Chinese friends and business acquaintances. The *baijiu* is flowing freely, and people are getting a bit loud. The host of the dinner is the elder person at the table, and your boss. He fills everyone's glasses and offers a toast. You enjoy an occasional drink but are a generally light drinker. Worse, you don't really enjoy the taste of *baijiu*. What should you do?

Ⓐ Say thank you, but no thank you to the host
Ⓑ Be polite and take the drink
Ⓒ Dump the drink in a nearby plant
Ⓓ Sip the drink and then leave it on the table

Comments

There certainly isn't anyone who wants to argue that forcing someone to drink alcohol is the right choice. This is a sticky situation in which you have to make a choice based on context. The polite thing to do, of course, is to accept the drink (answer B) and make a toast, then figure out how to avoid drinking further. Offers of alcohol, especially during a celebration, can be a bit forceful in China, with people sometimes holding a cup up to your lips. If you are aware of the situation going in, you can better prepare how to beg out of long evenings of excessive drinking by making an excuse such as poor health.

DOS AND DON'TS

DOS

- Be respectful of Chinese patriotism and responsibility to the Communist party
- Avoid discussing Chinese politics with those you do not know well
- Be aware of cultural norms like face
- Build guanxi with everyone you meet, including government officials
- Go above and beyond to meet expectations
- Express criticism or concern in private, not in public
- Do business over lunch and dinner
- Offer small honorifics and gifts to hosts and colleagues
- Place elderly and senior guests at the head of the table
- Use serving chopsticks to take food from shared bowls (when available)
- Carry business cards and remember to accept them with two hands
- Make your best effort to use Chinese passably
- Remove your shoes when entering the home
- Give a red envelope to those who work for you (secretaries, *ayis*, drivers) during the Chinese New Year holiday
- Remember that luck is an important concept in China

DON'T

- Criticize colleagues publicly
- Get on the bad side of local government officials
- Push for quick and direct resolutions to problems
- Give large gifts that can be construed as bribes or graft

- Create an imbalanced relationship with your colleagues
- Cause the Chinese to lose face
- Be overly expressive with those you don't know well
- Criticize the government publicly
- Address Chinese by their first names until told to do so
- Give ultimatums

GLOSSARY

BASIC WORDS

English	Pinyin
Hello	*ni hao*
How are you?	*ni hao ma*
Good morning	*zao*
Good night	*wan an*
Thank you	*xie xie*
You're welcome	*bu ke qi*
No thank you	*bu xie xie*
Goodbye	*zai jian*
Sorry	*bao qian*
Okay, fine	*hao* (usually repeated)
Right (used as okay, yes)	*dui*
Stop	*ting* (useful in taxis)
Official receipt (invoice)	*fapiao*
Fake market vendors	*shanzhai*
Foreigner	*wai guo ren* (not pejorative)
Foreigner (more common)	*laowai* (pejorative, but common)
Friend	*peng you*
Colleague	*tong shi*
Household help	*ayi* (literally "auntie")

COUNTING

One	*yi*
Two	*er*
Three	*san*
Four	*si*
Five	*wu*
Six	*liu*
Seven	*qi*
Eight	*ba*
Nine	*jiu*
Ten	*shi*
Eleven	*shi yi* (ten and one)
Twelve	*shi er* (ten and two)
Twenty	*ershi* (two tens)
Twenty-one	*ershi yi* (two tens one)
Thirty	*san shi* (three tens)
Thirty-one	*sanshi yi* (three tens one)
Forty	*sishi* (four tens)
Fifty	*wushi* (five tens)

SHOPPPING

One of . . .	*yi ge or zi yi*
Two of . . .	*liang ge*
Three of . . .	*san ge*
Do not want	*bu yao*
Don not have	*mei you*
Do have	*queshi you*
I want	*wo xiang yao*

Eyeglasses	*yan jing*
Traditional Chinese Dress	*cheongsam*
Silk	*si*

FOOD

Chopsticks	*kuai zi*
Cheers	*gan bei*
Alcohol	*jiu*
Chinse liquor	*bai jiu*
Coffee	*kafei*
Tea	*cha*
Green tea	*lu cha*
Black tea	*hong cha*
Oolong tea	*wulong cha*
Rice	*mi*
Water	*shui*
Chicken	*ji*
Beef	*niu rou*
Crab	*xia*
Hairy Crab	*mao xie*
Tofu	*dou fu*
Apple	*ping guo*
Banana	*xiang jiao*
lychee	*lizhi*
Mango	*mang guo*

RESOURCE GUIDE

SHANGHAI EMERGENCY NUMBERS

- Ambulance 120
- Auto Accident 122
- Fire 119
- Police 122
- Shanghai Hotline 962288

THE SHANGHAI EXPATRIATE ASSOCIATION (SEA)

The Shanghai Expatriate Association (SEA) is a membership organization for all expats from countries outside China and is one of the best ways to make immediate friends in Shanghai. A one-year membership typically runs about ¥300 (US$43) per person and comes with a subscription to their quarterly publication and calendar of events. SEA opens up a world of travel and cultural activities for new arrivals, including day and weekend trips for members as well as cultural learning experiences through classes in Chinese cooking or Chinese brushwork. The organization also provides opportunities to join spin-off groups such as mahjong, book clubs, and weekly coffees. Dinner events are on the regular agenda. Within the larger organization, many smaller nationality specific groups run their own activities. For more details, see their website. http://www.seashanghai.org

SAFE TRAVEL TIPS

The U.S. State Department's International Travel website provides a host of useful information about travel in China, including their free *Smart Traveler Enrollment Program* that provides U.S. citizens with the latest security updates from the nearest U.S. Embassy or consulate. Both the British and Australian Consulates also offer their citizens *Smart Traveler Programs* via their consular websites. Enrollment in these programs comes with the added benefits of allowing embassies or consulates to know where and how to contact you in the event of an emergency. In Shanghai, you will also receive regular texts from the Shanghai Safety Authority and the Civil Affairs Bureau, sometimes about safety issues, other times about philosophical issues.

All foreign consulates suggest keeping contact details for your nearest embassy with you at all times. In planning for a crisis or power outage, consider creating a plan to use social media platforms as an alternate means of communicating with family and friends.

INTERNATIONAL CONSULATES IN SHANGHAI

- **Consulate General of the Republic of Argentina**
  http://www.cshan.mrecic.gov.ar
  Suite 1202, Golden Finance Tower
  58 Yan'an Road East
  Shanghai 200002, China
  Tel: (86-21) 6339 0322
  Fax: (86-21) 5350 0058
  Email: cshan@mrecic.gov.ar

- **Australian Consulate-General**
  https://shanghai.china.embassy.gov.au/
  Level 22, CITIC Square
  1168 Nanjing Xi Lu,
  Shanghai 200041, China

Phone: (021) 2215 5200
Fax: (021) 2215 5252
Email: consular.shanghai@dfat.gov.au

- **Consulate General of Austria**
  www.bmeia.gv.at/gk-shanghai/
  Qi Hua Tower 3A
  1375 Huai Hai Zhong Lu, 200031
  Shanghai, China
  Phone: (+86) (21) 64740268
  Fax: (+86) (21) 647 11 554
  Email form on website

- **Consulate General of Belarus**
  http://shanghai.mfa.gov.by/ru/
  1702F, 2299 Yan'an Rd (W)
  Shanghai, China 200 336
  Phone: + (86 10) 65 32 16 91
  Fax: + (86 10) 65 32 64 17

- **Consulate General of Belgium**
  https://china.diplomatie.belgium.be/ en/contacts/
  consulate-general-shanghai
  Wu Yi Road 127 200050
  Shanghai, China
  Phone: +86-21-64376579 / 64376772 / 64376628
  Fax: +86-21-64377041
  Email: Shanghai@diplobel.fed.be

- **British Consulate-General**
  https://www.gov.uk/world/organisations/british-
  consulate-general-shanghai

The British Centre
17F Garden Square
968 West Beijing Road 200041 Shanghai
Phone: (+86) (21) 3279 2000
Fax (General)+86 (0) 21 3279 2005
Fax (Consular)+86 (0) 21 3279 2009
Email form: https://www.contact-embassy.service.gov.
uk/?country=China&post=British per cent20Consulate per
cent20General per cent20Shanghai

- **Consulate General of the Republic of Bulgaria**
  https://www.mfa.bg/en/embassies/chinagc
  Unit 1416, 14th Florr, Bldg. B
  Far East International Plaza
  317 Xianxia Road
  Shanghai 200051, China
  Phone: 86 21 6237 6183, 86 21 6237 6187
  Fax: 86 21 6237 6189
  Email: Consular.Shanghai@mfa.bg

- **Consulate General of Cambodia**
  http://www.cambodiaembassy.ch/english/embassies.php
  Huasheng Commercial Building 9th Floor,
  Hankou Road 400 Shanghai, China
  Phone: (8621) 63616681, 63600949
  Fax: (8621) 63611437
  E-mail: tangjx@online.sh.cn

- **Consulate General of Canada (Shanghai)**
  https://www.canadainternational.gc.ca/china-chine/
  offices-bureaux/shanghai/index.aspx?lang=eng
  ECO City Building

8th floor, 1788 Nanjing Xi Lu, Jing An District
Shanghai, 200040, China
Phone: (+86-21) 3279-2800
Fax: (+86-21) 3279-2801
Email: shngi@international.gc.ca

- **General Consulate of Chile**
  http://www.chile.gob.cl/shanghai
  Suite 2501, Shanghaimart Office Tower
  2299 Yanan Rd,
  Shanghai 200036 China
  Phone: 86 (21) 62360770
  Fax: 86 (21) 62361318
  Email: shanghai@consulado.gob.cl

- **Consulate General of the Czech Republic**
  https://www.mzv.cz/shanghai/en/
  808 New Town Center
  83 Loushan Guan Road
  Shanghai 200336, China
  Phone: 8621-6236 9925
  Fax: 8621-6236 9920

- **Royal Danish Consulate General**
  http://kina.um.dk/en/about-us/danish-representations-
  in-china/royal-danish-consulate-general-in-shanghai/
  Room 3101, Shanghai International Trade Centre,
  No. 2201, Yan'an Xi Lu,
  Shanghai 200336, China
  Phone: +86 21 8025 0600
  Fax: +86 (21) 6209 0878
  Email: shagkl@um.dk

- **Ecuadorian Consulate**
  http://shanghai.consulado.gob.ec
  317 Xianxia Lu, Torre B
  Floor 17, Office 1701
  Shanghai 200051, China
  Phone: (+86 21) 6235 0532, 6235 0536
  Fax: (+86 21) 6235 0539
  Email: cecushangai@cancilleria.gob.ec

- **Consulate-general of the Kingdom of the Netherlands in Shanghai (Dutch Consulate)**
  Dawning Center Tower B, Floor 10
  Hongbaoshi Road no. 500
  Changning District
  Shanghai 201103, China
  Phone: +86 21 2208 7288
  Fax: +86 21 2208 7300
  Email: sha@minbuza.nl

- **Consulate General of Egypt in Shanghai**
  https://www.egyptembassy.org/location/china/egypt-consolate-shanghai/
  Qihua Building, 19th Floor, A&B
  1375 Huai Zhong Road
  Shanghai, China
  Phone: (86 21) 6433 1020 / 6433 0622
  Fax: (8621) 6433 0049
  Email: egyptian.consulate.shanghai@gmail.com

- **Consulate General of Finland in Shanghai**
  http://www.finland.cn/Public/Default.aspx
  CITIC Square 2501-2505

2 th floor, 1168 Nanjing Xi Lu
200041 Shanghai China
Phone: +86 21 52929900
Fax: +86 21 52929880
Email: sanomat.sng@formin.fi

- **Consulate General of France**
  https://cn.ambafrance.org/-Consulat-Shanghai-
  Soho Zhongshan Plaza,
  Building A, 18th Floor
  1055 Zhongshan Xi Lu
  Shanghai 200051, China
  Phone: 8621 61032200
  Fax: 8621 61352089
  Email: info.shanghai-fslt@diplomatie.gouv.fr

- **Consulate General of Germany**
  https://china.diplo.de/cn-de
  181, Yongfu Road
  Shanghai 200031, China
  Phone: (8621) 3401 0106
  Fax: (8621) 6471 4448

- **Consulate General of Greece (Hellenic Repuoblic)**
  https://www.mfa.gr/china/en/consulate-general-shanghai/
  Suite 2201 & 2202, Citic Plaza
  1359 Sichuan Road (North)
  Shanghai 200080, China
  Phone: (8621) 6698 2790 6
  Fax: (8621) 6698 5502
  Email: grgencon.sha@mfa.gr

- **Consulate General of India**
  https://www.cgishanghai.gov.in/
  1008, Shanghai International Trade Centre
  2201 Yan An West Road
  Shanghai 200336 China
  Phone: 86-21-6275 8885
  Fax: 86-21-6275 8881

- **Consulate General of Ireland**
  https://www.dfa.ie/irish-consulate/shanghai/
  Suite 700A, Shanghai Centre (West Tower)
  1376 Nanjing Road West
  200040 Shanghai, China
  Phone: 86 21 6010 1360
  Fax: 86 21 62798739

- **Consulate General of Israel**
  http://www.isconshanghai.org/
  13F, No. 318 Fuzhou Road,
  Shanghai 200001, China
  Phone: 86-21-6010 2522
  FAX: 86-21-5168 5099

- **General Consulate of Italy**
  https://consshanghai.esteri.it/consolato_shanghai/it
  The Center, 19 Floor
  989 Changle Road
  200031 Shanghai China
  Phone: 86 21 669 659
  Fax: 8621 64716977
  Email: info.shanghai@esteri.it

- **Consulate General of Japan**
  www.shanghai.cn.emb-japan.go.jp
  http://8 Wan Shan Road
  Shanghai, China
  Phone: (86-21) 5257-4766
  Fax: (86-21) 6278-8988

- **Consulate General of Luxembourg**
  https://shanghai.mae.lu/en
  907-908, No. 1788 Nanjing Xi Lu
  Shanghai 200040, China
  Phone: (+86 21) 63390400
  Email: Shanghai.Visa@mae.etat.lu

- **Consulate General of Malaysia**
  www.kln.gov.my/web/chn_shanghai/
  Units 01, Block B - 9th Floor
  Dawning Centre
  No. 500 Hongbaoshi Road
  Changning District
  Shanghai 201103 China
  phone: +86 21 60900360
  +86 21 60900390 (Passport & Visa)
  +86 136 1176 3879 (After Office Hours)
  Fax: +86 21 60900371 (Consulate General),
  Email: mwshanghai@kln.gov.my

- **Honorary Consulate of Monaco**
  https://www.consulate-info.com/consulate/333/Monaco-in-Shanghai
  Thomson Commercial Building
  710 Dong Fang Road,

2F Pudong New Areal
Shanghai China
Phone: 8621 58314008
Fax: +86 21 5058 4833
Email: hsufeng@monaco.org.cn

- **New Zealand Consulate-General**
  https://www.mfat.govt.nz/en/countries-and-regions/north-asia/china/new-zealand-embassy/new-zealand-consulate-general-shanghai/
  2801-2802A & 2806B-2810, Corporate Avenue 5
  150 Hu Bin Road Huangpu District 200021
  Shanghai
  Phone: 8621-5407-5858
  Fax: 8621-5407-5068
  Email: shanghai.enquiries@mft.net.nz

- **Royal Norwegian Consulate General**
  https://www.norway.no/en/china/norway-china/shanghai/
  Room 1701, Bund Center
  222 East Yan'an Road
  Huangpu District
  200002 Shanghai, China
  Phone: 86-21-6039-7500
  Phone from Norway: 47 2395 8400
  Fax: 86-21-6039-7501
  Email: cg shanghai@mfa.no

- **Consulate General of the Islamic Republic of Pakistan**
  http://www.mofa.gov.pk/shanghai/
  Room 1111, Tower A
  SOHO Zhongshan Plaza

1055 West Zhongshan Road
Changning District, Shanghai, China
Phone: 86 21 6237 7000
Fax: 86 21 6237 7066
Email: cgpakshanghai@yahoo.com

- **Consulate of the Republic of Peru**
  http://www.consulado.pe/es/shanghai/Paginas/
  Contactenos.aspx
  Suite 2705 Kerry Centre
  1515 Nanjing West Road
  200040 Shanghai, China
  Phone: (86-21) 5298 5900
  Fax: (86-21) 5298 5905
  Email: conperu@conpersh.com

- **Consulate General of Philippines**
  http://www.shanghaipcg.dfa.gov.ph/
  Suite 301, Metrobank Plaza Building No. 1160 Yaan
  West Road (corner Fanyu Road) Changning District,
  Shanghai China
  Phone: 8621 6281-8020
  Fax: 8621 6281-8023
  Email: shanghai.pcg@dfa.gov.ph
  shanghaipcg@hotmail.com

- **Consulate General of the Republic of Poland in
  Shanghai**
  http://www.szanghaj.msz.gov.pl
  618 Jianguo Xilu
  Shanghai 200031, China

Phone: (86-21) 6433 9288
Fax: (86-21) 6433 0417
E-mail: shanghai@msz.gov.pl
E-mail to Visa Section: shanghai.visa@msz.gov.pl

- **Serbian Consulate General of the Republic of Serbia**
http://www.shanghai.mfa.gov.rs/
Rm, 302, No.1 Lane 60, Lyon Garden, Ronghua East Road
Gu Bei New Area
Shanghai 201103, China
Phone: 86-21-62081388 / 62081899
Fax: 86-21-62087412
Email: onsulate@srbshanghai.org

- **General Consulate of the Republic of Singapore**
https://www.mfa.gov.sg/shanghai
89 Wan Shan Road
Shanghai 200336 China
Phone: 8621-62785566
Fax: 8621-6295-6038
Email: singcg_sha@mfa.sg

- **Consulate of the Slovak Republic**
https://www.mzv.sk/web/cgshanghai-en
Qi Hua Tower 4A
1375 Huaihai Central Road
Shanghai, 200031 China
Phone: (86-21) 6431-4205
Fax: (+86-21) 6471-3604
Email: cg.shanghai@mzv.sk

- **South African Consulate**
  http://www.dirco.gov.za/shanghai/contacts.html
  27th Floor, Room 2705/6
  222 Yan An Road East
  Shanghai 200002 China
  Phone: 86-21-53594977
  Fax: 86-21-63352980
  Email: dhashanghai@rsaconsulate.com

- **General Consulate of the Republic of Korea**
  http://overseas.mofa.go.kr/cn-shanghai-ko/index.do
  No.60, Wanshang Road
  Shanghai, China
  Phone: 86-21-62955000 / 62952639
  Fax: 86-21-62955191 / 62952629

- **Consulate-General of Sweden**
  https://www.swedenabroad.se/en/embassies/china-shanghai/current/news/welcome-to-the-new-official-website-of-the-consulate/
  1521-1541 Shanghai Central Plaza
  381 Middle Huaihai Road
  Shanghai 200020 China
  Phone: 8621 5359 9610
  Fax: 8621 5359 9633
  Email: generalkonsulat.shanghai@gov.se

- **Consulate General of Switzerland**
  https://www.eda.admin.ch/countries/china/en/home/representations/embassy-in-beijing/consulate-general-shanghai.html
  22F, Building A, Far East International Plaza,

319 Xianxia Road, Shanghai, China
Phone: (86-21) 62700519 / 62700520
Fax: (86-21) 62700522
Email: shanghai@eda.admin.ch

- **Royal Thai Consulate-General**
  http://www.thaishanghai.com/th/
  Crystal Century Mansion 15 Floor
  No. 567 Weihai Road, Shanghai China
  Phone: (86-21) 62883030
  Fax: (86-21) 62889072

- **Consulate of the Republic of Turkey**
  http://shanghai.cg.mfa.gov.tr/Mission
  SOHO Zhongshan Plaza
  1055 West Zhongshan Road
  8F, Unit:806-808
  Changning District
  Shanghai 200051 China
  Phone: 86-21 6474-6838 / 6839
  Fax: 86-21 6471-9896
  Email: consulate.shanghai@mfa.gov.tr

- **Consulate-General of Ukraine**
  https://shanghai.mfa.gov.ua/en
  W402, Sun Plaza,
  88 Xian Xia Rdoad
  Shanghai China 200336
  Phone: 86-21-62953195
  Fax: 86-21-62953171
  Email: gc_cns@mfa.gov.ua

- **United States Consulate General Shanghai**
  https://china.usembassy-china.org.cn/embassy-
  consulates/shanghai/
  Westgate Mall
  1469 Huai Hai Zhong Road
  (Near Wulumuqi Nan Lu)
  200031 Shanghai, China
  Phone: 86-21 8011-2200
  Fax: +(86)(21) 6148-8266
  Emergency After-Hours Telephone: +(86)(10) 8531-4000
  Email: ShanghaiACS@state.gov

- **Consulate General of Uruguay**
  http://www.conurushang.com/
  Unit 2403 Hong Kong New World Tower 300 Huai Hai
  Zhong Road
  Shanghai 2000021 China
  Phone: 86 21 6335 3927 / 3521
  Fax: 86 21 6335 3741
  Email: info@conurushang.com

HEALTH CARE RESOURCES

This list focuses primarily on medical services that
cater to the expat community. Shanghai also has a
large number of Chinese hospitals which may be closer
and more accessible during an emergency. Western
languages, especially English, are widely spoken in
international hospitals but not necessarily in Chinese
hospitals that serve the local Shanghai community.

DENTAL CARE

- **DDS Dental Care (HuaiHai Rd., HongQiao, Lujiazui, Tianlin)**
  http://www.dds-dental.com/

- **The French Dentist**
  (Shanghai Mart, 2299 Yanan Rd, Changning)
  http://www.frenchdentist.cn/

- **Parkway Health Dental (Jingan, Pudong Jinqiao)**
  http://www.parkwayhealth.cn/medical-services/dentistry.php

- **United Family Health (Changning)**
  http://shanghai.ufh.com.cn/en/medical-services/dental-clinic/

- **DeltaWest Clinic Dental (Hongqiao)**
  http://www.deltahealth.com.cn
  Ren'ai Dental (Xuhui)
  http://en.renai.cn/servers/mouth/

- **Global Health Care (Puxi Jingan)**
  Nanjing West Rd, Pudong Lujiazui WFC
  http://www.ghcchina.com/programs-a-services/dental-services/cosmetic-dentistry

- **Raffles Dental (Xuhui, Hongmei Rd.)**
  http://www.rafflesmedicalgroup.com/shanghai/shanghai-medical-centres/rafflesmedical-dental.aspx
  CAD Dental Care
  (Puxi Huai Hai Central Rd.)
  http://www.caddental.cn/

- Tokushinkai Dental (Japanese and English) (Pudong, Jingan, Changning)
  http://www.tokushinkai.com.cn/

- New York Dental Gubei, Pudong Century Park
  http://newyorkdentalchina.com

- J Smiles (Jingan)
  https://www.jsmiles.com/

- Pure Smile (Hongqiao, Pudong Jinqiao Biyun)
  http://puresmile.com/

- Kowa Dental (Jingan, Pudong Lujiazui)
  http://en.kowa-dental.com/

- Arrail Dental (Pudong Lujiazui, Luwan, Xujiahui)
  http://www.arrail-dental.com/en/index.html

INTERNATIONAL HOSPITALS AND CLINICS

- American-Sino Medical Group (OB/GYN/Pediatric Services)
  http://www.am-sino.com/en/
  Locations
  Shanghai DingXiang Outpatient
  2-3F, Block 6, Clove Apartment Building,
  800 Huashan Road, Shanghai
  Tel: 400-163-4482 (24h)
  OB/GYN 021-31752530 / PED 021
  31752520

- **American-Sino Women's & Children's Hospital (SongYuan)**
  No.155, Songyuan Rd., Near Hongsong, (E) Road
  Tel: 400-163-4482
  Hours
  OB/GYN Outpatient Clinic Hours
  9:00-20:00 Monday-Friday
  9:00-17:00 Saturday & Sunday

- **Pediatrics Outpatient Clinic Hours**
  9:00-20:00 Monday-Sunday (Dingxiang)
  24/7/365 (Songyuan)
  Website: http://www.am-sino.com

- **Delta Health Hospital**
  https://www.deltahealth.com.cn/english/Home.html
  109, XuleRoad, Qingpu District, Shanghai 201702
  Reservation Line: (021) 6015 1313
  Switchboard: (021) 6700 7777
  Fax: (021) 6700 7766

- **GHC Global Health Care**
  http://www.ghcchina.com/
  Hours
  Mon.-Fri.: 8am-7pm; Sat.-Sun.: 9am-5pm
  Puxi
  ECO City, Suite 303
  1788 NanJing West Road, Jing An District,
  Shanghai 200040
  For appointment: 86-21-5298 6339, 86-21-5298 5833
  Fax: 86-21-5298 6993
  Direct Dental Clinic: 86-21-5298 0593

Pudong

Shanghai World Financial Center, Shop 212
100 Century Avenue, PuDong New Area,
Shanghai 200120
For appointment: 86-21-6877 5093, 86-21-6877 5693
Fax: 86-21-6877 5393
Direct Dental Clinic: 86-21-6877 5993

- **New Vision Eye Clinic**
  https://newvisioneyeclinic.com/
  3rd Floor, Jin Kai Li Square
  758 Xizang Nan Lu (near Jianquo Xi Lu), Shanghai
  For appointment: +86 21 6437 7445

- **Parkway Health Clinics (PHC)**
  http://www.parkwayhealth.cn/shanghai-clinics.php
  Puxi: People's Square (PHC) Gleneagles Medical and Surgical Center
  http://www.parkwayhealth.cn/shanghai-clinics/
  Gleneagles-medical-surgical-center.php
  Tomorrow Square,
  389 Nanjing Xi Rd., 4th Floor
  Shanghai 200003

- **Puxi: Jing'an (PHC) Shanghai Centre Medical and Dental Center**
  http://www.parkwayhealth.cn/shanghai-clinics/
  shanghai-center-medical-dental-center.php
  203-4 West Retail Plaza,
  1376 Nanjing Xi Rd.,
  Shanghai 200040

- **Xin Tian Di (PHC) Specialty and Inpatient Center**
  http://www.parkwayhealth.cn/shanghai-clinics/xintiandi-specialty-birthing-inpatient-center.php
  170 Danshui Rd., 3rd Floor
  Shanghai 200020

- **Pudong Jin Qiao Medical and Dental Center**
  http://www.parkwayhealth.cn/shanghai-clinics/jin-qiao-medical-dental-center.php
  997, Bi Yun Road, Jin Qiao, Pudong,
  Shanghai 201206

- **Jin Mao Tower Medical Center**
  http://www.parkwayhealth.cn/shanghai-clinics/Jin-mao-tower-medical-center.php
  Podium Building, JinMao Tower, J-LIFE,
  88 Century Avenue, Pudong New Area,
  Shanghai 200120

- **Raffles Medical Shanghai**
  https://www.rafflesmedicalgroup.com/shanghai
  1801 Hong Mei Road
  Innov Tower level 2 (Capitaland) building
  Xuhui District, Shanghai 200233
  Tel: (86) 21 6197 2300 (Also, online appointment form)
  Email: enquiries_shanghai@rafflesmedical.com

- **St. Michael Hospital**
  http://www.stmichael-hospital.com
  388 Hongbaoshi Road, Changning District, Shanghai
  24/7 Emergency hotline: +86 21 6270 5300
  Patient Care (8:30am-6:30pm): +86 21 5155 1858

- **Shanghai East International Medical Center (SEIMC)**
  http://www.seimc.com.cn/
  150 Jimo Road, Shanghai 200120
  Pudong 24 hour Emergency: 5879-9999
  Alternative: 150-0019-0899

- **Shanghai Sky Clinic**
  http://www.shanghaiskyclinic.com/en
  An international hospital
  396 Hongbaoshi Road, Changning District, Shanghai,
  China 201103
  Tel (Hotline for 24 Hours.): 0086-21-5153-0222
  Fax: 0086-21-5153-0222
  Email: generalenquiry@shanghaiskyclinic.com
  (Get an appointment)

- **Shanghai United Health Care (SUH)**
  http://shanghai.ufh.com.cn/?lang=en

- **Shanghai United Family Hospital**
  1139 Xianxia Road, Changning District,
  Shanghai 200336
  Appointment Center: 400 639 3900
  24-hour Emergency Hotline: +86 (21) 2216 3999
  Tel: +86 (21) 2216 3900
  Email: shuptservice@ufh.com.cn

- **Shanghai United Family Pudong Hospital**
  http://shanghai.ufh.com.cn/locations/shanghai-united-
  family-xincheng-hospital?lang=en
  No. 1598, New Jinqiao Road, Pudong
  New District, Shanghai, China

Appointment Center: 400 639 3900
24-hour Emergency Hotline: +86 (21) 2216 3999
Tel: +86 (21) 2216 3999

- **World Path Clinic International**
  http://www.worldpathclinic.com/en.php
  309 North Nan Quan Road, Shanghai 200120
  Phone: 021-2020 7888
  Email: info@worldpathclinic.com

PETS

A surprising number of expats bring their pets with them to Shanghai. Dogs and cats will have to be transported overseas via specialized pet transportation services and may require up to a month of quarantine when they land in China. Pet transportation services will provide lists of necessary vaccinations and paperwork needed before transporting your pet to Shanghai. Check with the management of your apartment complex or villa community to make sure pets are allowed. Many expats have their *ayis* care for their pets when they vacation, but boarding services are available in Shanghai too.

VETERINARY SERVICES

- **Doctors Beck & Stone (Changning)**
  Daily, 9am-7pm, 24 Hours emergency available
  500 Weining Lu, near Changning Lu
  Phone : 3250 6721 For review of services, see:
  http://www.smartshanghai.com/venue/6266/Eagle_
  Valley

- **Dog and Cat**
  377-379 Weihai Lu, near Shimen Lu
  Phone: 6340 1581 Cat For review of services, see:
  http://www.smartshanghai.com/venue/7057/Dog__Cat

- **Paw Veterinary Clinic (Pudong)**
  Daily, 9am-6pm, Appointment Only
  www.pawivs.com
  No.1-11, 1755 Donglu Lu, near Jingao Lu
  5043 5620 Full-service clinic with English-speaking
  doctors (pricey) For review, see: http://www.
  smartshanghai.com/venue/6918/PAW_Veterinary_
  Clinic_Pudong)

INTERNATIONAL SCHOOLS

The number of international schools in Shanghai seems to grow annually; new international schools seem to open every year. This list is not exhaustive, but does focus on larger, established schools whose reputations have been proven. Most schools are located either in Pudong or Puxi, and many of the largest schools maintain separate campuses in both locations. When schools have two campuses, they are listed under both headings Puxi/Pudong.

PUXI SCHOOLS
- **British International School of Shanghai, Puxi**
  https://www.nordangliaeducation.com/our-schools/
  shanghai/puxi
- **Dulwich College Shanghai, Puxi**
  https://shanghai-puxi.dulwich.org
- **Fudan International School**
  https://en.wikipedia.org/wiki/Fudan_International_School
- **German School Shanghai**

http://www.ds-shanghai.de
- **Lyceé Francais de Shanghai, Pudong**
  http://www.lyceeshanghai.com
- **Montessori School of Shanghai**
  http://www.montessorisos.com
- **Shanghai American School, Puxi**
  https://www.saschina.org
- **Shanghai Community International School**
  https://www.scis-china.org/about/campuses-and-facilities/
- **Shanghai Japanese School**
  http://english.pudong.gov.cn/2017-07/19/c_84917.htm
- **Shanghai Korean School**
  http://www.skoschool.com
- **Shanghai Livingston American School**
  http://www.laschina.org
- **Shanghai Singapore International School, Puxi (2 campuses)**
  https://www.ssis.asia
- **Yew Chung International School of Shanghai, Puxi**
  https://www.ycis-sh.com/en/about-ycis/campus-and-facilities
- **YK Pao School**
  http://www.ykpaoschool.cn

PUDONG SCHOOLS

- **Concordia International School Shanghai**
  https://www.concordiashanghai.org
- **Dulwich College Shanghai, Pudong**
  https://shanghai-pudong.dulwich.org
- **Lyceé Francais de Shanghai, Puxi**
  http://www.lyceeshanghai.com

- **Nord Anglia International School of Pudong**
  https://www.nordangliaeducation.com/en/our-schools/shanghai/pudong
- **Shanghai American School, Pudong**
  https://www.saschina.org
- **Shanghai Community International School**
  https://www.scis-china.org/about/campuses-and-facilities/
- **Shanghai High School International Division**
  http://www.shsid.org
- **Shanghai Japanese School**
  http://english.pudong.gov.cn/2017-07/19/c_84917.htm
- **Wellington College International School of Shanghai**
  https://www.wellingtoncollege.cn/shanghai/
- **Yew Chung International School of Shanghai, Pudong**
  https://www.ycis-sh.com/en/about-ycis/campus-and-facilities

CHAMBERS OF COMMERCE

Much like the expat association, international Chambers of Commerce usually require membership in order to make use of their services. The benefits of membership often include invitations to seminars and presentations about culture, business, and regulations in China as well as subscriptions to publications and email news.

- **American Chamber of Commerce**
  www.amcham-shanghai.org
  Shanghai Centre, Suite
  568 1376 Nanjing Xi Lu
  +86 21 6279 7119
  amcham@amcham-shanghai.org

- **Australian Chamber of Commerce (AustCham)**
  www.austchamshanghai.com
  Suite 1101B,
  Silver Court, 85 Taoyuan Lu, by Xizang Nan Lu
  +86 21 6248 8301
  admin@austchamshanghai.com

- **Benelux Chamber of Commerce**
  www.bencham.org
  Room 919,
  638 Hengfeng Lu, by Chang'an Lu
  +86 21 3220 0573
  shanghai@bencham.org

- **British Chamber of Commerce**
  www.britishchambershanghai.org/en/home)
  863 Nanjing Xi Lu
  Marks & Spencer Building, by Shimen Lu
  +86 21 6218 5022

- **Canadian Chamber of Commerce**
  www.cancham.org.sg/business/canadian-chamber-of-
  commerce-in-shanghai/
  Room 2805 172 Yuyuan Lu
  +86 21 6075 8797 / +86 21 6075 8798 /
  +86 21 6075 8799
  info@cancham.asia

- **Czech Trade Office (CzechTrade)**
  www.czechtrade-china.cn
  Suite 611, Oriental Center
  699 Nanjing Xi Lu

+86 21 3218 1955
shanghai@czechtrade.cz

- **Danish Chamber of Commerce**
  www.dccc-shanghai.com
  Tianan Center, 338 Nanjing Xi Lu
  +86 21 138 1811 4020
  mail@dccc-shanghai.com

- **European Union Chamber of Commerce**
  www.europeanchamber.com.cn
  Unit 2204, Shui On Plaza
  333 Huaihai Zhong Lu
  +86 21 6385 2023
  shanghai@europeanchamber.com.cn

- **French Chamber of Commerce (CCIFC) 2/F,**
  www.ccifc.org
  Mayfair Tower
  83 Fumin Lu
  +86 21 6132 7100
  ccifc-shanghai@ccifc.org

- **German Chamber of Commerce**
  www.china.ahk.de/membership/east-china/
  29/F Gopher Center
  No. 757 Mengzi Road
  200023 Shanghai
  Tel.: +86-21-5081 2266
  chamber@sh.china.ahk.de

- **Israel Chamber of Commerce (ISCHAM) 5/F**

http://shanghai.lps-china.com/partners/ischam/
The Luxury Properties Showcase Ltd.
North 2F, Bldg. 4, No. 223 Xilang Road
Jing'an District1452 Hongqiao Lu, by Yili Lu Metro
Station
+86 21 5269 0223
info@ips-ichina.com

- **China-Italy Chamber of Commerce**
  www.cameraitacina.com
  Room 1604, Xincheng Mansion
  167 Jiangning Lu
  +86 21 5407 5181
  infoshanghai@cameraitacina.com

- **Spanish Chamber of Commerce**
  www.spanishchamber-ch.com
  Huaihai Zhonghua Tower
  885 Renmin Lu, by Huaihai Dong Lu
  +86 21 6326 4177
  shanghai@spanishchamber-ch.com

- **Swedish Chamber of Commerce 12/F**
  www.swedishchamber.com.cn
  Sail Tower, 266 Hankou Lu
  +86 21 6217 1271
  shanghai@swedishchamber.com.cn

- **Switzerland Chamber of Commerce (SwissCham)**
  www.swisscham.org/sha
  Room 1133, 11th Floor, Carlton Building
  21 Huanghe Road, Huangpu District

Shanghai 200003
+86 21 5368 1236
info@sha.swisscham.org

HELPFUL CELL PHONE APPS

Most foreign cellphone apps work best if downloaded prior to arriving in China—primarily because download times are extremely slow on the mainland. You may occasionally find that some apps cannot be updated while you are inside mainland China.

- Alipay
- WeChat
- Sherpas (food delivery)
- Expat Express
- Didi (ride hailing/taxi)
- Map Apps
  The iphone maps app works in Shanghai
  Baidu maps/English version
- SH Metro (metro maps)
- Speak&Translate
- iTranslate and iTranslate Voice
- Papago (translation)
- Google Translate (works without a VPN)
- SmSH (Smart Shanghai)
- BeijingAirQuality App (offers air quality for multiple Chinese cities)
- Sh**t!I Smoke (air quality)

RETAIL GROCERY STORES IN SHANGHAI
Carrefour

The French multinational retail chain *Carrefour* has more than twelve locations spread out across Puxi and Pudong. Stores are typically large, big-box style shopping marts with huge grocery sections that sell both Western and Chinese food and produce. Most Carrefour stores also sell household wares and goods such as small appliances, towels, kitchenware, and school supplies. Additionally, DVD players, telephones and other types of audiovisual equipment are also sold at most Carrefour shops.

City Shop

City Shop has at least three locations in Shanghai selling gourmet food, including Asian and Western-style products. The most expensive of the retail grocery chains, City Shop is a good place to buy specialty imported items that can be difficult to find, such as cheese or Greek yogurt. Don't do your daily shopping here since prices are exorbitant.

Big-Box Wholesale Markets

While Metro has had a longer-standing presence in Shanghai, Costco entered the Shanghai market in 2019, opening its first location in Huacao Town, Minhang. Most things at Metro and Costco are sold in large quantities—toilet paper and paper towels are good bets. Families may want to visit these stores to buy imported items such as cases of boxed milk that don't have to be refrigerated or freezer items that can keep for a long time. They also have a large section of household appliances such as vacuum cleaners, crockpots, and rice cookers.

Tesco

This British chain has multiple locations throughout Shanghai and also sells groceries along with household items.

RT Mart

A Chinese version of Walmart, RT Mart is everywhere in Shanghai but is most convenient for those living in the outer ring areas such as Minhang.

ONLINE GROCERY STORES

The convenience of buying groceries online and having them delivered to your door is very popular choice for working people. It's especially helpful for those who don't have the luxury of drivers and can't carry groceries in one walking trip. A bit more expensive than buying food at a brick and mortar store, these online groceries offer a wide range of local and imported foods in addition to locally sourced and organic produce.

- **Kate and Kimi**
  http://www.kateandkimi.com
- **Fields**
  http://www.fields.com
- **Tesco**
  http://elegou.cn.tesco.com
- **Epermarket**
  http://elegou.cn.tesco.com

LOCAL GUIDES

The following individuals offer private and small group tours of sights in and around Shanghai, including nearby water towns as well as cities and villages in neighboring provinces.

Tracy Lesh: Shanghai and Beyond
WeChat ID: shanghaiandbeyond

Website: https://shanghaiandbeyond.com
Email: Tracy.Lesh@yahoo.com
Phone: +86 139 5724 0650

Lisa Zhu (China Travel Consultant and Tours)
WeChat ID: Lisa_haiyu
Website: http://www.shanghailisa.com
Email: Lisa_haiyun@hotmail.com
Phone: +86 139 1839 8254

Yo Ho Guide (Yo Ho Tour)
WeChat ID: yuexinstudior
Follow on WeChat at Yoho
Website: http://www.yoho-guide.com
Emaill: yohoguide@189.cn
Phone: +86 189 1765 9228

LIFESTYLE WEBSITES

- **AirQuality Monitoring:** U.S. Consulate Website
  https://china.usembassy-china.org.cn/embassy-consulates/shanghai/air-quality-monitor-stateair/
- **AmCham Shanghai.** American Chamber of Commerce in Shanghai.
  https://www.amcham-shanghai.org/
- **China Daily Online.** China's leading English-language daily newspaper:
  http://www.chinadaily.com.cn/
- **China Incidentals**
  https://chinaincidentals.com
- **Expat.com**
  https://www.expat.com
- **Health and Medicine**

https://www.healthandsafetyinshanghai.com/

- **Expat Essentials.** Hundreds of tips for living in Shanghai
  https://expatessentials.net/category/shanghai/
- **Jobs in Shanghai.** Job openings for English-speaking professionals
  http://www.jobsinshanghai.com/
- **Meet in Shanghai.** "The official Shanghai China travel website.".
  www.meet-in-shanghai.net/events.php
- **Sapore di Cina.** How to rent an apartment in Shanghai.
  https://www.saporedicina.com/english/rent-in-shanghai/
- **Shanghai Expatriate Association.** SEA "provides a social and cultural network for expats and their families in Shanghai."
  http://www.seashanghai.org
- **Shanghai, China.** Shanghai government
  http://www.shanghai.gov.cn/shanghai/node23919/index.html
- **Shanghai Daily Online (Shine).** News and views.
  http://www.shanghaidaily.com/
- **Shanghaiist – China in bite-sized portions.** For expat news and commentary on all things
  http://www.shangaiist.com
- **Smart Shanghai.** News, nightlife, current events
  http://www.smartshanghai.com/
- **Smart Shanghai.** Veterinary listings
  http://www.smartshanghai.com/listings/services/veterinary/
- **That's Shanghai.** Shanghai news, bars & restaurants, lifestyles.

https://www.thatsmags.com/shanghai
- **Time-out Shanghai.** Shanghai news and entertainment guide
  http://www.timeoutshanghai.com/

LANGUAGE LEARNING WEBSITES

- **7 Days Mandarin Pronunciation with Xaoqian**
  http://chineseonthego.com/7-days-mandarin-with-xaoqian-lesson-1/
- **Learn Chinese Pinyin Vowels**
  https://www.echineselearning.com/blog/learn-chinese-pin-yin-vowels
- **Chinese Pronunciation (audio of vowels)**
  https://www.echineselearning.com/blog/learn-chinese-pin-yin-vowels

FURTHER READING

Little Soldiers by Lenora Chu

China in Ten Words by Yu Hua

Falling Leaves by Adeline Yen Mah

Last Boat out of Shanghai by Helen Zia

When We Were Orphans by Kazuo Ishigaro

Life and Death in Shanghai by Nien Cheng

Remembering Shanghai, A Memoir of Socialites, Scholars and Scoundrels by Claire Chao

Street of Eternal Happiness by Rob Schmitz

Shanghai in 12 Dishes – How to Eat Like You Live There by Antony Suvalko and Leanne Kitchen

Girl at the Baggage Claim by Gish Jen

Chinese Business Etiquette by Scott Seligman

Shanghai 1937: Stalingrad on the Yangtze by Peter Harmsen

Shanghai Girls by Lisa See

A Guide to Soup Dumplings in Shanghai (available in Shanghai) by Christopher St. Cavish

The Path: What Chinese Philosophers Can Teach Us About the Good Life by Michael Puett and Christine Gross-Loh

Between Two Worlds: Lessons in Shanghai by Betty Barr

Shanghai Boy, Shanghai Girl by Betty Barr

China Rules by Tim Clissold

The Rape of Nanjing by Iris Chang

The Art of War by Sun Tzu (Chinese classic, 5th century BCE)

Journey to the West by Wu Cheng'en (Ming Dynasty Chinese Classic)

ABOUT THE AUTHOR

Sharol Gauthier has worked as a teacher and writer for a nonprofit organization. In 2014, she moved with her family to Shanghai, where she taught high school English at Shanghai American School, Puxi. While in Shanghai, Sharol created the blog *China Incidentals* where she explored life as an expat in China. In 2019, she returned to the U.S. where she teaches English, podcasting, and Chinese-American literature at an independent school in the greater Seattle area. She continues to travel back to Shanghai regularly.

INDEX

Titles in the CultureShock! series:

Argentina	France	Philippines
Australia	Germany	Portugal
Austria	Great Britain	Russia
Bahrain	Greece	San Francisco
Bali	Hawaii	Saudi Arabia
Beijing	Hong Kong	Scotland
Belgium	Hungary	Sri Lanka
Berlin	India	Shanghai
Bolivia	Ireland	Singapore
Borneo	Italy	South Africa
Bulgaria	Jakarta	Spain
Brazil	Japan	Sri Lanka
Cambodia	Korea	Sweden
Canada	Laos	Switzerland
Chicago	London	Syria
Chile	Malaysia	Taiwan
China	Mauritius	Thailand
Costa Rica	Morocco	Tokyo
Cuba	Munich	Travel Safe
Czech Republic	Myanmar	Turkey
Denmark	Netherlands	United Arab Emirates
Dubai	New Zealand	USA
Ecuador	Norway	Vancouver
Egypt	Pakistan	Venezuela
Finland	Paris	Vietnam

For more information about any of these titles, please contact the Publisher via email at: genref@sg.marshallcavendish.com or visit our website at: www.marshallcavendish.com/genref